SURVIVING
the
STORM

INVESTMENT STRATEGIES
THAT HELP YOU MAXIMIZE PROFIT AND
CONTROL RISK DURING THE COMING
ECONOMIC WINTER

Who do you listen to and why?

Respectfully,

1-800-800-6364

JAMES O. LUNNEY
WITH LARRY CHAMBERS

NEW YORK   CHICAGO   SAN FRANCISCO   LISBON
LONDON   MADRID   MEXICO CITY   MILAN   NEW DELHI
SAN JUAN   SEOUL   SINGAPORE   SYDNEY   TORONTO

Copyright © 2008 by The McGraw-Hill Companies, Inc. All rights reserved. Printed in the United States of America. Except as permitted under the United States Copyright Act of 1976, no part of this publication may be reproduced or distributed in any form or by any means, or stored in a data base or retrieval system, without the prior written permission of the publisher.

1 2 3 4 5 6 7 8 9 0 DOC/DOC 0 9 8 7

ISBN-13: 978-0-07-149604-9
ISBN-10: 0-07-149604-1

This publication is designed to provide accurate and authoritative information in regard to the subject matter covered. It is sold with the understanding that the publisher is not engaged in rendering legal, accounting, or other professional service. If legal advice or other expert assistance is required, the services of a competent professional person should be sought.
>   —From a declaration of principles jointly adopted by a committee of the
>   American Bar Association and a committee of publishers.

McGraw-Hill books are available at special quantity discounts to use as premiums and sales promotions, or for use in corporate training programs. For more information, please write to the Director of Special Sales, Professional Publishing, McGraw-Hill, Two Penn Plaza, New York, NY 10121-2298. Or contact your local bookstore.

Library of Congress Cataloging-in-Publication Data

Lunney, James.
  Surviving the storm : investment strategies that help you maximize profit and control risk during the coming economic winter / James Lunney with Larry Chambers.
      p. cm.
  ISBN-13: 978-0-07-149604-9 (hardcover : alk. paper)
  ISBN-10: 0-07-149604-1

  1. Investments. 2. Finance, Personal. I. Chambers, Larry. II. Title.
HG4521.L8625 2008
332.6–dc22

                                        2007016930

CONTENTS

PREFACE AND ACKNOWLEDGMENTS

In its heyday in the 1800s, Butte, Montana, was one of the largest and wealthiest boomtowns in the American West. It had hundreds of saloons, boasted an infamous red-light district, and had a population of 115,000 at its peak. But that was then.

Two years ago, my wife and I decided to take our family on a vacation to Flathead Lake near Kalispell, Montana, where we enrolled our two daughters—both of whom are serious horse enthusiasts—in a riding event. On our way to the lake, we planned to stop over at my in-laws' house in Butte.

The night before we left for Montana, my 12-year-old daughter fell off her horse and broke her leg. The doctor set her leg and said she could still go on the trip, but he recommended that we pick up a wheelchair along the way so she could travel more easily and avoid a lot of pain. When we reached my in-laws', we asked around and learned that there was an easy-to-find health care equipment store in downtown Butte.

We headed downtown on an early Saturday morning. The area initially appeared so quiet that it seemed abandoned—until I noticed a congestion of cars, pickup trucks, and shoppers in front of what turned out to be the health care equipment store. Customers were emerging from the store pushing beds and wheelchairs and carrying commodes and walkers. The place was hopping.

After renting a wheelchair, we stopped at a coffee shop for breakfast, where I struck up a conversation with an elderly gentleman. I told him I had grown up in Montana but didn't remember seeing so many empty, unkempt houses—and didn't realize that 25 percent of the houses were for sale.

"Son, people don't paint their houses when their knees hurt," he replied.

I then asked him about the new multistory building I'd seen going up in town. "Why would they build something that big when so many of the houses are for sale?" I remarked.

"Yes, sir," the man said. "That's the new retirement living center, and she was sold out before they even put a shovel in the dirt. As a matter of fact, most of the buyers already owned their houses, but that's not why they moved."

"Why?" I asked.

"When you get to be my age, you just want to be around your friends, playing cards, and doing things together," he said. "Besides, there's not much of a market for those houses, because there are so few young people living here to buy them."

"They left town to join the military?" I asked.

"No, son, there are no young people here, because they were never born!" he finished.

Butte, Montana, is not an isolated case. The basic economic and social ingredients found there mirror other American cities and towns, as well as those in other countries with aging populations. The entire modernized world is aging.

I know we're all tired of reading about the baby-boom generation and how it's about to transform into the largest elderly population in human history. But it's critical to understand that what's really being discussed are the effects of a baby *bust* that immediately followed a boom.

In Butte, I had the opportunity to see firsthand what American cities could look like in the next few years. But I had another realization sitting in that coffee shop—one that literally changed everything in my life. It affected both the way I work and offer financial advice, and it caused me to write this book. I realized that all past performance which is used to predict future investment returns, pick investment properties, buy homes and businesses, and even choose colleges for our kids was about to become complex and misleading.

This book is about three profound ideas, which, if you understand and take them to heart, will give you the power to look into the future and create an extraordinarily exciting and successful life. Ignore them, and you will likely join the hundreds of thousands of investors who pour money into failed retirement plans or the many others who struggle along simply trying to survive.

Butte painted a graphic picture of what's headed our way. This has led me on a three-year journey which you are about to experience. I've been to the future—and it's Butte, Montana.

* * *

I'm blessed to have had so many wonderful and talented people come in to my life over the years. Without each of those collective experiences, I would not have had the references, vision, or direction to complete this project.

This book's ultimate success will mostly rest on the writing talents of Larry Chambers. His ability to transfer my thoughts, concepts, and ideas to words has taken patience and understanding. I am grateful to Larry for his support.

I am grateful for having been part of a wonderful network of investment advisors over the past several years, The H.S. Dent Advisers Network. Each one of these dedicated advisors is committed to learning and understanding investment theory, reality, strategy, and structure, all of this in an effort to honestly help investors achieve better results. I am a much better investment advisor to my clients from this association. Thank you to each of the members for letting me be part of your team.

Thank you to Harry S. Dent. Your willingness to share your investment experiences of the past and insights into the future has had a positive impact on those who listen.

Rodney Johnson, president of H.S. Dent Investment Management, is the most "fair and reasonable" person you could hope for when it comes to sharing incredibly helpful research and ideas. Thank you, Rodney.

Harry Cornelius, at H.S. Dent, continues to seek out the most appropriate investment alternatives based on the important demographic data outlined at the beginning of this book. Thank you, Harry, for helping our advisors and clients to have the best investment choices.

I'm also grateful to Alex Schwartz at McGraw-Hill for taking the time to listen to the message outlined for this book and understanding how important and impactful the message is. Thank you, Alex, for your positive can-do attitude and approach, even when things didn't seem so positive or do-able.

I would also like to thank Alex Ramsey at Loadstar International for helping me dig deeper for the meaning of the message in this book, a message that so many can benefit from.

During those times when I needed to be away from the office to work on this project, Mark Trevenna, my office partner, was always there to cover for me. Mark has been hugely helpful and supportive over our 20-plus-year working relationship. Thank you, Mark, for your help and friendship.

Lori Keating and Lisa Valdez have been gracious with their varied assistance over many years. I honestly don't know how I could have juggled our daily workload and this "temporary" workload without their contribution. Lori, thank you for always making our work consistently accurate, on time, and pretty. Lisa, not only do I thank you, but our clients thank you for making everything behind the curtain seem so seamless, sensible, and easy. We all know it isn't, and that it is you who makes it that way.

To each of the professionals in The Wealth Strategy Group Solution Network™, thank you for supporting the work we do. You, too, make the results seem so effortless and easy. I know how much time, effort, and concentrated thought it takes to create the results we deliver for clients and we all appreciate your efforts.

I started in the investment business in 1981. It has been a wonderful career, full of learning, growing, and always looking for what is next. I love it and it would not have been possible if Don Eder at RBC Dain Rauscher hadn't made the decision to bring me on board. Thank you, Don Eder, the gift is cherished.

I'm especially grateful to Elaine, Tiffany, and Brittany for their love and support.

My parents are not here to share and enjoy this completed project, but the result of their parenting is. Without the value and belief systems they built in me, this book and the peek into the future it describes would not be in your hands.

To my wife, Elaine, thank you for sharing 31 fabulous years of your life with me. And to our daughters, Tiffany and Brittany, thank you for letting me be your father. I couldn't be a papa without each of you.

THE MORE YOU PREDICT, THE BETTER YOU'LL MANAGE

Any serious discussion about the management of wealth; investing for retirement; or buying, selling, or running a small business should begin with a basic understanding of human behavior—of when and why people do things. The study of human behavior may be the most overlooked and least understood factor in the world of investing. Our behaviors are both measurable and predictable, a simple concept that's meaningful and understandable to all intelligent people, regardless of their level of experience.

If we know the size and demographics of a population—for example, the population of the United States—we can then quantify, calculate, gauge, and predict probable outcomes based on the makeup of that population.

If predictable spending patterns affect company earnings, and company earnings are then reflected in the price of company stock, the observation of these patterns can provide a window into the future. So why then has the investment industry not used this knowledge to manage clients' wealth? Because the industry is stuck in a regulated world that doesn't allow advisors to make investment decisions by predicting future returns but does allow investment decisions to be made based on past performance.

The practice of making investment choices based on past performance has become so entrenched within the investment profession that most advisors and investors have never even considered its ineffectiveness. In fact, this is a misguided practice that's leading hundreds of thousands of members of the investment public straight toward disaster.

What if you own (or want to own) a small business? Here's what one of my business-owning clients recently told me: "If I thought about the economy, I would never do anything but worry! I can't stop long enough to even worry about it." This very attitude is the reason why many businesses become unmanageable and unpredictable.

Just look at the numbers. Businesses start up and fail in the United States at an increasingly staggering rate. Every year, over a million people in this country start a business of some sort. Statistics tell us that by the end of the first year at least 40 percent of them will be out of business.[1] Within five years, more than 80 percent of them—800,000—will have failed. And the rest of the bad news is that if you own a small business that has managed to survive for five years or more, you still can't breathe a sigh of relief. Why? Because 80 percent of the small businesses that survive the first five years fail in the second five.[2] Why is it that with all the information available today on how to be successful in business, so few people really are?

If just one idea in this book saves some readers from losing a portion of their assets, or one suggestion helps to strengthen their portfolios, or one example gives small business owners information that is critical to their decision making, then this book will be worth many, many times its cost or the time spent reading it.

Unfortunately, for the everyday, hard-working person who is trying to make enough to feed his or her family while saving and investing for retirement, a few major components are missing from all that financial information concerning past performance that he or she has been getting (such as 401[k] plan reports). Namely, consumer spending and demographics (such as a large group of consumers moving through a specific time period) aren't taken into account when looking at investment performance. They're not factored in in the traditional risk return graph, style analysis model, linear forecasting, time series forecasting, Monte Carlo simulation, or five-star ratings reports. The financial tools advisors and planners use are missing the most important cause of economic growth, booms, busts, and financial trends. Their charts show only snapshots of the past with no explanation of spending patterns or economic seasons.

The investing public has no idea that consumer spending is a critical factor in creating the past performance numbers that advisors tout. My agenda for this book is to open your eyes and make you aware of this information and to illustrate how to use it to predict financial outcomes.

As members of a free society, we're privileged to have total disclosure and availability of information. But information can also include exposure to worthless opinions as well as biased marketing propaganda. My goal is to educate readers and clients so that they can discern bad advice and make intelligent investment decisions. By the way, you will not find the information presented in this book by studying modern academic theory or by reading popular best-selling investing or how-to business books.

When I titled my book *Surviving the Storm: Investment Strategies That Help You Maximize Profit and Control Risk during the Coming Economic Winter,* I knew that it would evoke a conditioned response reaction from the buy-quality-and-hold-forever disciples of tradition. They would be offended but, hopefully, it would get their clients to wonder, "Why hasn't my broker or advisor shown me this information?"

I look around me every day and can only conclude that most investors and their advisors have no idea what causes markets to move up, down, build, or stall. They never address the source— those fundamental factors that create dynamic expansion and growth. But as the industry shifts from investment advisors to wealth managers, they'd better start to learn.

Many books begin with an approach such as: "There have been a great number of books written on this subject, many of them very helpful, but none have organized the principles into an easy-to-understand form. I therefore saw the need to fill this great void, and thus ... etc., etc." Sound familiar?

Well, I'm going to set a different tone for *Surviving the Storm* early on by telling you that even though there have been a multitude of books written on economics, investing, and how to run a business, I don't think that many of them have been very helpful. In fact, most of them (including some of the most famous best-sellers) have been very harmful to the millions of readers who have blindly followed their rhetoric, because the expounded principles do not stand up to the realities of life.

Most advice books specifically avoid these realities, and, for the life of me, I can't understand why. I have long contended that after you strip away all of the complexities, they're little more than carbon copies of one another. It has occurred to me that the average reader—the person who invests in the stock market, starts a small business, or speculates in real estate who must then face the hard realities—might be fed up with the fantasies described in most investment books.

There are three kinds of readers who will not relate to the contents or ideas presented in this book and who will completely miss the whole point. First, there are the dilettantes, who pretend to have deep knowledge of all economic principles and who rationalize away whatever doesn't fit their agendas. They don't want to be presented with anything that might conflict with whatever they imagine success to be. Second, the lemmings, who blindly follow along in regimented masses, hoping that someone knows where we're headed. And third, the academic purists, the rule-keeping traditionalists who will simply think I'm a nut. And that's OK with me.

Three Key Wealth Factors

Without asking you to make a leap of faith or understand complex formulas, charts, or theories, I'll reveal three easy-to-understand wealth factors that influence, shape, and predict everything we do in the economy: *Birthrate, Predictable Spending Patterns,* and *Seasons of the Economy.* If you know the birthrate of a country, you can calculate decades in advance when new generations of consumers will move through predictable earning and spending cycles.

These three wealth factors already exist in the study of economics, but are actually hidden. Many people talk about the economy, but few take the trouble to find out exactly how it works. My definition of *economics* is simply the "study of how human behavior interacts with distribution and consumption." The first factor, Birthrate, is merely the number of people born at any given point in history. Why is this important? Because the birthrate of a particular place and time is a fixed number, it can be used to determine the size of a population or a generation.

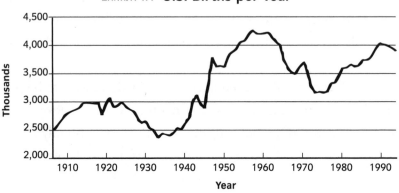

Exhibit I.1 **U.S. Births per Year[3]**

WHAT YOU'RE LOOKING AT: The growth of our population. That dramatic bulge in the middle is the baby-boom generation. The horizontal bar represents the year of birth. The vertical line represents measurement of growth.

The National Center for Health Statistics (NCHS) tracks how many people are born every year. The NCHS has been tracking birthrates since 1909, which is when birth data first began to be collected on a yearly basis. Birthrate also tells us when populations have peaked. There was a peak in the birth cycle in 1921 that has been dubbed the "Bob Hope" generation, and another in 1961, which is well known as the "baby-boom" generation.

WHAT THIS TELLS YOU: Because the birthrate is known, we can calculate and determine probable economic trends based on the predictability of the population. We know people buy and do things at very predictable periods of their lives, such as when populations enter the workforce, or when people are spending money on houses, cars, travel, health care, etc.

WHAT THIS MEANS: The boomer generation is notably over four times the size of the previous generation and overshadows its own offspring generation.

●●●●●●

From Exhibit I.1 alone, you can begin to understand how birthrate data are one the most important factors missing from the traditional financial planning model.

WEALTH INSIGHT: You can see the Consumer Expenditure Survey online at www.bls.gov/cex/.

According to the U.S. government, our second factor, Predictable Spending Patterns, drives 70 percent of our economy. The U.S. Department of Labor (DOL) conducts an ongoing Consumer Expenditure Survey that measures how much people spend per year, down to the penny, on over 1,000 different items. Likewise, this collection of numerical data shows how consumers greatly reduce spending in very predictable ways and at predictable ages, as shown in Exhibit I.2.

Have you noticed how many sleeping pill, health care products, and pain management commercials have started airing on mainstream news programs in the last five years? Marketing companies have always used population demographics to decide which products fit best into the various time slots. What you're witnessing every night on your television set with so many prime-time prescription drug commercials is evidence of aging baby boomers moving into a health-care cycle.

The Consumer Expenditure Survey information can show us exactly when family spending starts, levels off, and begins to decrease. When the kids reach maturity and move out, a big house is no longer needed; there's less need to replace furnishings and appliances, and grocery bills diminish. When kids leave home, parents find that their costs can suddenly drop by as much as half. This translates into more money to save and invest.

For retail companies to prosper, they need to know more than who their customers are. They also need to know the numbers of customers that live within shopping distance and whether those numbers are increasing or decreasing. Without this data, they must wing it—and that's no way to run a business. By the way, this type of comparison can be done for any industry and any product. The information is available to anyone.

Exhibit I.2 **Average Annual Family Spending by Age (Five-Year Age Groups)**

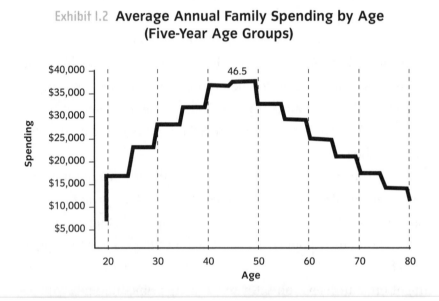

WHAT YOU'RE LOOKING AT: A plot box chart depicting a predictable spending pattern of the average American family.

WHAT THIS TELLS YOU: A quick look at the chart reveals an instant picture of the annual spending habits by age. By scrutinizing what consumers are buying and not buying, researchers are able to paint a very clear picture of what the future will entail. The knowledge of precisely when specific populations enter the workforce; when predictable changes in the workforce take place; and when specific age groups buy houses and cars, travel, and reach their peak spending allows demographers to predict areas of spending with a high percentage of accuracy.

WHAT THIS MEANS: If you were about to start, buy, or even sell a small business you need to know about this factor.[4]

• • • • • •

When we examine what people are buying, and observe where those products and services are in their product life cycle, we begin to see a series of economic cycles. The classic economic business cycles are Growth, Boom, Bust, and Recovery. What I've found is that these business cycles act similarly to nature's own growing seasons. Certain times of year are better for planting, growing, and harvesting than others. For instance, real estate properties climbed in the early 1970s (growth), crashed in the mid-1980s (bust), then started climbing back in the 1990s (recovery). A small business owner can track product cycles through each boom and bust of the economy out into the future and see if it's time to sell.

These economic spending cycles give us a way of looking at how asset classes fit into consumer spending cycles. When we overlay these cycles, we get the third Wealth Factor: the Seasons of the Economy.

Whether you're an individual managing your personal assets or a financial advisor managing a pool of client assets, this knowledge is invaluable. With this information, you can avoid relying on out-of-date tactics such as life stage allocation charts that suggest that age, emotional state, or time horizon are valid criteria for making investment choices or determining appropriate risk. You will also quit using past performance as a guide. These traditional tactics will likely decimate your own portfolio or your clients' portfolios. Past performance doesn't reflect current population spending cycles; it only shows where they were. Making investment decisions based on past performance is just guessing.

Frustrated clients will leave advisors who continue to manage using backward thinking. Real estate speculators will walk around dazed and confused about whether they should unload or hold. Even the franchise business owner—the golden model of the 1990s that reported success rates of 75 percent in contrast to the 80 percent failure rate of all businesses—will implode should people quit buying their services or products.

Success over the next two decades will depend upon understanding the current economic season or economic cycle and the season that will follow. The successful investors and their advisors will be the ones looking at what's coming next.

Bulletproof Your Future

Although there are no magic bullets, and any financial decisions will remain difficult, understanding the three fundamental economic factors will provide you with a new code with which to interpret the relationship between you and the economy; safety and risk, success and failure. By understanding how these three wealth factors interrelate and interconnect, you will get past the guards, pull back the curtain, and observe firsthand the levers and dials that affect our world.

Let's get started with Chapter 1, where I begin to give you an even clearer picture of how to use this knowledge to build, protect, and predict your financial future.

1. Department of Commerce.
2. *The E-Myth Revisited: Why Most Small Businesses Don't Work and What to Do About It*, Michael E. Gerber, New York: HarperBusiness, 1995, p. 2.
3. The HS Dent Foundation: *The Secret of Asset Allocation*, Special Report, 2005.
4. Ibid.

FOCUSING ON FACTORS THAT MATTER

Before you can construct a new building on the same site as an old one, you have to raze the existing structure. And that's exactly how I'm going to begin this book: by tearing down old, inefficient investment structures that have been taught to people for generations.

It'll be easier to explain why I developed my philosophy if I first share with you what I've learned about existing investment philosophy and why it doesn't work.

Advisors May Hinder More than Help

According to a new study that evaluated the performance of all mutual fund investments made by individuals and financial intermediaries during a seven-year period[1], intermediaries as a whole do a poor job of allocating client assets to mutual funds. The study, titled *Assessing the Costs and Benefits of Brokers in the Mutual Fund Industry*, was conducted over a two-year period by finance professors at the Harvard Business School in Cambridge, Massachusetts, and the University of Oregon in Eugene.

Study results showed that financial advisors and brokers can actually impede investors' overall portfolio performance. The study revealed that funds purchased through intermediaries had a 2.9 percent net average annual return (with the exception of upfront loads and redemption costs) over the study period, which included both a bull and bear market cycle. The average annual return of funds purchased directly by investors during the same period was 6.6 percent.

These conclusions may surprise you—but not me. That's because the primary objective of Wall Street brokerage firms is to make a profit, and most stockbrokers earn their money from commissions, not performance. They are often encouraged to drive transactions by pushing their clients' emotional hot buttons. A well-informed public could dramatically cut into the profits of these brokers.

WEALTH INSIGHT: As children, we learned the trick that if your mom says you can't go out to play, then you ask your dad (or vice versa)—thus nearly doubling your chances of being allowed out. Investment companies use a similar tactic to get you to buy their products. They present distorted information designed to motivate you to take actions by pushing an emotional hot button. A recent example is the hedge fund industry. The hot button is the investor's desire for an increased return. Such is the case of the hedge fund industry, which has grown to nearly 9,000 hedge funds managing over $1.2 trillion in assets.

Exhibit 1.1 is a comparison bar graph that shows what investors are doing and what they plan on doing in various investment products.

Financial planners and advisors often feel that the best way to keep the commissions coming in is to select next year's winner.

Exhibit 1.1 **Investor Activity in Various Products**

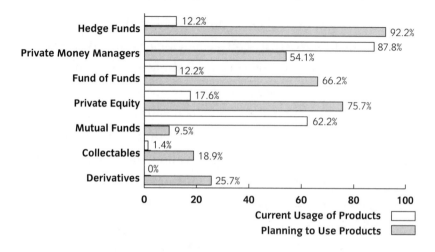

WHAT YOU'RE LOOKING AT: A comparison bar graph that shows what investors are doing and what they plan on doing in various investment products.

WHAT THIS TELLS YOU: The clear bars are how investors are investing currently. The shaded bar shows what investors are planning to do.

WHAT THIS MEANS: Hedge funds are expecting significant growth. Investors are moving out of traditional investment products such as mutual funds.

• • • • • •

They become so focused on this that they can't see the proverbial forest for the trees. There are approximately 16,580 mutual funds (and that's a lot of trees). Strategies that produce the least positive results in the management of investor wealth, such as the constant emphasis on the next big thing, are the very strategies typically preferred by advisors.

High Activity Doesn't Equal High Performance

Above all, the most popular investment strategy embraced by advisors is that high activity equals high client value. Advisors may try to remain extremely active by obsessively analyzing mountains of data about the latest products. But no amount of analysis in the world will do them—or you—any good unless it's viewed in the context of the economy's seasons. Until advisors understand this, they're still just winging it, operating without any real comprehension of how events and asset classes interconnect.

To make themselves appear more active than the competition, Wall Street firms spend billions of dollars each year trying to out-promote themselves over their rivals. Part of this approach is to provide many financial vehicles and tools to help their advisors sell more products. It's big business, but as we've already observed in the study results above, unfortunately it doesn't work well for investors.

WEALTH INSIGHT: This more-is-more approach became the norm because, again, most advisors haven't studied the economic seasons, believing the good times will never end. Many focus on high current income, and some are motivated almost exclusively by product payout, that is, their commissions. If they can get an 85 percent payout, they're thrilled, failing to understand that they could get 95 percent if they used more effective strategies. Too many advisors have learned to gorge themselves on big houses, sports cars, boats—whatever is showy or trendy. Little, if any, of their earnings go back into their businesses or savings—or are used for protective strategies such as paying off their mortgages.

The fever-pitch marketing effort by Wall Street firms has resulted in a world of look-alike competitors, and the average consumer can't tell those who are competent from those who aren't. They all use the same titles. Even the products look similar, which makes it more difficult for investors to find any objective reason to choose one advisor over another. When the alternatives are basically similar, investors will default to basing their judgment on activity, swallowing the mass message that they've been fed: The more activities advisors perform, the greater their value.

The big firms then continue to reinforce this dynamic of high activity, retaining clients by offering more and more products and services. Even though the investing public has been taught to believe that this activity equals value, it isn't true. Unless production is measurable, value is subjective. Growing up on a feedlot in Montana, we had a saying for people like that: "Big hat, no cattle."

Don't Be Fooled by High Activity Tools

The following are common high activity tools used by average advisors hoping to select, reposition, and uncover investment products. The first, shown in Exhibit 1.2, is what I call the *Star Rating Game.*

Exhibit 1.2 **Morningstar Box Grid**

Large-cap Value	Large-cap Blend	Large-cap Growth
Mid-cap Value	Mid-cap Blend	Mid-cap Growth
Small-cap Value	Small -cap Blend	Small-cap Growth

WHAT YOU'RE LOOKING AT: The Morningstar box grid is what most financial advisors, planners, and consultants widely accept, use, and follow as the investment management standard. A Chicago-based company called Morningstar created this grid to help make the investment advisor's job a bit easier.

WHAT THIS TELLS YOU: The grid is based on a star rating system that's designed to categorize asset classes and investment managers, to diversify, and to monitor fund performance. Three academic studies[2] that examined the efficacy of the grid found that:

1) The characteristic boxes weren't asset classes as traditionally defined and did *not* aid in portfolio diversification.

2) Many advisors falsely believe that the grid flows from and is part of Modern Portfolio Theory (MPT).

3) Investment consultants who work with pension plan sponsors and high net worth investors often cite the underlying size and value growth effects as a way of capturing an equity manager's style and as the most important reason for accepting the characteristic grid. (However, they found no evidence that this approach produces the best results for investors.)

4) In order to produce superior returns, managers must be allowed to pursue their unique style and have access to the entire universe of stocks, which means that portfolios will experience drift and that constraining drift sets the stage for underperformance.

WHAT THIS MEANS: Not a lot. As you read in point 4 above, the nine-box grid is basically a constrained system created to detect style drift.

• • • • • •

When choosing an asset manager, 59 percent of investors consider a consistent investing style to be the most important factor.[3]

WEALTH INSIGHT: Fifty years ago, Harry Markowitz, a graduate student at the University of Chicago with exceptionally keen insight, developed the principle called Modern Portfolio Theory (MPT). The principle held that risk (which he defined as volatility) must be the central focus for the whole process of investing. What Markowitz found was an investment world blindly living in a paradox. While it was accepted that human beings, by their nature, are risk-averse, investing had essentially ignored the interrelationship between risk and return. What he had also discovered was that if you have two investments, and they both have the same average rates of return, the one with lower volatility would have a higher compounded return. The basics behind MPT are set forth in a 15-page paper entitled "Portfolio Selection" authored by Markowitz in 1952. Investment managers began to apply techniques of the theory in the late 1960s, and by the l970s, these techniques had become fixtures in the investment world.

Wall Street's top analysts study a barrage of economic data: currency exchange rates, trade imbalances, jobless claims, continuing claims, and capacity utilization. But even with all of the quantitative models, advisors are still wrong most of the time.[4] There are just too many variables in economic data that change too quickly to accurately represent the current economic state or to forecast future changes.

The next so-called strategy, which I call the *Life Stage Chart Game*, should be against the law. It could potentially be the most damaging to you should you become a victim of it. Less sophisticated advisors still use oversimplistic charts and archaic financial planning principles in making investment decisions for their clients. For example, based on an investor's age and tolerance for losing money (risk), an advisor will label that individual as aggressive, moderate, or conservative. The advisor then maps the label to the investment strategies listed under the corresponding categories in his or her so-called life stage chart, like the one in Exhibit 1.3.

Media Circus Creates Investment Uncertainties

Based on all of their misinformed approaches and just plain bad advice, it's tempting to blame advisors for most of investors' problems. But there's another very tangible enemy out there that plays a significant (and often detrimental) role in investors' decisions: the media.

Exhibit 1.3 **Life Stages Chart Game**

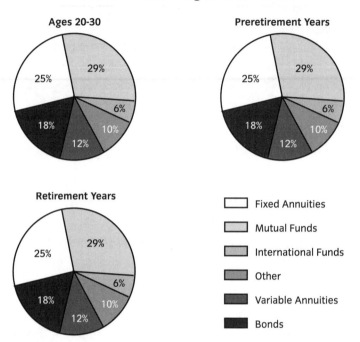

Ages 20-30

Preretirement Years

Retirement Years

Fixed Annuities

Mutual Funds

International Funds

Other

Variable Annuities

Bonds

WHAT YOU'RE LOOKING AT: The pie graphs show typical investment allocations at different life stages.

WHAT THIS TELLS YOU: The strategies in these charts are normally prescribed by an aggressive promoter of an investment company. The charts themselves suggest that an investor's decisions should be based on a time horizon and should match specific investment vehicles. For example, the charts might suggest that as you get closer to retirement, you should shift your allocations from equities into fixed-income investments. Or, if you are conservative, you should be heavily invested in bonds.

WHAT THIS MEANS: It all may sound logical and sensible, but this type of profiling could decimate your portfolio, because it doesn't take unforeseen and unavoidable circumstances into account, such as a sudden, drastic change in the economic season. Here's an example of what could happen:

Suppose you're about to retire and still want to experience growth in your portfolio. The life stage chart says that you should diversify into real estate, foreign and domestic equities, and a small amount of fixed income. Unfortunately, neither you nor your advisor have any warning that a long economic winter is on its way, during which all of your financial assets, including your real estate, will drop in value—no matter what your age or risk profile tells you.

• • • • • •

You may be asking yourself, "Aren't magazines and TV shows in business to help investors make informed decisions?" The answer is *No*. The motivation of these media outlets is to make money for their owners and advertisers. The media thrive—actually, they make the most money—in times of volatility and uncertainty. If everyone knew how to invest appropriately, there would be less volatility and less need for media gurus. Sales of magazines and newsletters would plummet. Media profits would suffer.

Back in the 1980s, you may remember hearing this well-documented factoid around the water cooler: "A 40-year-old single woman is more likely to be killed by a terrorist than to marry." That little gem all started as a research study at Yale and Harvard about Americans' marriage patterns and the relationship of those patterns to the age structure of the country's population. The study reached a preliminary conclusion that a 40-year-old unmarried woman had just a 1.3 percent probability of ever getting married. The figure was mentioned in 1986 in a small college newspaper article that was subsequently read by a journalist at *Newsweek*—who then went on to write a story about how a 40-year-old single woman was more likely to be killed by a terrorist than to marry.

It didn't matter that the *Newsweek* claim was unfounded. Simply because it appeared in print, it became a "fact" and was repeated in popular media and around the water cooler for years. In addition to being hurtful toward women, causing unnecessary panic and implying that marriage was every woman's number-one goal, *Newsweek*'s claim was completely false.

Jeffrey Rosenthal, a University of Toronto professor in the Department of Statistics, wrote a book titled *Struck by Lightning.* In it, he writes that even taking 2001 into account, only about one American in 94,000 has been killed by terrorists, which is equivalent to 0.001 percent. This is a much smaller figure than even the 1.3 percent probability of marriage that the Harvard–Yale study claims. (Of course in the years before 2001, terrorist actions on American soil were practically nonexistent, so the corresponding probability would have been even smaller.) So, there was simply no logic or accuracy whatsoever to *Newsweek's* claim. Despite the huge publicity surrounding the original study, these corrections and clarifications were mostly ignored.[5]

That's the whole problem with the news. They tell us all these facts, and a lot of them aren't even true. But even if they are true, they don't give us any context so we haven't got a clue as to what the facts mean. Our next step is to have the right framework and perspective before we invest.

Consumer Spending Governs All

There's a lot of evidence that points to deceptive advisor and media tactics. In the face of all that evidence, the question is, How do the securities industry and the media continue to get away with regularly misleading investors by using these destructive tactics to manage and direct clients' wealth? And why can't we mention the words *predict* and *future,* yet nearly every advisor I've ever met has based investment decisions on past performance?

I believe that the answer to the first question is Investors cannot let go of the age-old idea that advisors ultimately want to help them. And I'm convinced that the answer to the second is Historical trends are easy to summarize, explain, and sell to clients.

These answers enable advisors to comfortably maintain their practice of bad tactics. All of their tactics completely ignore the most dramatic force behind the U.S. economy or any economy: consumer spending. On average, this force drives 70 percent of our economy. The dollar's core strength depends on spending at home and on demand for goods and products overseas. Most corporate business owners understand and capitalize on this knowledge, relying on spending and demographic data from the Consumer Expenditure Survey (which I cover in more detail in Chapter 2) to inform their efforts. Wall Street marketing departments base their advertising decisions on this very same data—which their investment advisor counterparts overlook in the management of clients' assets.

Prepare for Change in Consumer Spending Habits

We're all familiar with the signposts of changing seasons, for example, summer fades into fall, the leaves turn colors, the days become shorter, the nights colder. But do you know the tell-tale signs of the changing *economic* seasons?

Let's say we're on the verge of a deflating economy—the equivalent of a bad winter. During this type of economic season, bonds will more than likely go up, at least in the first stages, and real estate will drop in value. The worth of financial assets, including stock, could also be expected to drop.

If you had only paid attention to the greatest indicator of our economic health—consumer spending—you would have been able to predict this forthcoming winter and would have prepared for it by protecting your assets. And only when you embrace the fact that data *are* available to help you anticipate these scenarios *before* they occur, can you prepare for impending risk to your wealth.

The succeeding chapters of this book will help you with that preparation. For example, I'll tell you about effective Wealth Planning Strategies, such as creating and monitoring a visual plan that shows how and when these cycles will affect your investments. I'll also cover how correct ownership structures can protect your wealth, title your business, or hold ownership in your properties. The correct structure will place your assets in the most advantageous configuration—meaning, how each asset is owned, titled, and controlled. Structure is also a major component in how assets transfer to the next generation.

In addition, I'll discuss the process of investment management, where you'll learn that if your process monitors both the season of the economy that we're in and the season that we're headed toward, you can eliminate a lot of the guesswork involved in selecting investments and allocations. Finally, I'll tell you how to divest from your holdings and implement logical alternatives to long-term holdings.

At this point, you may be wondering how you can possibly prepare yourself for every potential scenario. True, the possibilities are many and varied, but they all have one thing in common in each case. Traditional investment advice is not going to help if you don't understand the season of the economy in which you are currently living.

Let's move on to Chapter 2, where I'll focus on the three factors that really matter—and eliminate the ones that don't.

1. This seven-year period was from 1996 to 2002.
2. "The Characteristic Grid Is Not Part of Modern Portfolio Theory," 2005, Thomas Howard, Ph.D., and Craig T. Callahan, DBA; "Evolution of the Characteristic Grid," September 2005, Thomas Howard, Ph.D., and Craig T. Callahan, DBA; and "The 'Problematic' Style Grid," July 2005, Thomas Howard, Ph.D., and Craig T. Callahan, DBA.
3. Cerulli Associates, *Financial Planning* magazine, August 2006.
4. Just before the 2000 market crash, Wall Street analysts' buy recommendations outnumbered sells by 37 to 1. Five out of 40 economists surveyed in June 1990 forecasted that year's recession, and 63 percent of large-cap fund managers couldn't beat an S&P 500 index fund over the past decade (*MONEY* magazine's "Why We Can't Believe Predictions," June 22, 2006, Pat Regnier).
5. For example, writes Professor Rosenthal:

    The U.S. Census Bureau reported that in 1970, of all American women between 40 and 44 years old, 4.9% had never married. In 2001, it reported that of the 8,851,000 American women who were over 75 years old, 366,000 (4.1%) had never married. A woman who was 40 in 1970 turned 70 in the year 2000, so these two statistics refer to essentially the same group of women. (Of course, they are not precisely the same group, due to immigration, emigration, and death.) But we could say that the fraction of women who were unmarried at 40 but who were wed by age 75 is about 0.8% and if you divide that by 4.9%, it equals 16.3%.

    In other words, of those American women in the year 1970 who were between 40 and 44 years of age and who had never married, about 16.3% eventually will be married. This is quite a large percentage, especially if you consider that many of the women might not have wanted to get married. Furthermore, this figure is over 12 times larger than that claimed by the Harvard–Yale study, and over 15,000 times larger than the chance of being killed by terrorists, even during the 9/11 attacks. And, a 40-year-old woman today is probably even more likely to marry than was her 1970 counterpart. The original Harvard–Yale study figure of 1.3% was entirely incorrect, and that *Newsweek* analogy to being killed by a terrorist was way off base.

Jeffrey Rosenthal, *Struck by Lightning*, Joseph Henry Press, 2006, pp. 120–122.

CHAPTER 2

SEASONS OF THE ECONOMY AND WEALTH FACTORS

You may know Jeff Hawkins as the guy who invented the Palm Pilot. In 2005, he co-wrote a bestselling book called *On Intelligence,* in which he discusses how the human brain doesn't work in quite the same way that most scientists have traditionally posited. Rather, Hawkins asserts that the primary function of the brain is to make predictions—and that human behaviors are best understood as by-products of those predictions.

According to Hawkins, the way that the brain makes predictions is to create a memory-based model of the world. Everything that a person knows and learns is stored within this model. By recognizing what does *not* belong in the model, the brain constructs predictions of future events.

I had a big "Aha" insight—you know, one of those powerful moments in which the tangle of confusion suddenly clears—when I realized that predicting the economic future is much like the process that Hawkins describes.

We all have the same preconceived vision of the ideal economic world burned into our brains. This utopian vision includes growth, prosperity, and generally positive performance in the major financial sectors. Yet when we hear about a circumstance or event that doesn't fit into our perfect economic picture, we begin to predict that our ideal world may be moving beyond our reach.

The key, as Hawkins points out, is not to let these predictions pass without examining their importance. In this chapter, we'll talk about the three core factors—*birthrate*, *predictable spending patterns*, and *seasons of the economy*—that you should always look to as important "predictors" of our economic future.

Wealth Factor One: Birthrate

The first factor, *birthrate*, is defined as the ratio between births and individuals of a population at any given point in history. Birthrate is fixed; it's how we form new generations. It expands as new generations of consumers and workers move through a very predictable earning and spending cycle.

Birthrate is critical. When you can track the population into the future, you can calculate and determine probable economic trends based on the numbers of people that affect a given aspect of the economy, for example, education or health care. The time-value chart in Exhibit 2.1 represents a kind of demographic instrument panel.

The baby-boom generation has been called "a pig moving through a python." It's over four times the size of the generation before it and so massive that everything it does has stretched our society and economy to extremes. Why are baby boomers important to you today? Because this very large group of people is now reaching its peak spending years, and when its spending inevitably begins to decline in the not-too-distant future, you may witness a longer-lasting pullback in the U.S. economy. Birth charts such as this one tell us decades in advance when new generations of consumers, like the baby boomers, will move through predictable spending cycles.

Exhibit 2.1 **U.S. Births per Year**

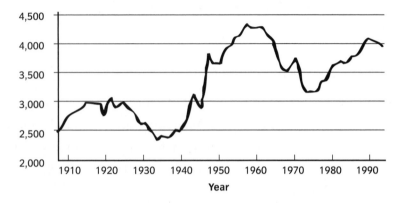

Year

WHAT YOU'RE LOOKING AT: Like a cockpit panel that shows pertinent aircraft statistics, this "demographic instrument panel" shows birth pattern stats since 1909—the point at which the United States began collecting birth data on a yearly basis.

WHAT THIS TELLS YOU: We can see that new generations emerge about every 40 years. For example, notice that the birth cycle peak of the so-called Bob Hope generation occurred in 1921. Then, note the size of the massive baby-boom generation, which experienced the peak of its birth cycle in 1961. These two peaks are exactly 40 years apart.

WHAT THIS MEANS: You can look decades in advance and see when consumers, such as the baby boomers, will move through predictable spending cycles.

• • • • • •

WEALTH INSIGHT: In 1980, my writing partner, Larry, was also a real estate speculator building hundreds of resort condominiums in Park City, Utah. Unfortunately he made a colossal mistake by assuming that people would buy up resort properties in the area. What he failed to realize at the time was that the real buyers of resort condos had not yet reached the age when they would buy.

"The whole time I was building the condos, my gut was screaming 'NO,'" Larry has since told me. "But the messages I was getting from my immediate environment were saying the opposite. The media and local experts were all claiming that inflation was going higher and that these units would be worth a million apiece."

Back then, Larry had never considered birthrate as a factor. He was not aware of the seasons of the economy (which I discuss later in this chapter) or the role that spending plays in it.

Noise Covers Up Real Causes

We've established that the birthrate factor serves as a hard-and-fast indicator of economic trends. Yet a lot of investors (and society in general) tend to ignore this strong factor and instead fall prey to *noise*—misleading information that obscures the true underlying factors behind trends.

The media is responsible for a great deal of the noise out there, largely because it distorts much of what happens at the Federal Reserve. The Fed's job is to keep hold of the steering wheel in the economy, from the government's perspective. It's legally mandated to do three things:

1. Promote maximum employment

2. Support stable prices

3. Moderate long-term interest rates

The Fed has a number of tools that it can use to effect these things. One of these tools is the fact that it controls the amount of money in circulation by buying and selling bonds.

If the Fed wants more money in the economy, it simply buys back U.S. government bonds. It employs bond traders who go into the bond market to buy and/or sell the bonds. The traders create more money in the economy by buying (creating liquidity, which simply means converting an asset to cash) or they take money out (liquidity evaporates) by selling at the Federal open window in New York.

Most people don't follow the numbers that tell you how much money the economy currently has, yet knowing the amount of money that's floating around out there is precisely the opposite of *noise*. If you look up the Federal Reserve Bank of St. Louis online (www.stlouisfed.org/), you'll see a lot *of reports* on money at zero maturity and money in the marketplace. That's a great way to track how much liquidity exists.

> **WEALTH INSIGHT:** The Fed has pushed liquidity a number of times, with the last time occurring after 9/11.

Before 9/11, the biggest push on liquidity that I had ever seen was Y2K. Remember all the fears surrounding it? The media told everyone to hoard cash because the end was near. *NOISE*.

You can imagine what ensued: a hundred million adult Americans took an extra $1,000 out of the bank. By December 31, 1999, our system was awash in money as the Fed prepared for what it thought might be a drawdown of everything that people had on deposit—all at one time.

None of the predictions came to pass, but we did have a lot of liquidity in the market that the Fed had to take care of. When it eventually started taking money back in, it constricted the amount of money that was able to flow—and that put pressure on all the markets.

Noise Distorts Birthrate in Two Historical Examples

There are two strong historical examples of the way that noise has distorted the birthrate factor. The first occurred in New York City during the 1990s, when the city's leadership wrongly assumed that crime disappeared because of repairs to windows and subways.

In 1965, there were 200,000 crimes in the city, and from that point, the number began to rise sharply. The incidence of crime doubled in two years and continued to climb until it hit 650,000 crimes a year in the mid-1970s. It remained steady at that level for the next two decades, then plunged downward in 1992—not tapering off or gently decelerating, but jamming on the brakes— more rapidly than it had risen 30 years earlier. People were quick to both celebrate and theorize, with the prevailing hypothesis coined the Broken Window Theory.

WEALTH INSIGHT: The Broken Window Theory goes something like this: When a broken window is left unrepaired, people conclude that no one cares about fixing it. Soon, everyone becomes accustomed to the sight until it no longer looks out of place or seems to matter. As other windows are broken, they, too, are left that way. This sense of abandonment then gives way to anarchy, when windows are intentionally broken, trash accumulates, and the area is otherwise defaced. People have the general impression that no one is watching, and the situation escalates—eventually reaching epidemic proportions.

The second example came about in Washington, D.C., from June 7 to July 30, 1993, when approximately 4,000 people assembled for the National Demonstration Project. The project included participation in the Transcendental Meditation and TM-Sidhi programs of Maharishi Mahesh Yogi. District of Columbia officials hypothesized that the programs would lead to a substantial reduction in the levels of violent crime in the area during that period.

Upon completion of the project, a 27-member Project Review Board comprised of independent scientists and leading citizens approved a research protocol to review whether the crime levels had in fact dropped. Weekly crime data were derived from database records provided by the District of Columbia Metropolitan Police Department. Statistical analysis of this data considered the effect of weather variables, daylight, historical crime trends and annual patterns in the area, as well as trends in neighboring cities.

WEALTH INSIGHT: The weekly crime data used by the Project Review Board are the very same data used in the FBI's Uniform Crime Reports.

The results of the analysis showed that crimes dropped significantly during the project and seemed to correspond with increases in the project's size. Ultimately, the Project Review Board claimed that the endeavor would have a long-term effect of reducing crimes by 48 percent.

The problem with conclusions in both the New York City and D.C. cases was that analysts neglected to consider one key variable: the possibility that the criminals were never born in the first place. As Steven Levitt and Stephen Dubner suggested years later in their book *Freakonomics: A Rogue Economist Explores the Hidden Side of Everything*, the real reason behind these crime drops may have been that the criminals weren't there. Levitt and Dubner made the point that *Roe v. Wade* made abortion not only legal, but available, affordable, and safe. This allowed many women who were not in a position to adequately parent a child to have abortions, thereby reducing the population within a specific socioeconomic group and ultimately lowering crime.

What Levitt and Dubner's book does *not* say, but should, is that there was a natural rhythm to the population, whereby we peaked in births with the boomers; had terrific crime problems 20 to 25 years later; went through a birth drop (Generation X); and consequently had fewer people overall in the age range of the common street criminal. This approach suggests that street crime should begin to increase again as the echo-boomers reach this age range, with higher numbers observed in the 2010s.

WEALTH INSIGHT: The New York State Office for the Aging provides interesting population info at www.aging.state.ny.us.

Noise Throws Analysts Off-Track

A general example of how noise distorts true causes took place during the 1960s, when a researcher noticed a strong correlation between the sales of television sets and the incidence of heart attacks in Great Britain. The two curves followed remarkably similar contours. In fact, the shapes of the graphs mapped peak-for-peak and valley-for-valley, almost identically.

It seemed reasonable to assume that as people bought more television sets, they spent more time sitting in front of those sets, which caused them to get less exercise. It would follow that the physical condition of these people subsequently deteriorated, rendering them more likely to have heart attacks.

But even this argument, if valid, can't explain the uncanny exactness with which the two curves followed each other, year after year. If television watching really did cause heart attacks, a lag effect would have shown up between the curves—but there was none.

The truth was that no strong correlation existed between television sales and heart attacks, a fact that would have become apparent simply by adding relevant factors into the survey. For instance, maybe television buyers suffered heart attacks because their sets emitted electromagnetic fields that caused immediate susceptibility to a heart attack. Or people who had already suffered heart attacks may have been advised by their doctors to avoid physical exertion while recovering, and this caused them to buy television sets to help pass the time. Or was the entire phenomenon merely a coincidence?

At times, behavioral scientists rummage around for nonexistent cause-and-effect explanations, growing increasingly frustrated as statistical data pour in that demonstrate the existence of a correlation but give no clue as to its cause. Applied to economic and social theory, this sort of correlation-without-causation can lead to scary propositions like chaos theory.

WEALTH INSIGHT: *Chaos theory* suggests that the answers to certain questions are just because that's the way it is.

Yet simply because two events (like heart attacks and television sales) tend to go together (in other words, are correlated), that doesn't necessarily prove that one causes the other. A study may convincingly demonstrate a correlation, but it doesn't necessarily establish the underlying causes. Once again, correlation does not imply causation.

A simple misunderstanding of the causes behind correlations may have grave consequences. The challenge is to dismiss available data that simply are not accurate and examine the fixed variables that count, such as birthrates. Those who do are more likely to see through the mysteries and, like my writing partner, save themselves from losing millions in the wrong investment area at the wrong time.

Too Much Information

When typical economists make predictions, they begin by looking at leading economic indicators to decipher where the economy is headed. (See Exhibit 2.2.) These indicators are important because they tend to move in advance of the overall economy. The indicators often turn downward before the overall economy starts to cool and turn upward in advance of an overall economic expansion.

Perhaps the best-known leading economic indicator is the aptly named Index of Leading Economic Indicators (LEI). Published each month by The Conference Board, a New York–based private research group, the LEI is really a compilation of 10 different component statistics, each of which has a separate weighting within the index.

The largest LEI components are M2 money supply, the interest-rate spread between the 10-year Treasury note and the federal funds rate, and the average hourly manufacturing workweek. Together, these statistics account for over 80 percent of the total accepted leading economic indicators, but of course everyone in the financial community has a different opinion on their usefulness.

WEALTH INSIGHT: Leading Economic Indicators

The following is a summary of some of the more popular leading indicators and where to find them.

Exhibit 2.2

Indicator	What It Tells Us	Where to Find It	Frequency
Gross Domestic Product	Growth in the overall U.S. economy	www.bea.doc.gov/bea/dn /home/gdp.htm	Quarterly
Durable Goods Orders	Future manufacturing activity	www.census.gov/ indicator/www/m3/adv	Monthly
Factory Orders	Manufacturing orders and sales	www.census.gov/ indicator/www/m/prel/ index/htm	Monthly
Business Inventories	Domestic business sales and inventories	www.census.gov/mtis/ www/mtis.html	Monthly
Industrial Production	Domestic industry output and available capacity	www.federalreserve.gov/ releases/g17/current	Monthly
ISM Manufacturing Survey	Leading indicator of manufacturing strength	www.ism.ws/ismreport/ index.cfm	Monthly

Index of Leading Economic Indicators	Leading indicator of future economic strength	www.globalindicators.org /us/ latestreleases	Monthly
New Housing Starts and Building Permits	New housing construction and permits	www.census.gov/const/ www/newresconstindex. html	Monthly
Existing Home Sales	Sales of previously owned single-family homes	www.realtor.org/research. nsf/pages/ehsdata	Monthly
New Home Sales	Sales of new single-family homes	www.census.gov/ newhomesales	Monthly
Federal Reserve Beige Book	Domestic economic strength	www.federalreserve. gov/frbindex.htm	Twice/ Quarter
Current Account Balance	International trade	www.bea.doc.gov/bea/ rels.htm	Quarterly
Consumer Price Index	Price inflation in retail goods and services	www.bis.gov/cpi/	Monthly
Producer Price Index	Inflation in prices paid by businesses	www.bis.gov/ppi	Monthly
Employment Cost Index	Domestic labor costs	www.stats.bis.gov	Quarterly
Productivity and Costs	Changes in worker efficiency	www.bis.gov/lpc	Quarterly

Because there are so many opinions and so much information out there, we tend to get overloaded with info clutter. Yet at the end of the day, all that extra information isn't an advantage—it's simply a distraction.

WEALTH INSIGHT: Remember Pareto's principle, or the 80/20 rule? Pareto's idea wasn't widely known until Joseph Moses Juran renamed it the "Rule of the Vital Few" in his 1951 tome *Quality Control Handbook*, in which he separated the vital few from the trivial many. The 80/20 rule itself states that 80 percent of results flows from 20 percent of causes. In other words, most of the universe consists of meaningless noise, which can drown out those few forces that are tremendously powerful and productive. And if you isolate and harness those powerful forces, you can exert incredible influence.

A case in point was in Malcolm Gladwell's bestselling book *Blink*, where he writes about an emergency room physician named Lee Goldman. Goldman discovered that too much information was causing doctors to make mistakes in the ER by missing a heart attack or failing to recognize when someone was on the verge of having one. He found that a person could walk into an ER with chest pain and get advice that was all over the map. A patient might be sent home by one doctor or checked into intensive care by another.

Goldman fed hundreds of cases into a computer, looking for things that could predict a heart attack. He came up with a standard equation that took the guesswork out of treating chest pain. The equation included three urgent factors: (1) Is the pain felt by the patient really unstable angina?, (2) Is there fluid in the patient's lungs?, and (3) Is the patient's systolic blood pressure below 100?

Goldman then drew up a decision tree that recommended a treatment option for each combination of the three risk factors. Ironically, a big chunk of the funding for this research didn't come from the medical community but from an unlikely source—the U.S. Navy. The Navy supported the project for the most arcane of reasons: If you're the captain of a submarine, snooping on the enemy at the bottom of an unfriendly ocean, and one of your sailors gets terrible chest pains, do you risk giving away your position by surfacing and then evacuating the sailor—or do you just give the sailor an antacid and hope he or she doesn't die?

Of course, the medical community eventually did its own research (though more to disprove Goldman than to determine methods for more accurately diagnosing heart attacks). After evaluating years of research, it found that Goldman's three rules were 70 percent more likely to lead to an accurate diagnosis than the old established methods.

Not only did Goldman's results help to diagnose and treat more heart attacks, but they also proved that having large amounts of data does *not* necessarily make for an accurate heart-attack prediction. As in so many cases, the extra information wasn't an advantage—it was a distraction.

Goldman's simple formula eliminated unnecessary details and resulted in the essential criteria to make an accurate diagnosis. This reasoning is the same rationale behind the three wealth factors. Why is this anecdote important to you? Because we assume that the more information we have as decision makers, the better off we are. This assumption is not always accurate.

Wealth Factor Two: Predictable Spending Cycles or Patterns

A few years ago, many economists predicted that we would now be living under dire economic circumstances for a number of reasons—the massive federal deficit, which totaled $500 billion in January 2005, being chief among them.

We've also spent enormous amounts on the wars in Afghanistan and Iraq and experienced the devastating Hurricanes Katrina and Rita, all of which helped push oil prices up to an astronomical $72 a barrel. With a gallon of gas over $3, most industry watchers assumed that consumers would be unable to spend money at even the most stalwart American institutions, like Wal-Mart.

Yet one month after the hurricanes, Wal-Mart saw reduced earnings of just one penny per share, with several other U.S. companies demonstrating similar standings. The S&P 500 has also had the highest earnings in history, and the budget deficit has dropped from nearly $500 billion to $148 billion in 2007. In the face of what many believed were certain indicators of a downturn, how do we explain our seemingly inexplicable economic growth?

The explanation lies largely in a single factor: consumer spending. This one factor drives 70 percent of our economy. The U.S. government has acknowledged the importance of consumer spending by establishing the Consumer Expenditure Survey program, which is directed by the Bureau of Labor Statistics.

The program is comprised of two survey types: a quarterly interview survey and a weekly diary survey, in which participants track all of the purchases they make each day for two consecutive one-week periods. The results of these surveys offer insight into the buying habits of American consumers, including data on their expenditures, incomes, and consumer unit (families and single consumers) characteristics.

Results from the Consumer Expenditure Survey consistently prove that consumers in various age groups exhibit very predictable spending patterns. Spending patterns are important because they affect company earnings, and company earnings are reflected in the price of publicly held stock. By observing those patterns, we can look around corners and see into the future of a company. If you know exactly when populations enter the workforce; when changes in that workforce take place; and when age groups buy houses and cars, travel, save, or invest, you can start to make some predictions about spending patterns with a high degree of accuracy.

The fundamental factor that drives the boom-and-bust cycles of our economy in a predictable manner is *consumption*—how the average family spends money in predictable patterns over time. See Exhibit 2.3.

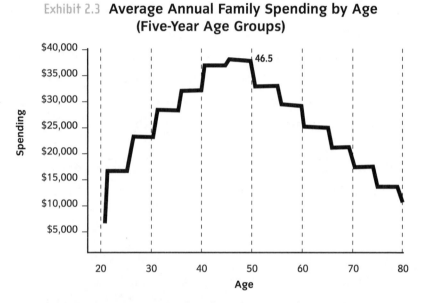

Exhibit 2.3 **Average Annual Family Spending by Age (Five-Year Age Groups)**

WHAT YOU'RE LOOKING AT: The information came from HS Dent Foundation/U.S. Department of Labor, U.S. Bureau of Labor Statistics Consumer Expenditure Survey.

WHAT THIS TELLS YOU: The predictable spending cycles of the average American family.

WHAT THIS MEANS: All families, including yours and mine, go through very predictable spending cycles. On average, we enter the workforce at age 19 and get married at age 26, when we buy our first new cars and move into apartments that we furnish. Two years later, we have our first child.

• • • • • •

The Consumer Expenditure Survey shows us that the average person goes on to buy a starter home at age 34 and purchases all of the furnishings to go with it. By age 43, that person trades up to the family's largest home and furnishes it. At age 47, the kids leave for college or go to work.

After age 48, the average family spending decreases sharply, because the kids are gone and they no longer need the big house or more furnishings, appliances, cars, and car insurance. They also don't need to buy trendy tennis shoes and designer clothes or have a refrigerator crammed with food. Parents typically mourn this loss of their kids until they realize that they are at the top of their earnings cycle yet simultaneously they experience a massive drop in financial obligations. They still have the fixed costs of a home and furnishings, but their variable costs suddenly drop by as much as half.

Now that we can pinpoint the types of products and services that consumers buy at certain ages, we can determine the *quantities* of those products and services that will be bought and sold by studying U.S. census data. The data reveal the percentage of our population in each age group. Add these percentages to Consumer Expenditure Survey data, and the results show how many people will buy specific products and services now—as well as what those people will be buying as they grow older.

Many American businesses are already capitalizing on the data gathered from the Consumer Expenditure Survey program. For example, major grocery chains use the data to determine when to open new stores in a particular area, when to close stores in others, and which products to sell in each store as their local shopping populations mature. A huge number of teenagers live in my own neighborhood, and within a $2^1/_2$-mile radius, we have a Super Safeway, a Super King Market, and a Super Albertson's.

Ironically, investors are not using this same information as they develop their investment strategies, but rather are overlooking the concrete economic predictors that we have shown do exist.

WEALTH INSIGHT: The same sequential spending pattern of the average American family is exhibited in an important moment in our nation's history—the Great Depression.

The history books tell us that the ultimate cause of the Great Depression was a run on banks. Since the U.S. government hadn't insured those banks, they were unable to provide sufficient payouts, leaving people penniless. However, these events encompass only the end of the story, the beginning of which may be traced to immigration.

Between 1820 and 1914, the U.S. population exploded, primarily due to a rapid influx of immigrants. From the Ellis Island records, we know that the average age of these immigrants was 30. When World War I began in 1914, the United States abruptly ended its immigration program. For the next 16 years, the economy prospered until 1929. What was missing was the huge group of immigrant consumers who would have fueled the economy with their peak spending habits. The Great Depression ensued.

Spending Cycles Close to Home (or Why Most Small Businesses Don't Work)

To get a precise estimate of the age breakdown in your own neighborhood, go to www.factfinder.census.gov, where you can generate a spreadsheet of the demographics of the area, and even a population distribution, by entering your address, county, and zip code. It will work for your hometown or anyplace else.

The FactFinder Web site also enables you to compare U.S. population data to your local area. For example, you can compare the population of Fresno, California, to the United States in general and learn a tremendous amount about Fresno (in less than two minutes). What you discover is that Fresno has a very high population of people in the 50 to 64 age range, very few in their 40s, and even fewer kids. From that information, you can surmise, for example, that lawn mowing services run by kids probably make a fortune in Fresno due to the lack of competition.

So with consumer spending pattern information in mind, you can then look at what the people in Fresno are potentially doing now and will be doing next. You can examine those services and products that should be doing well in Fresno compared to those that are doing well across the country in general. You can compare populations to get a sense of what's going on locally.

Now, let's look at another town—Clovis, California—which seems like an emerging nation compared with Fresno. There are very few people in the 55 to 59 age range. The bulk of the population in Clovis is primarily young people who are doing very different things than the people in Fresno.

A good strategy to use when determining spending cycles is to create a timeline for the period that interests you. For instance, my very simple timeline of when people peak in their spending tells me that they buy new cars at age 54, and their wine consumption peaks at age 56. Why? Because at age 56, the doctor says no more hard alcohol—just two glasses of wine a day. Dry cleaning peaks at 56. Catering bills increase at age 57. Again, why? Because children are getting married, people are hosting 30-year wedding anniversary celebrations, etc. Campers peak in purchasing at 58, and there is an increase in newspaper purchases at 74.

> **WEALTH INSIGHT:** A great business idea for today would be to have a newspaper with larger or bolder print. And that paper would include just the stories from subject areas you select—not all the other stuff.

Once you create a timeline of when people buy consumer goods, you can look at the population of the year that you're interested in and create a spending cycle based on these products. You can also create a timeline within a local area, tracking spending on different products and services. Business owners already know that this works and charities are very interested in this type of data. The chart in Exhibit 2.4 shows spending waves in our economy.

Spending Cycles Move in Waves

Exhibit 2.4 **Peak Spending versus Family Formation**

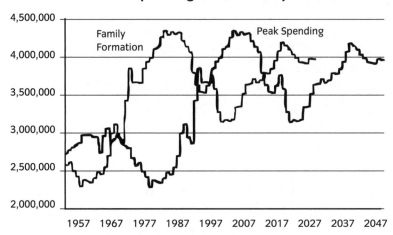

WHAT YOU'RE LOOKING AT: The exhibit comes from HS Dent and shows spending waves in our economy.

WHAT THIS TELLS YOU: When spending should grow, stall, and decline almost five decades out.

WHAT THIS MEANS: By studying spending waves, you can make a prediction about the future. You don't have to make a big leap of faith in order for spending waves—or any of the three factors—to work. And the more you can predict, the more you can manage.

• • • • • •

WEALTH INSIGHT: For a small retail business to be successful in the old days, you needed three things: location, location, and location. For success in today's world, you need information on the ages of your customers, their spending cycles based on age, and what season of the economy you're in. Along those lines, I'll tell you the following story:

Years ago, my family went on vacation to Palm Springs. As we walked down the main street in town, I remarked to myself that in a town which generally conjures up images of old, wealthy people, there were tons of baby and children's stores. The reason why was not, of course, that old people have babies, but rather that grandmas shop for grandkids. And so as I walked down the street in Palm Springs, I had the gut feeling that there was something terribly wrong with a place that had five baby stores and all old people. But once I understood the three factors at work, *click*—I knew what was going on.

I then looked specifically for men's clothing stores—and there were none. Again, I knew from the three factors that men over age 55 spend virtually nothing on clothes. So if you were a tailor or a clothing retailer and you thought to yourself, "Gee, I'm going to open a men's clothing shop in Palm Springs and really deck out those old, rich people," you'd likely go bankrupt.

Again, the factors tell us precisely when populations begin to work; when the face of that working population will change; and when large age groups buy houses and cars, travel, and spend at their peak. It follows that we may predict spending patterns with a level of accuracy as high as 92 percent, and that our demographic spending trends should peak and begin to decline around 2010.

The Common Sense Machine

Imagine that you have access to a hypothetical machine that is designed to read and record traditional investment data. Only this machine has an additional feature: a *Common Sense* meter, which makes a loud buzzing sound when something doesn't compute.

You set the instrument to record different investment sectors, the average returns of those sectors, volatility and risk, short-term swings in the market, and the average volatility of each sector as it moves up and down over different time periods. You are attempting to compare patterns of volatility, trying to determine which sectors have similar price movements. The machine should show you different asset allocation models, depending on the level of risk you're willing to take in order to get the return you desire.

You flip the machine's switch, but all the warning lights start flashing.

You recheck your data, thinking, "This can't be right. All of my programming is based on the classic asset allocation strategy established by Harry Markowitz in the 1950s and used extensively by Roger Ibbotson and others during the last 20 years," which you assume means that on a risk-adjusted basis, you should have outperformed the S&P 500. The problem is that the machine's red warning light began flashing—meaning, you didn't.

Buzz, buzz, buzz ... buzz. Buzz.

How could this be? The answer is because for the first time in history, a large population is being followed by a smaller one.

You reenter all past investment returns, their degree of correlation or similar movements, their risk, and their standard deviation for each time period.

Buzz, buzz, buzz ... buzz. Buzz. Wrong again!

You refeed this data back into your machine once again, then sit back and wait for it to crunch the numbers, make comparisons, and arrive at your recommended asset mix. But something still goes wrong. You even recheck your numbers yet another time. Did it apply classic asset allocation going back to the 1920s? Check. You did everything right.

WEALTH INSIGHT: Big problems come from using 70 years of data for positioning a portfolio for the next 10 years or so. Our economy went through many extreme seasons during those 70-plus years. Having the same portfolio strategy through all of these economic seasons would be

like wearing a light raincoat year-round in New York because the average
weather forecast is 50 degrees with 0.2 inches of rain daily.

Buzz, buzz, buzz … buzz. Buzz.

As the Common Sense buzzer keeps blaring, a visual printout explains that your data have four fundamental flaws:

1. No human beings alive today have the 70-year investment horizon included in the classic asset allocation model.

2. The average of the economic conditions of the last 70 years doesn't take into account dramatically different long-term seasons in our current economy.

3. The data that you input do not give a precise picture of the economic conditions for the next 10 years.

4. The asset classes used in classic asset allocation were too broad.

With these four points in mind, you feed a new timeline into the machine, reflecting the current average investor's horizon of three to five years, and you hope to measure the success of an investment strategy within that time frame and then adjust accordingly.

Sadly, the buzzer blares and a red light flashes as the machine spits out another data challenge. The printout explains that the reason analysts have traditionally used the very broad asset categories of large cap, small cap, fixed income, and international is that these are the only categories for which they have data that goes back several decades.

Yet there are many large sectors—some that have emerged only in recent decades—that are very suitable for diversifying risk. These sectors, which include technology, financial services, health care, and Asia, represent the best sectors of returns in the 1990s and should continue to outperform in the coming decade due to predictable demographic trends.

Consumer Expenditure Survey Captures Spending Cycles

As I discussed earlier in this chapter, consumer spending habits are predictable by age. On average, consumers purchase goods and services at set times in their lives. This information is compiled by the U.S. government in its Consumer Expenditure Survey, which studies the spending habits of thousands of consumers. The exhaustive survey is conducted annually and asks consumers to compile a diary of expenditures, including items as small as vending machine purchases. This information is free to anyone.

CASE STUDY: Peter Johnson

DENTIST

One of my favorite clients, Peter Johnson, ran a pediatric dental practice in North Denver that was struggling to the point where Peter wondered, "This is a growing area—why don't I have more business?" He was right—the area was growing—but not (yet) in the way he needed. Peter's business required kids, but all of the growth at the time was in young adults who didn't yet have those kids. Children don't need a pediatric dentist until around age six, and the young adults weren't going to become parents for two to four more years, so he was still eight to ten years away from a profitable patient base.

I suggested to Peter that we pull the demographic data for that zip code and compare it to other zip codes. I pulled up the information and found an area called Lonetree (a suburb south of metro Denver) that looked promising in terms of a pediatric patient population. Peter's business was currently located a bit north of metro Denver. I said, "Peter, if you look down in Lonetree, the area has roughly four times more kids in the age group that would need a pediatric dentist." Being a bright guy, he sold the place up north, started a new practice in south Denver and had so much business that he had to add other dentists to the practice.

Peter just didn't have the numbers—he didn't have the factors. But I had the factors, and when we put them together, it became obvious where the business would and wouldn't grow. Now's the time to make sure your advisory team understands your current and future businesses and investments in businesses.

All of us have goods and services that we need or want at certain times. We consume certain things at certain ages: higher education around age 18 to 22; multifamily housing in the form of apartments between 18 to 26; marriage-related services around age 26; and baby-related products at 28.

At about age 31, we purchase our first house, incurring our highest amount of debt so far as a percentage of our income. We trade up to our most expensive home at around age 42, with our largest mortgage by age 42, and we peak in our spending between 46 to 50, or 48 on average. Our first round of vacation homes comes at about age 48; resort travel around 54; and a second round of vacation and retirement homes around age 63.

Exhibit 2.5 reflects this type of information taken from the Consumer Expenditure Survey.

Exhibit 2.5 **Consumer Expenditure Life Cycle (Key Consumer Expenditures and Investments)**

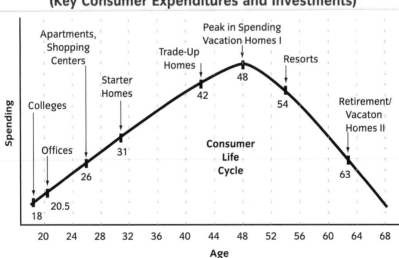

WHAT YOU'RE LOOKING AT: The exhibit comes from HS Dent and shows spending patterns over a consumer's life cycle.

WHAT THIS TELLS YOU: The ages when people make large purchases.

WHAT THIS MEANS: The histogram enables us to deduce certain behaviors at certain points in a person's life.

• • • • • •

An extremely simple example is that we can assume that on average, Americans spend the most on potato chips when they're 42 years old. They're not buying potato chips for themselves, of course, but for their teenage kids.

Yet it's not enough to know that 42-year-olds spend the most on potato chips. We also need to know how many of those 42-year-olds there are in the population, and whether the number is increasing or decreasing. These same types of behaviors take place in products, which also have a life cycle that is strongly correlated with spending. See Exhibit 2.6.

Exhibit 2.6 **The Classic S-Curve**

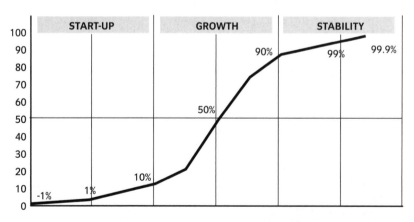

WHAT YOU'RE LOOKING AT: What is commonly known as the classic S-Curve, which is sometimes referred to as the product life cycle display.

WHAT THIS TELLS YOU: It has three distinct sections: start-up, growth, and stability. Each of these sections takes approximately the same length of time to complete—so generally speaking, if a product takes 14 years to move through start-up phase, from 0.1 percent market penetration to 10 percent market penetration, then it will also take approximately 14 years to move through the growth stage, from 10 percent market penetration to 90 percent market penetration. Finally, it will take another 14 years to move through a stability phase, from 90 percent to maximum market penetration.

The S-Curve in the exhibit is closely related to the stages of another curve—the Product Diffusion Curve—that describes four different classes of buyers or users: early adopters, early majority, late majority, and laggards.

WHAT THIS MEANS: That each group has specific attributes and adopts a product or service at a different point on the curve.

••••••

Exhibit 2.7 shows the classic S-Curve in cars.

Exhibit 2.7 **The S-Curve in Cars**

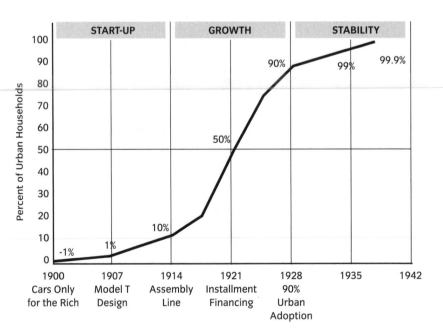

WHAT YOU'RE LOOKING AT: The product life cycle of the automobile.

WHAT THIS TELLS YOU: You can trace the start-up phase to the point when the car became stable as a product. Look at cell phones as another example. During the 1980s and early 1990s (the innovation phase for this product-service), the cost of the technology was very high, and the ability to connect was very low because there were so few cell towers available. At that time, everyone was jockeying for position.

If you want to feed these details into your hypothetical machine to forecast an economic change, you start by combining the demographics and the product life cycle. Once the information is combined, you then develop a forecast of (1) long-term economic seasons and (2) what areas of the economy should be outperforming for years to come.

WHAT THIS MEANS: Not only do you know what people most likely will be buying, but you also know where those products and services are in their product life cycle. You can see how this knowledge is invaluable when added to the investment process.

••••••

Think back over the last two decades, and you'll remember that large-cap stocks had their best periods in history—while international stocks underperformed, and small caps lagged. The point here is that the two leaders of the 1980s and 1990s were the same ones as in the previous cycle. Small caps outperformed large caps by one of the widest margins ever in the previous cycle; many international sectors like Japan outperformed due to a very different generation spending cycle; and many emerging countries benefited from rising natural resource prices. Real estate had wonderful performance in the 1970s, as it represented a leveraged hedge against inflation, and the baby-boom generation was moving strongly into its commercial, multifamily, and starter home cycle of spending.

Why do these different sectors perform so differently over time? Because every product and company has a life cycle, and the variable is when each sector of the population predictably spends its earnings on the different products.

But What about Inflation?

Most people don't really understand inflation; they believe that it's caused by the government printing money. While that's true in the short term, it's not true in the long run.

Inflation is simply a monetary phenomenon, a natural mechanism in our economy. Inflation correlates most closely with the entry of new generations into the workforce, which happens at age 20, on average. How could this be? Because it's not just the family paying for kids, it's also the government paying to educate them and businesses paying to incorporate them into the workforce. But after their initial introduction into the workforce, those newly minted employees become productive citizens—earning, producing, and spending more.

Did you know that our U.S. inflation rates peaked around 19 years after the peak in baby-boom births? *Click*—have you ever considered that inflation may be a direct result of the birthrate factor? If this knowledge was widely known in the years preceding the 1970s, we could have predicted that the decade would be a terrible era for long-term bonds (as interest rates went up and bond prices dropped), and that 1981 to 1995 would be a great era for bonds (as interest rates dropped and bond prices increased). It would have shown that valuations on large-cap stocks would fall in the 1970s and rise from the early 1980s into the late 1990s.

All the bright young people drive this trend, particularly those emerging from college at age 22 who join companies or start their own. Small-cap stocks benefit the most from the new innovations that emerge, as these companies are faster to respond to new technology and product trends.

WEALTH INSIGHT: Large companies are less likely to—or take longer to—accept innovation. They're better at exploiting mainstream markets, not new niche markets.

Armed with this knowledge, we can address the question: "What's the best time to buy small-cap stocks?" Answer: "At the bottom of the worst crashes and in the very early stages of the next boom." And when do large caps do the best? When products are moving out of niche markets into mainstream markets, as the generation moves up its spending cycle into its peak at about age 48. In other words, large companies perform best when their economy of scale efficiencies allow them to dominate and take over what until then would've been small-growth niche markets. This low-cost distribution model allows them to dominate profitably.

Throughout this section, we've explored how a person's spending and/or investing surges to its peak from ages 38 to 54. But remember, unlike spending, investment is a cumulative process. Your net worth expands as you move into your mid-sixties; after that, you begin to spend what you have saved to finance your retirement. Imagine an entire generation moving through this age range.

Wealth Factor Three: Seasons of the Economy

The third—and perhaps the most important—wealth factor to consider is what is referred to as the *Seasons of the Economy*, which are represented visually in Exhibit 2.8. To understand this factor, I like to use the metaphor of weather, which provides parallels that can help you predict the future of our economy. Like the seasons of the year, we have four economic seasons that comprise the basis of the financial world. Each of the seasons has a different set of characteristics that can affect your investment assets. These seasons of our economy dictate which businesses or investment categories you should own.

Exhibit 2.8 **Understanding the Economic Seasons**

| The Seasons of the Economy

Know what causes investments to go up or down during the different economic seasons | Spring

Planting | Summer

Growing | Fall

Harvesting | Winter

Protecting |

WEALTH INSIGHT: To predict the weather, today's typical meteorologist uses billions of bits of data and the fastest conceivable parallel computers. Why, then, does the Farmers' Almanac consistently prove to be much more reliable? How can this 189-year-old publication continue to predict long-range weather forecasts with amazing 85 percent accuracy? Because weather patterns are predictable. The authors avoided the use of too much information when making predictions, relying instead on only the most salient factors. Keep this in mind when forecasting your own economic future.

Spring

In spring, everything begins to heat up again after lying dormant during the winter season. New products and technologies emerge into the economy or "blossom" after their invention or incubation stage in the preceding winter, which occurs following the decline of the last growth cycle. Growth and demand rise from the new technology cycle, but that also extends the applications of older, maturing technologies. At first, supply may lag behind growing demand, needing time and investments to ramp up. Waning productivity from the larger, older industries also trumps the rising productivity of the smaller, newly emerging industries. Finally, inflation rises more substantially than it slows.

Summer

Summer is marked by exponential growth and increasing inflation rates, as demand rapidly outstrips supply. This is the period in which businesses grow and expand. It's also a period of rising prices that encourage expanding investments to build up capacity, eventually leading to overexpansion and falling rates of inflation as the season moves into autumn.

Autumn

When economic temperatures begin to cool, inflation rates flatten or drop at first, and a brief recession from overexpansion occurs due to slowing growth rates. This is followed by a boom into the maturity stage, which sees full penetration of the new technologies into society and the economy, much like the final colors of the autumn season in the Northeast as the days grow shorter. During autumn, growth rates tend to plateau, and a period of disinflation is also possible. The strongest booms tend to take place later in this season. That combination creates the best environment for stock prices and valuation of most investment assets, including real estate. This is when we see bubbles in the stock market due to the irrational exuberance about the potential of the new technologies.

Winter

Winter can be a hard and uncertain time—a period of slowing or perhaps no growth at all. For business, it can be a period of plummeting profit margins. Only the strongest survive these periods of lengthy consolidation. Those that do would be expected to dominate into the future. The many growth companies and competitors from the spring season continue to narrow down to become the few dominant leaders.

If you study these economic seasons and their associated "weather" patterns, you will know when an economic winter is coming and when the winds of change are likely to start blowing in. You can then plan sufficiently for economic seasonal events. You don't need to cut the old tree down in May—it will provide shade in June, July, and August. But come September, before the winds start blowing, you want the tree to come down. This doesn't mean that you shouldn't diversify or use asset allocation. But roughly around the summer of 2009 into 2010, you may want to have your systematic liquidation strategy ready to implement. I present a specific systematic liquidation strategy with a timeline in Chapter 10.

WEALTH INSIGHT: An economic winter is a good time to send kids to college, as applications to top universities tend to drop off when parents can't afford the extra expense of tuition. It's also possible that tuition costs may stop increasing or even drop.

The most important insight here is that different seasons clearly favor some sectors of investments and disfavor others. The 1990s were characterized by low inflation, high productivity, and strong economic growth (as we are projecting from the present until 2010–2011). The 1980s saw growth with strong disinflation, exploding debt ratios, and lower productivity rates. The 1970s was a season of recessions, stagnant productivity, and the highest inflation in modern history.

It goes all the way back to classic Keynesian economics as to how people spend money—and they spend based on their standard of living. We will do anything to protect this standard; after all, it's easy to go up, hard to go down. So while consumers may feel like they're getting poorer if their 401(k) values and their stock portfolios are going down, they won't start spending less until they either don't need to spend more or simply can't spend more.

WEALTH INSIGHT: Do you remember where you were when you first heard about 9/11? I was in my office when a friend called me and asked, "Did you hear what just happened? A plane accidentally hit the World Trade Center."

"No way," I thought, "planes don't hit the World Trade Center." Yet I turned on the news, and there it was. Then the second plane hit, and everything shut down, including the bond market. Some really good trades were put on that morning right before the second plane hit, and there were a lot of people buying the safety of U.S. Treasuries.

The markets were shut down for four days. You couldn't buy or sell anything. There wasn't a lot to do except watch the news and worry. But you and I did something pretty amazing—we kept spending money. In fact, we've spent more money every single quarter since 9/11/2001. Behaviorists suggest that people spend less when they are fearful. I don't know anybody who wasn't fearful after 9/11; yet we kept spending.

The Season of Today's Economy

Today, it appears that we've just been through a normal seasonal shakeout, and now we're seeing brilliant and colorful summer growth as we move toward the winter season.

The demographic data have guided us accurately to this point. Our three wealth factors have helped to keep us on track. We knew when and how many people were born, so we could conclude that they would keep spending, as well as how intensely they would spend. We currently have record corporate earnings and productivity, with the highest household net worth and some of the lowest unemployment rates in history. We know that we as consumers are spending money, or these data points couldn't exist. And we know this trend will go on for a certain number of years. In fact, we can foresee the trend lasting for three or four more years, because the people who are causing it—the baby boomers—haven't yet hit the peak of their spending. From the Consumer Expenditure Survey, we expect that will happen in roughly 2009–2010.

> **WEALTH INSIGHT:** Here is a simple test that you can do to determine the heath of the economy: become a social scientist.
>
> The next time you go to the local mall, notice how full the mall's parking lot is. Last year, I went to a mall in southwest Denver. I can usually park reasonably close to the structure at a distance of about 50 yards. But on that day, I couldn't even get into the lot. I had to park at a different lot across the street. I had the same problem at another major mall in town, where I had to park about half a mile away and take a shuttle bus to the mall. My sister, who lives in Hawaii, recently told me that she had experienced the same problem in her area.
>
> When you get inside the mall, take note of what people have in their hands. Is it a purse or backpack—or is it a bag from a store like Lord & Taylor, Nordstrom, or the Gap? Today, people's arms are most likely overflowing with merchandise from all of those stores. People don't go shopping if they don't have any money. So I knew from my sample at the mall, when I saw the vast majority of people spending a lot of money, that the economy was pretty healthy.
>
> Start to look at your own life through social scientist glasses and make observations about the everyday activities around you. Then, overlay these observations onto the wealth factors we've discussed in this chapter. Then you can predict both the season we're currently in and where we're likely headed in the future.

Early Warning Indicators That Winter Is Approaching

Right now, I think we're in the really wonderful growth state of late summer. You could say there's a fine line between this period and early fall, when all is in full bloom and growing—a very enjoyable period. But let's say you start to see spending beginning to slow. That will mean that companies will make less money, which ultimately means that the economy will contract, and it's likely that employees will be laid off. This drop in consumer spending is a warning that the seasons are transitioning toward winter...so you need to be transitioning your portfolio in advance of that.

The following is a list of The Seven Winter Warning Signs to keep in mind as you attempt to determine when the next seasonal change is in process. I go into more specific detail on each of these signs in Chapter 10.

1. Personal Consumption Expenditures (www.bea.gov) drop for three consecutive months or more.

2. Big institutions begin to move their money. Is it flowing into or out of various sectors?

3. Leading Economic Indicators (LEI) trend down for three to four months. (You can find the LEI at www.businesscycle.com.)

4. Employment rate: A flattening then downward trend in non-farm employment with a flattening to decreasing after-tax income (www.bls.gov).

5. Durable goods spending flattens and/or decreases for two or more quarters. (You can find this information at www.census.gov/indicator/www/m3.)

6. Two down quarters of S&P 500 earnings-per-share growth. (This is reported in all major newspaper business sections.)

7. Changing inflation and/or deflation numbers: an interruption to the consistent but modest increase in the cost we all pay for goods and services (www.bls.gov/cpi).

Does all of this mean that you can predict your own future? I believe that you can start to get very close, if you focus on the wealth factors, stop listening to the noise in the media, and think for yourself.

CHAPTER

CORRECTION PROTECTION

Exhibit 3.1 **Correction Protection**

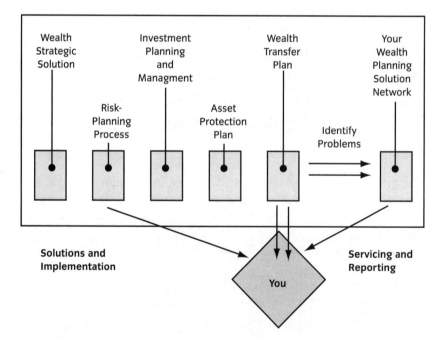

WHAT YOU'RE LOOKING AT: The essential factors involved in protecting yourself against economic corrections.

WHAT THIS TELLS YOU: The matrix indicates that there are several considerations to take into account when developing a protective plan for your assets—there's no one-factor-cures-all approach.

WHAT THIS MEANS: Clearly, there's a lot to consider, so start your planning as early as possible.

• • • • • •

recently asked one of my clients, "What has to happen over the next five years for you to feel satisfied with your progress?"

"I work for the next five years, retire, and then move," he said.

"Do you have a forecast on how the economy might impact your actions?" I asked.

He replied: "No. I guess it's just too much to think about."

My client failed to follow the fundamental law of nature: protection of the nest egg. How does nature protect it? In the most basic form, the tree protects the nest, and the nest protects the eggs. Nature uses a double protection structure to ensure its future—and you should, too.

WEALTH INSIGHT: On May 15, 2006, the *Los Angeles Times* ran an article discussing the investment practices of past winners of the Nobel Prize for economics. The *Times* found that a number of Nobel Laureates didn't follow even basic financial planning concepts when investing their own nest eggs.

Perhaps most surprising was their discussion of Nobel Prize winner Harry Markowitz, who is generally credited as being the father of Modern Portfolio Theory (MPT), an investment discipline that stresses diversification among various asset classes to reduce portfolio risk. In 1952, Markowitz scientifically proved the old adage "You shouldn't put all of your eggs in one basket." In 1990, he won a Nobel Prize for his efforts.

The *LA Times* article pointed out that Markowitz, however, has been less than diligent in practicing what he preached. Even though the MPT recommends wide diversification, Markowitz split all of his money right down the middle, with half in a stock fund and the other half in a conservative, low-yield investment. He now admits that he should have allocated more of his assets to stocks when he was younger, but the fact remains that he wasn't very good at following his own advice—and he's not alone among his peers.

George Akerlof, a 2001 winner of the Nobel Prize in economics, currently has a significant percentage of his investments in money market accounts, which have very low returns. He confesses, "I know it's utterly stupid." Nevertheless, his personal investment strategy seems to fly in the face of discoveries by prior Nobel Prize winners.

In all, the *LA Times* surveyed 11 Nobel Prize winners in economics from this decade and several others from the 1990s, and many admit that they fail to manage their retirement savings properly. The most often found faux pas was that they had too much of their money invested in low-yielding, conservative investments rather than in stocks that have historically provided better returns.

The *Times* went further and asked Harvard University about the investment habits of its faculty. The paper found that an estimated 50 percent of Harvard's faculty and staff put all or most of their retirement savings into low-yield money market accounts. In many cases, contributions were left in money market funds simply because the faculty and staff didn't bother to provide any investment direction (advice) for their accounts.

Let's recap what we've discussed so far. Tens of millions of baby boomers will turn 60 by 2009, and the ensuing decade will see vast numbers of these boomers retiring, or at least leaving their current full-time careers. We've seen proof of how the baby boomers drive 70 percent of the economy, leading us to ask ourselves, How will their upcoming mass migration out of the workforce affect us, our children, and our retirement? And what are we doing to plan around it?

WEALTH INSIGHT: It's interesting to note that many of today's companies have downsized and cut out the middle, leaving them with the following organizational structure: a huge group of older people—the baby boomers—who are nearing retirement, a lot of young people in their 20s and early 30s, and not enough people in between. According to David W. DeLong, a research fellow and head of the workforce unit at the Massachusetts Institute of Technology's Age Lab (as well as the author of *Lost Knowledge: Confronting the Threat of an Aging Workforce*), companies most at risk from the coming brain drain are those "with established, traditional cultures where people have spent 20 years or more."

We've also come to understand that the way retired baby boomers will spend their money is going to determine the next *season of the economy*—the economic spring, summer, winter, or fall in which the "climate" mirrors the characteristics of the corresponding season in nature (for example, an economic winter includes rough times with plummeting profit margins, which would in turn cause reduced equity prices). Before each season ends, you need to have a map that overlays the new season's factors onto your life, so that you can anticipate what will happen next and plan accordingly. As outlined at the end of Chapter 2, I call these changing economic signposts The Seven Winter Warning Signs, which I cover in more detail in both Chapter 10 and on my Web site, www.wealthstratgroup.com.

So far we know what's on the horizon for consumer spending: the single largest spenders in the nation—baby boomers—will soon be retiring en masse and therefore spending less money as well as spending money in different ways. We also know what entities to avoid—traditional advisors and the media—when developing our plan to protect ourselves against any negative repercussions of this spending shift.

Preventive Planning Starts with
The Wealth Planning Strategy™

Armed with this information, you're now ready to begin building out your protection plan. Let's start by outlining some concrete strategies that you can use to formulate your plan. I'm going to focus on what I call *correction protection*, which is occasionally referred to as wealth preservation planning. The core ideas behind this concept are as follows:

1. Correction protection is the basis of wealth protection. It involves identifying exposure to the risk of loss of capital, evaluating methods of preventing and protecting against such loss, and ongoing monitoring of both risks and solutions.

2. Correction protection planning encompasses a wide variety of conservative investment activities.

3. There are several effective techniques that you can use to protect your assets against unforeseen events.

A personal correction protection program focuses on minimizing risks to one's property, life, health, and assets as well as risks faced by family and dependents. The development of a sophisticated risk management solution requires input from an experienced team of professionals—*not* the average investment advisor (salesperson) who is motivated simply by the number of products sold and commission received.

This experienced team, whom I refer to as The Solution Network™, will consist of selective professionals who truly understand the core concepts behind effective protection planning and have mastered the complexities of various techniques. By helping the investor to identify and quantify possible losses in this way, the team enables the investor to gain a better overall picture of his or

Exhibit 3.2 **The Wealth Planning Strategy**

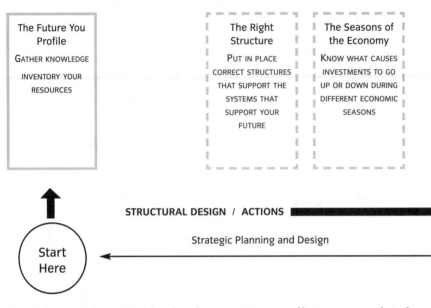

her risks and the critical role of prevention. I talk in greater detail about the wealth management dream team in Chapter 4.

The Wealth Planning Strategy is my term for all of the steps that lead to a successful wealth management plan. At our firm, The Wealth Strategies Group, we begin to develop this plan by collecting comprehensive details about a client's life. The details include significant life events and timelines. We then marry this information with investments that work best during different seasons of the economy. Finally, we put all of this information into a hardbound book that becomes our client's customized wealth road map. I've found that this holistic approach provides clients with the confidence to help them make the right investment decisions throughout their lives.

The information in Exhibit 3.2 is the eight-step, trademarked course of action that I use when working with a client, and what your own team of advisors should use to create your Wealth Planning Strategy:

The Wealth Maximizer	The Asset Protection and Estate Transfer Process	Legal Transfer Strategies	The Solution Network
MATCH THE CURRENT YOU TO THE FUTURE YOU	PUT IN PLACE WHAT IS NEEDED TO PROTECT ASSET FROM WRONGFUL LAWSUITS	UNDERSTAND WHAT IT TAKES TO TRANSFRE WEALTH EFFECTIVELY	CONSULT WITH OUTSIDE EXPERTS TO ENSURE SUCCESS
WHAT TYPES OF INVESTMENT STRATEGIES DOES IT TAKE TO GET YOU THERE			

Execute, Observe, and Repeat

Endless Family Progress
You now have a road map in place that can keep you on track and show you what's next

WHAT YOU'RE LOOKING AT: The eight steps involved in The Wealth Planning Strategy.

WHAT THIS TELLS YOU: The eight steps are named:

Step 1: The Future You Profile™

Step 2: The Right Structure

Step 3: The Seasons of the Economy Advantage™

Step 4: The Wealth Management Maximizer™

Step 5: The Asset Protection and Estate Transfer Process

Step 6: Legal Transfer Strategies

Step 7: The Solution Network™

Step 8: Endless Family Progress

WHAT THIS MEANS: Your best bet for creating an effective correction protection approach is to follow a thorough, sequential series of steps, rather than simply trying to plan piecemeal.

●●●●●●●

Step 1: The Future You Profile

What difference does it make how much you earn or accumulate if you forfeit all (or a large percentage) of your asset base to frivolous lawsuits or unnecessary federal estate taxes? Developing a Future You Profile is the first step in shielding that base, enabling you to articulate the critical life information and goals that you'll need to create the underlying structure for your asset protection plan.

To develop your Future You Profile, write down the details of a compelling "future." These details include answers to questions such as, What are my personal life goals? What are my financial goals and objectives? What is my vision for myself and my family in one, three, five years, and beyond? Until now, what has been my financial strategy to achieve that vision? At this stage, you also identify any potential roadblocks, setbacks, dangers, opportunities, and/or strengths in your life.

CASE STUDY: Anna Chatham

SURGEON

My prospective client, Anna Chatham, a successful surgeon, had built up an impressive net worth. Our Wealth Strategies Group started working with Anna and her husband by having the Future You Profile discussion. Together, we identified their future dangers, opportunities, and strengths.

The couple identified reduced future cash flow, out-of-date estate documents, and uncertainty about their many scattered investments as potential dangers. They also believed that there may be economic opportunities for them outside of medicine—namely, a small business. They felt that the confidence they had from the dollar amount of the assets they had built up over the years was their biggest strength.

Step 2: The Right Structure

Structure is a large part of the Wealth Planning Strategy creation process. This step is so important to your overall plan that I've dedicated all of Chapter 4 to discussing it in more detail. For now, I'll simply tell you that the wrong structure can keep you stuck in a rut whereas the right one can liberate you. In fact, the right structure in any system is often more important than the individual components that make up the system.

Make a Life Map

Once you complete the Future You Profile, you must then begin to synthesize the profile's most important points into a working structure for your financial future. To help reveal the essential information that you need for your structure, you can put the written details of your Future You Profile into a visual map. The visual experience is often the most effective way to learn, so by creating this map you can better absorb the importance of what you'll do and where you'll go throughout your life.

WEALTH INSIGHT: Nobel Prize–winning physicist Murray Gell-Mann has said that the most valuable personal trait in the twenty-first century is the ability to synthesize information. This capacity to decide what information to heed and what to ignore often reveals nonobvious relationships within big-picture complexity. All the needed pieces of information may be close at hand, but they're often hidden from view.

Making a visual representation of cause-and-effect connections can help you to thoroughly think through all possible sources of a problem. This representation becomes a navigational aid that you can use to see, plot, and organize information and dates. Narrative lists, on the other hand, tend to be one-dimensional. Collecting and even prioritizing all activities in lists doesn't always demonstrate causality or connections—or how events contribute to a desired outcome. However, when you plot activities on a visual chart, an overall plan becomes apparent.

The exercise of creating a visual map uncovers high and low value asset protection activities while at the same time revealing unexplored opportunities. Finally, it supplements the Future You Profile as another permanent record of your investment path.

Exhibit 3.3 **The Moving Parts of Master Life Mapping**

WHAT YOU'RE LOOKING AT: A representation of the many moving parts at play in the master map of your financial life.

WHAT THIS TELLS YOU: This visual representation of the various demands on your money really drives home the point that there are many complex life factors to take into consideration when planning your financial future.

WHAT THIS MEANS: Plan early—and often!

••••••

Your visual strategy map should resemble the example in Exhibit 3.3. You can see how the life goals and objectives are clearly called out in the map, making it much easier to determine how various types of investment portfolios will perform relative to these goals and objectives—and then to make decisions or adjustments accordingly. By visually monitoring your steps using your own map, you'll clearly see when your actions aren't meeting your expectations or are moving you in a different direction than your goals.

I adapted the concept of visual planning from effective project planning theory and NASA (National Aeronautics and Space Administration). By using this structure, you'll help to ensure that your plans are fully considered, well focused, resilient, practical, and cost-effective. Merely by shifting your thinking from the norm of linear, narrative-based planning to visually plotting on the map, you'll increase your overall awareness of your life circumstances and financial goals. You'll also learn from any mistakes that you may make and feed the knowledge that you've gained back into future planning and decision making.

WEALTH INSIGHT: NASA found that traditional planning methods were ineffective in formulating high-level projects such as moon landings, because these methods didn't allow complex systems to be integrated into the big picture.

The most important step in making a visual map is to establish criteria for what information to include and what to discard. Expand your awareness by allowing your mind to zero in on one strategy or activity, then pull back to see how that strategy or activity connects or relates to everything else. Don't allow yourself to be overwhelmed or distracted by unimportant details.

Once you see how the activities interconnect and identify what actually constitutes a successful outcome, you'll feel more confident about the course of future actions. For example, you may have a goal of liquidity, but the asset protection strategy being presented has a holding period of 10 years. And competing with that goal are issues such as minimizing the number of hours that you want to work. It's the resolution of these competing goals that characterizes the human decision process.

Stage 1: Choose a Central Theme

You'll establish the structural design of your visual map in two stages. The first is to choose a central theme. The more you shape your actions around one clear idea, the better your chances for success. (See Exhibit 3.4.) This theme anchors every activity and should resonate in every decision you make. After you choose your central theme, draw a circle in the center of a piece of paper, and write in the theme.

Exhibit 3.4 **Choosing a Central Theme**

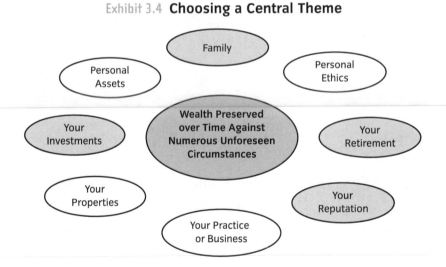

WHAT YOU'RE LOOKING AT: An example of what you'll do in the first stage of developing your visual map.

WHAT THIS TELLS YOU: This exercise helps you put a name to all of the things that may be affected by a change in your financial situation.

WHAT THIS MEANS: Your central theme becomes the unifying force that shapes your strategic choices and keeps your efforts on track. You may eventually encounter the stress of a divorce, lawsuit, or death of a spouse or other loved one. Or you may simply want to look more closely toward the future, seeking to better deploy your capital. For our example above, the controlling theme consists of one concise phrase: "Wealth preserved over time against numerous unforeseen circumstances."

● ● ● ● ● ●

Stage 2: Inventory Your Assets

In the second stage, you want to inventory your assets, collecting and reviewing your investments to evaluate whether they could be attracting liability. Gathering this information can be a daunting task. It requires two components: a method of organization and the patience to apply this method to the information. Information gathering also means going beyond the hard data to gain a clear understanding of your core values and objectives. Yet once the information-gathering process is complete, you can finally see the big picture.

Your primary goal in this stage is to find out where all your assets are. Compile copies of legal documents and other key documents: will(s); trusts (including revocable or irrevocable living trusts and charitable trusts); durable powers of attorney for assets and health care; divorce decrees as well as alimony and child support agreements; prenuptial agreements; stock purchase agreements; business buy/sell agreements; family limited partnerships; and your most recent tax return.

Regarding your investment accounts, ask yourself the following questions: What was your original objective in setting up the account? Are those goals being served? What has been your experience with the account? Are you happy with it? If you're contemplating a change, why do you feel the need for the change?

With these two stages complete, you can proceed with filling out the remaining sections of your visual map.

Step 3: The Seasons of the Economy Advantage

The next step along the way to creating a Wealth Planning Strategy is to select investment entities that fit the economic season. To learn more about which entities fit the particular season that we're in, you can go to my Web site at www.wealthstratgroup.com and view an educational slide presentation that will help you to determine both the current season and how you should plant (or harvest) your assets

Step 4: The Wealth Management Maximizer

Now that you know where you want to go in your financial future—and which investment entities best fit the economic season—you can synchronize the two, ensuring your optimal outcome. In this step toward your Wealth Planning Strategy, you take the "current you" and determine what must change to make the "future you" a reality. The result is a targeted investment strategy that matches your constraints for time, risk, volatility, and economic seasons.

Step 5: The Asset Protection and Estate Transfer Process

The objective of this step is to help you protect your assets from creditors and to deter attachment of your assets. It will be of particular interest to you if you don't want to be recognized as a high net worth, high income person. The main protection activity here is to transfer ownership of those vehicles from which you receive money and control to other entities, such as trusts, limited liability partnerships, or regular partnerships. Other forms of protection exist as well.

This strategy of various forms of ownership and structures is designed to discourage attacks from attorneys who file frivolous (or perhaps even legitimate) lawsuits against high net worth individuals. The most effective asset protection processes will reduce an individual's net assets to what I call the "human zero"—meaning that the person's assets are not attackable in the event of a settlement, since the individual has zero net worth.

For a closer look at asset protection structures, see Chapter 4, "Structure and Methodology," where I delve much deeper into the topic.

Step 6: Legal Transfer Strategies

This step is a continuation of the prior step, The Asset Protection and Estate Transfer Process. It's also the last step that's likely to be based on information which you included in the Future You Profile. At this point, you establish a structure for the most efficient legal transfer of wealth to those you love.

A primary transfer strategy that you can employ is to have your assets put into a trust. As I mentioned in the last step, this decision protects your assets as well. If you're sued, you're not liable, because you technically don't own the assets. Rather, since the assets are owned by the trust, there's nothing for the plaintiff to attack. The beauty of certain trusts, such as an irrevocable trust, is that they are vehicles which you may influence. In an irrevocable trust, you can potentially receive money out of it—but it isn't owned by you.

Legal transfer strategies can also be a big help when your investment plan works and yields a big nest egg, even if you haven't properly planned for future tax liability. A few minor structural changes in titling and ownership can legally save an average investor who owns a home and a life insurance policy thousands and thousands of dollars in unnecessary taxes.

To learn more about how to avoid a huge tax hit, take a look at Appendix A, "The Life Planning Strategy Module—Legal Transfer Strategies," which covers my Tax Reduction Tool—a process that involves five levels of estate planning, which you can use depending on your particular objectives and circumstances.

CASE STUDY: Dan Wilson

BUSINESS OWNER AND ENTREPRENEUR

Dan Wilson, a long-time client and entrepreneur, wanted to restructure his company in an effort to segregate one operation of the company in order to take it public through an Initial Public Offering (IPO). As part of the preparation process, he engaged The Wealth Strategies Group to review the titling and ownership of the current structure.

Wilson's primary concerns were the effect that any changes in ownership would have on his current tax situation, as well as any federal estate tax (FET) that his family would face in the event of his passing.

Our group engaged members from The Solution Network™ (our virtual network containing tax, legal, and other investment professionals, which I cover in detail in Chapter 4), who determined that the current ownership structure was originally built to deter legal liability—a concern to most start-up operations. The Solution Network™ put additional tools in place to reduce Wilson's current income tax, capital gains tax, and future federal estate tax.

Wilson's shares in the "spin-off" portion of the company were put into an Estate Freeze Trust. The current corporate shares were exchanged for shares of equal value; however, the new shares wouldn't grow in value, that is, they were "frozen." His family beneficiaries were gifted preferred shares of the new entity where all future growth would be realized. Thus, the tax on future growth accrues to the preferred shares held by the heirs. Estates are required to pay taxes on unrealized gains, often forcing the business to be sold in a bad market or in a distress sale. With this strategy, Wilson had little or no estate tax while providing his heirs with the flexibility to continue operations or liquidate the company.

Wilson's non-spin-off assets were restructured in a Limited Partnership, in which he retained control as the general partner and the heirs as limited partners. This structure allowed him to transfer more assets to his heirs with less tax, as the ownership was a partial interest ownership. Partial interest assets can reduce the owner's estate value by as much as 30 percent and therefore reduce FET by approximately the same amount.

Any unrealized capital losses were taken to offset capital gains realized in the reconfiguration, resulting in a nearly nontaxable event. Finally, The Wealth Strategies Group suggested a Family Limited Partnership (FLP) to hold other illiquid real estate and private equity investments.

The recommended structure created a family holding company that convenes quarterly family board meetings, allowing the children to become involved and comfortable in the process of making financial decisions. The structure deters litigation through the ownership model. Transfer of assets to the next generation is assured by structure. The potential to continue as an operating business will not be interrupted from the need to sell for payment of Federal Estate Tax (FET). Current income tax and future Federal Estate Tax are greatly reduced leaving more of the assets for the heirs of our business owner.

Step

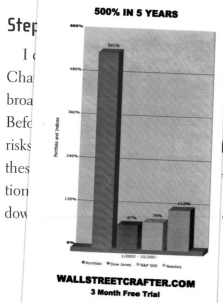

I ...   *ork*, and I discuss it in detail in
Cha...   are how this step relates to the
broa...   ssary, but how can we control it?
Befo...   take a look at the major kinds of
risks...   book to drill down into each of
thes...   , but if you'd like more information...   www.wealthstratgroup.com and
dow...   each topic:

1. *Rollover Risk:* I invented this term based on the negative effects of ill advice that I've begun to notice among my client base. There will be 75 million baby boomers retiring over the next 20 years—approximately one every 10 seconds. We're starting to see the very beginnings of taxation, penalization, and loss of stretch IRAs on what will amount to more than $13 trillion in rollovers from these boomers.

2. *Market Risk:* In this type of risk, the securities that you own will fluctuate because of changes in price levels. Most people associate market risk only in relation to the stock market. Stock prices can move up or down at random.

3. *Reinvestment Risk:* This risk includes the possibility that the return on your investment will not be reinvested as projected.

4. *Liquidity Risk:* This is the type of risk that occurs when you need your money now. It may come in the form of early withdrawal penalties or a low return due to a depressed market. The return on various investments may not be immediately available, could be subject to penalties, or may be subject to a reduced market price.

5. *Inflation Risk:* Possibly the most devastating type of risk, inflation affects all investments equally. To combat inflation, you must have an investment program that works during each economic season. Unless your retirement savings can continue to grow, you run the risk of receiving income with reduced purchasing power. That could mean a decline in your quality of life.

6. *Default Risk:* Investments made in specific companies or organizations are subject to default risk. The potential for default due to poor management, economic cyclical swings, or catastrophe will present a level of risk for any investment other than the

There have been many innovations in the health care industry over the years, as doctors seek higher salaries and consumers seek better, cheaper coverage. Some of the recent innovations in health care are the introduction of health savings accounts, boutique doctors, and even pet health insurance. While health savings accounts allow consumers to save for their own medical costs somewhat inexpensively, boutique doctors are more expensive but provide convenience and better service to patients. Surprisingly, 5 percent of companies already offer pet health insurance to employees. The big companies in the health care insurance industry include Kaiser Permanente, Blue Cross & Blue Shield, Aetna, and United Health Care.

Disability Insurance or Income Replacement Insurance

Disability insurance, which protects your ability to earn income, is another major component of risk management. It's also a critical need for many consumers, as nearly one in three Americans between ages 35 and 65 will suffer a disability that lasts more than 90 days. A three-month leave from work can be financially fatal to anybody; this is where disability insurance comes in. However, most consumers don't have disability coverage.

There are three types of disability insurance: "can't work at all," "any-occupation," and "own-occupation." Can't-work-at-all coverage uses the same standards as social security disability benefits. The title describes the coverage: You may only receive benefits if you cannot work at all. The criteria for this type of disability are very difficult to meet, and, subsequently, few claims are paid. However, this is the least expensive disability coverage. Any-occupation coverage only pays benefits if the policyholder cannot perform work that he or she is reasonably qualified for. This type of insurance is often referred to as income replacement insurance. The last type of disability insurance is own-occupation disability coverage. The owner of an own-occupation policy receives benefits only if he or she cannot perform his or her own specific occupation. This is the easiest type of disability to receive; however, insurers have backed away from offering it after there was an upsurge in claims by doctors in the mid-1990s.

Some of the big players in the disability insurance market are Guardian, Unum Provident, and Northwestern Mutual.

Long-Term Care Insurance

Long-term care insurance protects assets in the event of a medical situation that requires extended care, which includes home care, assisted living, and nursing home care. Long-term care is most needed by the developmentally disabled; those with catastrophic illnesses or who are involved in accidents; and people suffering from the effects of Alzheimer's disease.

One out of six consumers will require long-term care within his or her lifetime. Though this doesn't sound like a significant percentage, the risk of having to pay for the expensive care costs is most likely not worth it. The average cost of long-term care services has grown to nearly $75,000 annually, a number that has been rising steadily.

The way most people pay for long-term care is out-of-pocket. This is by far the majority, especially when the 58 percent paying out-of-pocket are compared to the 17 percent that is paid by Medicaid, and 13 percent paid by Medicare. Only 6 percent of consumers own long-term care insurance. In turn, long-term care is the least owned component of risk management among consumers.

Unlike health care and disability insurance, individual products make up the majority of long-term care sales. However, more and more employers continue to offer long-term care insurance. There are now nearly 6,000 businesses offering long-term care policies nationwide, compared to just 506 in 1992. Unfortunately, group benefits don't provide a true safety net against an employee's potential financial catastrophe, mainly due to low levels of employee participation.

There are two types of long-term care products, including reimbursements and indemnity. Reimbursement policies will pay back expenses up to a certain specified amount, whereas indemnity policies pay a certain amount per day. Indemnity policies typically range from $40 to $500 a day, or $1,000 to $8,000 per month.

Due to consolidation, there are now fewer companies selling long-term care insurance compared to a few years ago. As of this writing, there are 100 companies selling long-term care insurance. As a result, the top 11 long-term care companies make up over three-quarters of policy sales. In other words, there are 89 companies sharing just 19 percent of the long-term care market.

Some of the big long-term care companies are Genworth, Manulife Financial, and Met Life.

Liability Insurance

The fourth component of risk management insurance is liability management, or property and casualty insurance. The most notable types of property and casualty insurance include automobile and homeowners insurance.

Insurance claims have been rising in recent years due to increasingly costly hurricane seasons. Hurricanes are becoming more and more damaging, and it's estimated that by 2020 a single storm could cause losses of $500 billion.

Individual policies make up two-thirds of property and casualty products. This is most likely because most property and casualty products cover individual assets, and coverage varies depending on the individual.

Captive agents control more than half of the property and casualty market with 60 percent of sales. Independent agents sell about one-third of policies (32 percent).

Affluent clients require more coverage than average consumers, and their policies are often more complex. The first thing that most affluent clients insure is their jewelry. Jewelry is often extremely valuable and a favorite target among thieves. A lot of high net worth individuals also carry coverage for expensive collections, like wine or antiques. And some clients also need to cover multiple homes and yachts. As I mentioned earlier, umbrella liability is available to cover any additional claims arising from loss of property and is sold as an addition or add-on to basic policies.

Small business owners typically purchase insurance to cover assets, but contrary to individual property and casualty types, business owners must consider coverage against litigation, failed business attempts, and general liability. Product types include small business property and casualty, fleet auto insurance, workers compensation, errors and omissions (E&O), and commercial general liability.

Retirement Income Insurance

The next component of risk management insurance revolves around the need of many households for guaranteed retirement income. Many consumers worry about amassing enough money for retirement and how to make a limited pool of savings last for the rest of a lifetime. Nearly half of all consumers fear that they will outlive their savings, creating a large potential for retirement products.

There are two main reasons that consumers don't have retirement income protection. Many consumers are unaware of how much money they'll need during their retirement years, and others have money tied up in assets that inhibit their ability to purchase retirement income.

If you're considering retirement insurance, look for low-cost annuities. Income from an annuity is not taxed until withdrawals are made, but taxes are at the income tax rate rather than the lower capital gains tax rate. By annuitizing, investors can withdraw principal and interest together in small pieces to reduce taxes.

There are two types of annuities by funding mechanism: immediate income and purchase annuities. Immediate income annuities revolve around a lump sum contribution, which can be derived from other retirement plans, like a 401(k) distribution. Once this payment is made, the purchaser receives regular monthly payments for the rest of his or her life. Purchase annuities, on the other hand, involve annual contributions. Investors make premium payments over a period of time before receiving income payments.

There are also two types of annuity products by investment. These are fixed and variable annuities. Fixed annuity sales are traditionally driven by interest rate levels, and increased rates could spur sales. Returns are usually about 100 basis points (1 percent) higher than CDs; however, CDs can usually be bought for shorter periods. With variable annuities, investors can benefit from multiple fund managers and can switch between funds and money market accounts without having to pay taxes.

Multiple fees exist within the annuity market, which is a big deterrent among investors. Many of those who are educated about annuities are hesitant to buy for this reason. Some of the fees include management fees, 12b1 fees, and surrender charges. IRS Code 1035 lets you directly transfer an annuity policy to another company. If the swap is done directly between annuity issuers, no income taxes are due on the transfer. However, cashing out one annuity to buy another is a taxable event. This is not always in the investor's best interest. Switching annuities often requires longer surrender periods, higher surrender charges, and higher internal expenses. Annuities are often included in retirement plans, but the tax benefit is lost because retirement plans already have tax benefits. Annuities are also difficult to shop for, as vendors often tweak the features so that no two are exactly alike.

The top 25 annuity companies dominate the market with 85 percent of sales.[2] This is mainly due to the large portion of sales held by TIAA-CREF, which generates nearly one-third of annuity sales.

Life Insurance

The main objective of life insurance is to protect against financial hardship and replace an income source. Life insurance may play an increasingly important role for consumers in the future. Nearly 69 percent of consumers own some type of life insurance, yet 36 percent of U.S. households say that they need more.

Life insurance products can serve many different objectives for both individuals and corporations. There are four main objectives, which are satisfied by specific product types.

1. Income protection and replacement is the most common life insurance objective, and it can be fulfilled through the purchase of a single life policy.

2. Estate planning can be accomplished through second-to-die or survivorship policies. Payments from second-to-die policies are paid when the second of two specified people passes away.

3. Small business protection exists through key-person or buy-sell agreements. Buy-sell agreements are set up to provide immediate liquidity for a company upon the death of a key individual to alleviate the immediate need to buy or sell partnership interests.

4. Increasing executive compensation is achieved through corporate-owned life insurance. Employers are generally the applicant, owner, premium payer, and beneficiary of the policy.

There are two main types of life insurance: cash value life and term life. Cash value life insurance includes traditional, whole, fixed life, variable life, fixed universal life, and variable universal life. Term life insurance provides a set amount of insurance for a set period of time, usually greater than one year. This is the most basic type of life insurance and is convertible and renewable. However, there's no further value when the term expires, as there isn't any buildup of cash. There's also no payment to the beneficiary in the event of death if coverage lapses.

Beyond term, most life insurance can be referred to as cash value or permanent insurance. Cash value policy owners put more money in than what is needed to cover policy costs. The extra money is to earn a return for the policy owner. The untaxed return may be used in whole, or in part, to cover policy costs. If insufficient returns are earned to cover policy costs, the capital in the policy will be used to cover them. If the capital is used up by costs, the policy owner will have to pay more money into the policy, or the policy will lapse. Whole life, variable life, and universal life are all types of cash value policies.

Individual life insurance exceeds group life, as it makes up 56 percent of all life insurance in force. Because there are so many factors that go into each life insurance policy, it's easy to see why individual policies make up the majority.

Interestingly, more than 10 percent of life insurance companies operating in the United States are foreign owned. And the larger life insurance companies dominate the industry. Specifically, the top 25 life insurance companies account for close to $7 trillion, or 89 percent of all life insurance in force.

Step 8: The Ideal Strategy for Endless Family Progress

By this time, nearly all of the components in your Wealth Planning Strategy are present. The eighth and final step in creating your solution is something that I call The Ideal Strategy for Endless Family Progress™, which plays a major role in your financial success.

Now that you have wealth strategies in place and a process to get you where you want to go, you must focus on your family. At a minimum, you should sit down with them for an annual strategic meeting that evaluates the family's overall progress, reviews the structure of its goals, and repositions resources and assets to account for new goals and objectives. By doing this, each member of your family gains the tremendous benefits of direction, capability, and confidence.

By now you've come a long way. You've established the basis of your wealth management plan and are on the road to adequately protecting it. You'll continue down that road in the next chapter, where we dig deeper into asset protection structures, as well as learn how to choose the right wealth management team to help guide you in your efforts.

1. Source: Tiburon Investment Strategies.

2. Michael Lane, *Guaranteed Income for Life*, New York: McGraw-Hill, 1999.

4

STRUCTURE AND METHODOLOGY

In this chapter, I'll tell you about things to do *before* building a structure—the most important of which is to put together an outstanding wealth management team. Then I'll talk about methods to use for building the structure itself, including structural methodology (such as corporations and IRAs), transfer methodology, and separation methodology. And as I've done in previous chapters, I'll provide you with plenty of special Wealth Insights along the way.

> **CASE STUDY:** Mark Weisberg
>
> **BUSINESS OWNER**
>
> In Michigan, a nanny who worked for a man named Mark Weisberg, a wealthy business owner, was driving Weisberg's car—with his children inside—while talking on a cell phone. Distracted, the nanny ran through a red light, crashed into a car containing another family, and killed three people in all.

Michigan law states that in cases like this, both the driver *and* the owner of the vehicle are liable. So when the lawyers looked at the names on the car title, they found that both Weisberg and his wife were listed—as they were on all of their assets. They could have done everything else right in terms of investing, but this one structural oversight put all of the Weisbergs' assets in jeopardy.

Thankfully, most other circumstances involving litigation, even though financially devastating, are not this tragic. We live in a country where there's been a litigation explosion—where our legal system practically encourages people to file frivolous lawsuits. In the face of these global realities, the way that you structure your asset protection plan means everything to your investment plan. An ideal wealth protection structure also facilitates and enhances your ability to transfer wealth to future generations, in an effort to reduce Federal Estate Taxes as much as legally possible.

> **WEALTH INSIGHT:** One of the best asset protection strategies, and the simplest, is correctly titling your assets.

> **WEALTH INSIGHT:** If you think that your assets may someday be at risk because of your business or profession, you should begin to consider maximizing the use of contributing to certain asset classes and pretax accounts, including life insurance, annuities, pensions, and IRAs.

Three Key Considerations before Building a Structure

Before I get into detail about building your wealth protection structure, I want to call your attention to three key points to always keep in mind during the preplanning stage.

1. *Use multiple wealth protection safeguards, since no perfect structure exists that will protect all assets, all the time.*

No single line of defense will cover everything that you own, so you'll need to look at a variety of strategies and structures. We discussed some basic strategies in Chapter 3, and I'll also present you with additional safeguarding ideas in Chapter 6, "The Wealth Management Process." Remember, to be successful, you need to educate yourself, work with knowledgeable advisors, and heed their advice.

2. *Protect your assets* before *the need for protection arises.*

The basic principle of any protection strategy is that you do it before the need, not after. Don't put off getting the protection that is readily available to you to insulate your wealth because you didn't understand or didn't have time to learn.

3. *Hire a cohesive wealth management planning team.*

In the next few pages I'm going to talk about this point, because it's critical to the success of your asset protection structure. Successful people understand that in a complex world, you must surround yourself with experts in various fields. And successful investors understand that to achieve maximum output from an investment plan, you must seek out legal and financial expertise. Yet the way that the typical investor seeks out this advice is counter-intuitive to his or her overall best interests.

The Solution Network Team: All for One, One for All

As already mentioned, comprehensive wealth protection planning includes investment planning, financial planning, estate planning, ownership and/or management asset protection, and retirement planning. It's difficult to find one individual who has both the multidisciplinary knowledge and the interpersonal skills necessary to complete a comprehensive asset protection plan.

The average investor typically seeks out financial and legal expertise from individual sources, relying on separate providers for each product and service. A stockbroker takes care of the stock portfolio; an insurance agent writes life insurance policies; a lawyer handles trusts and estate planning; and an accountant computes the taxes. Rarely do these various financial providers interact.

Each product that is offered by these individual professionals is customarily promoted and sold separately, not according to its integral role in an overall financial plan. While the various professionals understand the concept of protecting against investment risk, they often have blind spots that lead to undesirable outcomes.

In this organizational model, investors often become the messenger, passing information among financial professionals who may not know each other. This often results in overlap and confusion, resulting in a situation where important information is not shared.

Worse, the lack of a cohesive team effort can even foster competition among professionals who should be working together in your best financial interests. Each advisor operates in a vacuum, and each is continually measured against the other's advice. They are evaluated on the basis of their professional expertise alone rather than on the basis of a combined outcome.

The ideal wealth management design focuses on building a collaborative team of experts that works together to achieve the investor's goals. In my practice, I refer to this concept as The Solution Network™. Under this model, the focal point for all team members revolves around the client's needs. Products and services are designed to satisfy and meet those needs.

The Solution Network dream team of wealth managers may include any or all of the following professionals.

The Facilitator (Your Financial Planner or Manager)

After the general decision to assemble a wealth planning team, the most important decision you'll make is to choose one individual—likely your financial advisor—to coordinate the various experts who comprise the team. The team leader must be: well versed in a cross-disciplinary approach to planning, able to direct the other team members to best serve your objectives, and have your confidence and trust.

Various financial services and/or investment advisors may use the title "financial planner." I recommend a Certified Financial Planner (CFP) Practitioner or Certified Public Accountant (CPA) educated in advanced financial planning. That includes an academic education in money, investments, estate transfer, retirement, tax, education and business structures, and planning. They are usually well versed in applying their academic training to assisting people with planning situations (such as business asset protection planning).

In light of the ever-increasing demand for a variety of different financial and legal services, it's becoming more difficult for one planner to competently offer the full array of services that clients want. As a result, the financial planner's role becomes one of managing a greater degree of cooperation and coordination among teams of professionals. The role is shifted from advisor to manager of the client's wealth, that is, a wealth manager.

I'll give you some more tips for choosing a financial manager in Chapter 7. The key here is to have your potential advisor share his or her personal plan with you. Whether the advisor will or won't—or even has a plan at all—will likely tell you all you need to know to make this investment decision. For now, let's move on to other members of the team.

Asset Protection Planning Attorney

Tax laws and asset protection planning rules are in a constant state of flux. It follows that your team must include a legal professional—most likely an attorney—who keeps abreast of changes in the rules. With these rules in mind, the attorney will review and revise your comprehensive wealth protection plan with you and your team on an annual basis. He or she will also ensure that your plan is correctly designed to protect you in the event of unforeseen circumstances such as a lawsuit, premature death, or disability.

Certified Public Accountant

A certified public accountant (CPA) who is well versed in your unique situation is an important member of your team. The CPA ideally retains a wealth of knowledge about the intricacies of comprehensive asset protection planning, which will greatly augment your planning and implementation process. At this point in time, it's important to note that many CPAs have been losing revenue to very good quality software tax computation programs from the do-it-yourself crowd. This has caused many to enter the investment arena as financial advisors, when in reality, they're trying to replace their lost revenue by becoming part-time investment advisors. As a quarter-century veteran of the investment world, I'd suggest the ultimate outcome of this will likely be a disadvantage to the CPA's client-investor. Just be aware of this reality and place a CPA on your team who's truly providing tax advice versus using CPA credentials to make a commissioned sale of an investment product to you.

Trust Officer

As you know by now, many wealth protection plans involve legal trusts. Each trust must designate a trustee to manage the assets of the trust. If you plan to use a corporate trustee (a bank or specific trust entity), you may be well advised to include a trust officer on your wealth management team. The experience and education of the trust officer may add an important dimension to your asset protection plan.

Banker

You may already have a working relationship with a knowledge-able banker—someone who has helped you make wise decisions regarding leveraged financing, production credit, and financial development. By including a banker on your team with whom you intend to have an ongoing relationship, you will have help clarifying your financial needs.

Insurance Agent

Much of a comprehensive wealth protection plan is designed to compensate for disastrous contingencies. One individual who can help you avert a financial disaster is an insurance agent. In the case of devastating events ranging from premature death or disability to litigation, an insurance agent who is knowledgeable about asset protection issues may be able to enhance your wealth management team.

Other Specialists

Under this format, the team can contract or expand to include nontraditional and nonfinancial specialists such as clergy, life coaches, eldercare specialists, and hospice caregivers. This ensemble also enables a small advisory firm to have the ability to offer clients a united set of recommendations similar to larger competitors. It also benefits the team leader, expanding his or her existing skills and capabilities by bringing in the specialists when needed and without expanding costs.

How to Assemble Your Wealth Team— and Keep It Working Well

Now that we've identified key roles on a wealth management team, how should you go about selecting your team members and encouraging them to collaborate on the path to your financial success? Here are a few points to keep in mind when attempting to assemble a dream team that will consistently work well together.

Choose Your Team Leader Wisely

Ironically, most people spend more time shopping for a new pair of shoes than they do shopping for a financial manager. Shoes are infinitely easier to find and far less expensive, yet we spend hours driving from one store to the next in search of the perfect pair. We'll try them on for size, and then we'll make sure we're getting the best price.

Finding the right advanced wealth manager to orchestrate the many facets of your asset protection planning process will be a big challenge. First, understand that cheaper is not necessarily better. If you want the best, you have to pay for it. As with other professionals—lawyers or doctors, for instance—the more you have at risk, the more you should be willing to spend on quality advice.

How do most people find a manager? Usually, it's in one of two ways.

The most popular way is to get a referral from a friend or relative. This isn't necessarily a bad way to go, and it's much better than another method—to pick a planner from an ad in the yellow pages. I don't recommend the latter; after all, anyone can pay for an ad.

The best method for finding the right wealth manager is to ask for a referral from other wealth management professionals such as your accountant or attorney. Keep in mind, though, that a truly savvy accountant or attorney will recommend that you find a manager before you even suggest it.

Whatever method you use, a thorough interview to determine whether the manager is right for you and your situation is critical to the success of your asset protection plan. Compatibility between you, your team, and your team coordinator is essential. The relationship between you and your wealth manager needs to be a partnership. Before you make the decision, clearly define what you expect of the individual.

The more complex your financial affairs, the more you need a team leader who can bring everything and everyone together for your benefit. You should choose a financial manager who can juggle many financial (and related) issues as well as provide a variety of solutions.

WEALTH INSIGHT: The following could be a job description for the ideal wealth protection plan manager:

Willingness to do the research and use the same due diligence that clients would use for themselves

Comprehensive wealth protection planning experience in money, taxes, estate, retirement, and financial planning

Thorough understanding of the intricate details of asset protection planning and the motivation to ensure that no details are ignored or unaddressed

Ability to pull other professionals together as a team to serve clients' specific objectives

Ability to intermediate and integrate discussions between clients and the team

Establish Realistic Expectations from the Get-Go

The most important first step for your wealth management team is to agree on a set of realistic expectations that you identify together through an educational process. This step will ensure the probability of reaching your target financial goals.

Success is determined by how well your team can fine-tune all of your known variables such as time horizon, savings, and expenditures. Together with your team, you can explore new possibilities and noninvestment solutions. You can fine-tune these variables to control where you're going. This forms the basis of a long-term strategic wealth management investment plan with the highest probability of reaching your financial goals.

Communication Is Crucial

The comprehensive wealth protection structure is built on a series of meetings and discussions led by the team's coordinator. The structure must thoroughly address all of the issues that you deem important to the protection of your assets.

Open communication throughout the wealth protection planning process is paramount to a successful result. There are many sensitive issues involved in the asset protection process. Contentious circumstances will be the rule rather than the exception. Therefore, the leader must be a full-time communicator, sometime arbitrator, and occasional therapist.

To foster frequent communication among team members, initiate annual meetings to review and, if necessary, revise your structure in accordance with current tax law, since changes in those laws are inevitable. Your initial investment of time, money, and effort will be wasted if your structure doesn't remain current. Your structure must be kept up to date in order for it to perform efficiently and effectively.

Set Goals at the Start—and Revise as Necessary

The goal of the wealth management team is to uncover what you truly want and need. To that end, your wealth managers should set target goals and fallback goals. A target goal is what you would like to have (if everything goes right), and a fallback goal is what you must have. After determining those goals, your wealth advisory team converts your financial goals into future liabilities. That way, you and your team can view these liabilities as money that you owe to yourself at some point in the future.

Again, your wealth management team can readjust your asset allocation percentages whenever they fall out of line with your future financial goals and risk tolerances. You should become an active part of this process. By setting these future dollar goals and understanding the risks inherent with various investments, your wealth management team can determine the probability of reaching your specific goals.

If this all sounds like financial planning to you—that's because it is. However, most investors will be able to tell merely from recalling their past efforts that what we're talking about here is a far more sophisticated (and effective) form of planning. If you've accumulated significant assets without a plan such as this, I'm surprised. With little or no network and no plan, you likely won't keep significant net worth. The lynchpin is the plan, so now's a good time to update yours or begin to create it.

Three Core Methods for Creating a Strong Structure

We've done a lot of good work so far in this chapter, learning about the critical elements to have in place before setting out to plan a wealth protection structure. Now let's talk more about how to build the structure itself.

The most effective wealth protection structures revolve around five central concepts. These concepts should inform everything you do while creating your structure:

1. *Safety or Low Risk:* Most investors don't understand all of the risks involved in asset protection structures. They decide that they only want to take risks for which the market rewards them, which in effect protects their assets.

2. *Enhanced Returns:* Everyone wants the best return available while maintaining security.

3. *Dependable Income Stream:* There was a time when CDs and T-bills represented two of the smartest investments a person could make. But rates on these investments are currently low—and are expected to stay that way for awhile. Plus, these investments offer little asset protection in case of attack.

4. *Liquidity:* No one wants to lock away assets so they can't be accessed in the event of an unexpected emergency. Many investors have faced this problem when their portfolio designs had no provisions for immediate liquidity.

5. *Simplicity:* This is a clear-cut concept: if a simple structure seems to best suit your needs, go with it.

WEALTH INSIGHT: In the fourteenth century, a European scholar named William of Ockham derived the principle *Pluralitas non est ponenda sine necessitate* (plurality should not be posited without necessity). Translation: The best explanation is the simplest one, and the most simplistic system is considered the best.

eBay President and CEO Meg Whitman attributes much of the company's success to this idea, maintaining that eBay thrives because its management spends less time on strategic analysis and more time trying and tweaking things that seem like they will work.

When building the structure itself, you'll rely heavily on at least two of the following three core methodologies:

1. *Structural Methodology*: Choosing and forming protection structures in a systematic way

2. *Transfer Methodology*: Transferring assets such as gifts, sales, and capitalization into those structures

3. *Separation Methodology:* Examining or possibly removing valuable assets from a liability-attracting operating business entity

The strongest asset protection structures employ a proactive combination of tools from various methods—particularly proven tools in the method category as well as innovative strategies that may have been overlooked altogether. I'll use the remainder of this chapter to explore the intricacies of each method.

Structural Methodologies

The following section describes the major types of structural methodologies that you can use in your asset protection structure.

The Domestic Corporation

Historically, the most commonly used asset protection structural methodology in the United States has been the *domestic corporation* (a corporation formed under the laws of one of the states). Even mutual funds—some of the largest repositories of wealth in the United States—are structured as domestic corporations.

Corporate law in the United States is well developed and, over time, has proved largely successful in insulating shareholders from corporate liabilities. As long as the corporation's separate identity is maintained and the corporation isn't used to perpetrate a fraud, the shareholders have little reason to fear that the corporate shell will be penetrated by creditors attempting to make shareholders personally liable for the corporation's debts. Even corporate officers and directors are shielded from corporate liability to a significant degree.

WEALTH INSIGHT: Be certain to consult with your legal advisor before forming a domestic corporation. The rules are long, complex—and there are many.

State of Incorporation

If a corporation holds real estate, the state in which the property is located is usually the logical choice for the state of incorporation, because a corporation must be registered in the state in which real estate is held. If the corporation is formed elsewhere, it must still be registered in the state where the real estate lies. Only in certain situations—such as where the added protections afforded by another state's laws outweigh the costs of having the corporation domiciled in one state and registered in another—would it be practical to register in a different state.

If the company fails to register in the state in which it's doing business, creditors may be successful in obtaining corporate assets based on the argument that the corporation shouldn't be protected in that state. However, an unregistered company may be doing sufficient business within a state such that it remains in the state's best interests to protect that corporation.

The issue of whether or not an unregistered company should be protected is sometimes difficult to resolve. For example, a creditor may have difficulty proving that the company is doing business in a state other than the state of incorporation. If a company is regularly entering into contracts in a particular state, and if its owners are concerned about liabilities arising from those contracts, then the company should likely be registered in that state.

Rights of Creditors

The biggest disadvantage to domestic corporations is that issues relating to shares of the corporation are within the jurisdiction of at least the state where the corporation is formed—and may be within the jurisdiction of other states as well. If the court makes a decision regarding share ownership, that decision is binding upon the corporation even if the shareholder and the physical share certificates are outside the jurisdiction of the court. A court can simply order that any change of ownership be entered on the books of the corporation.

The court can also give the equity in a corporation to a creditor, even if the court has no jurisdiction over the affected shareholder or the physical share certificates. The creditor can immediately become a shareholder of the corporation, with the full rights of any shareholder of that class of stock. From an asset protection perspective, this would be disastrous.

Under corporate law, the creditor has the right to inspect the corporation's books and records and to demand an accounting. The creditor can also bring a derivative action against the officers and directors of the corporation for any perceived malfeasance. As privately held corporations by their very nature often involve insider transactions, the remaining owners can personally become liable to derivative claims that would otherwise never have been asserted.

The Professional Corporation

The professional corporation encapsulates the liability from claims, such as employment practices claims made by staff and certain toxic materials claims. Additionally, the use of a professional corporation may later give tax planners some options if the corporation is eventually sold.

Because the corporate shell shields company owners from liability, most states will not allow professionals to operate their practices, such as medicine or law, from within a typical corporation. Instead, professionals are required to form professional corporations. These corporations are similar to typical corporations, but they may have only designated professionals as shareholders. In some cases, they may have nonprofessional shareholders, but they must be controlled by professionals.

Just as with any other corporation, a professional corporation doesn't protect an individual from liability for her or his own actions. In the same way that a shareholder who's at fault in an auto accident that occurs on company property is not protected from personal liability, neither is a professional who commits negligence. A professional corporation only shields the professional owner from the ordinary liabilities of the business, such as contractual liabilities for office supplies and equipment leases.

Insurance

As discussed in Chapter 3, insurance should always be one of your primary risk management methods, as it was designed to transfer the risk of loss away from the insured person and to the insurance company. If you're at risk of being sued, you should purchase as much insurance coverage as is economically practical, and your wealth protection planning should be closely integrated with the amount that is greater than the insurance coverage limits. Another benefit is that when insurance coverage is available to meet a plaintiff's claim, the plaintiff's attention becomes focused on the insurance company, since the insurance company has the proverbial deep pockets.

When an insurance company is on the hook for at least a portion of your liability to a creditor, you can make every attempt to transfer the onus of nonpayment to the insurance company and away from yourself. At the very least, every business should have a general liability insurance policy, and every household should have umbrella coverage in addition to homeowner and auto liability policies.

Although most states make proceeds from a life insurance policy unavailable to creditors, the cash surrender value doesn't enjoy the same protection.

Umbrella insurance plays an important role in making your wealth protection better insofar as it can often be taken into account if a court attempts a wealth analysis to determine whether you have proper coverage. Also, if litigation does arise, a plaintiff's attorney may well become fixated on chasing the limits of the umbrella insurance policy, to the exclusion of your other personal assets.

IRAs

The New Consumer Protection Act of 2005 has brought investment retirement accounts (IRAs) to the fore of structural methodologies. The good news about the act is that IRAs containing less than $1 million cannot be attacked by creditors, and rollover IRAs are excluded no matter how large they are. But the bad news is that, according to the act, if an IRA exceeds a debtor's need for support of him- or herself and dependents, it's not exempt. Who determines the extent of a debtor's need for support? The court does. And this opens the door for creditors to go after any money that exists beyond what the court has determined to be a debtor's need.

Employer-Sponsored Retirement Plans

Wealth protection structures like employer-sponsored retirement plans shouldn't be overlooked just because they're simple or obvious. If you have one of these plans—401(k), defined-benefit, defined-contribution, profit-sharing, or Keogh—you can generally breathe easy about it. As long as you comply with the federal Employee Retirement Income Security Act (ERISA), such plans are off-limits to creditors.

However, there are some loopholes. Say your plan belongs to you and your spouse only; that plan may not qualify under ERISA, because it discriminates against other employees, thereby leaving it unprotected. This is a good reason to add another employee to the plan and check with your attorney.

The Traditional Pension

The Pension Protection Act of 2006 was designed to close loopholes in the pension system and address problems for the roughly 34 million Americans covered by traditional pensions, also known as defined-benefit plans. The new law requires that pensions be fully funded by 2015. It also prevents companies with big pension deficits to skip annual contributions and still pronounce their plans healthy. Another major goal of the bill was to shore up the health of the Pension Benefit Guaranty Corporation (PBGC), which is running a $23.8 billion deficit. The agency assumes responsibility for terminated plans and pays benefits to retirees at a rate below what they were promised by their companies.

One problem that isn't addressed in the Pension Protection Act continues to affect millions of people of all ages (not just retirees): pension miscalculations. You are at risk anytime you change jobs or take a lump-sum pension cash-out. Women are especially vulnerable to pension mistakes because they tend to move in and out of the workforce more often than men. For the most part, pension mix-ups aren't intentional.

How would you know if there was an error that had been compounding for many years? How can you ensure that you'll get what's rightfully yours when you retire? It's up to you and your wealth management team to keep track of your own pension. Know your rights and monitor your retirement plan before the golden years creep up on you.

Educate yourself about how your plan works. Contact your company benefits officer and ask for a summary plan description. This will show how your pension is calculated. Request a personal statement of benefits, which will tell you what your benefits are currently worth and how many years you've been in the plan. It may even include a projection of your monthly check.

WEALTH INSIGHT: Most of the time, companies won't intentionally fudge their employee's retirement accounts. If you suspect that something's not right with yours, simple errors may be to blame. Here are eight common pension mistakes to watch for:

1. The company forgot to include commission, overtime pay, or bonuses in determining your benefit level.

2. Your employer relied on incorrect Social Security information to calculate your benefits.

3. Someone used the wrong benefit formula (that is, an incorrect interest rate was plugged into the equation).

4. The calculations are wrong because you've worked past age 65.

6. You didn't update your workplace personnel officer about important changes that would affect your benefits such as marriage, divorce, or death of a spouse.

7. The firm's computer software is flawed.

8. The company neglected to include your total years of service.

9. Your pension provider simply made a basic mathematical mistake.

You can protect yourself from these mistakes by creating a pension file. Keep all of your documents from your employer. Also, keep records of dates when you worked and your salary, since this type of data is used by your employer to calculate the value of your pension.

If you think something may still be amiss, ask for professional help from a qualified retirement specialist in your area. Contact the American Society of Pension Professionals & Actuaries (ASPPA), www.aspa.org, (703) 516-9300 or the National Center for Retirement Benefits, Inc., www.ncrb.com, (800) 666-1000.

Transfer Methodologies

From a wealth protection perspective, the method of transferring assets into a structure may be more important than the structure itself. This is because most of the laws that can negate asset protection planning primarily attack the transfer, not the structure.

If the choice is between a bad transfer into a good structure or a good transfer into a mediocre structure, the latter is preferred. If the transfer method is well planned, the structure itself may not be challenged, and the creditor may be out of luck. On the other hand, if the transfer is poorly planned, both the transfer and the structure likely will be challenged with a greater chance of success. The focus should fall on available methods of transfer at the same time as on available structures.

Trusts

One commonly used and typically effective transfer method is a trust, such as the charitable remainder trust (CRT) that is described in the following case study:

CASE STUDY: Joseph Basques

PROPERTY OWNER AND MANAGER

Joseph Basques was a client of mine whose greatest asset was a large apartment building in San Francisco worth $4 million. Basques was 84 years old and still doing his own property management on the building. He told me that he was growing tired of fixing leaky toilets and he and his wife were looking for a way out, but that the building had already been depreciated "down to nothing."

Basques also didn't want to get hit with the capital gains that would come from selling conventionally; neither did he want to go for the 1031 limited partnership craze currently going on (a 1031 allows for the exchange of one property for another, with some associated tax benefits). Basques wanted to simplify his life, not buy another apartment building. Yet his accountant never talked to him about anything other than the 1031.

After persuading his accountant and estate planning attorney that a 1031 wasn't the best option for Basques, we all worked together to map out a better choice: a charitable remainder trust (CRT), in which the title of the building was transferred through a gift to the trust. By keeping a portion of the building out of the trust and selling it directly, we were able to use the proceeds to fund a single-premium immediate annuity to help finance the couple's goals of setting up an annual gifting program (they wanted to help their kids and grandkids, and they also wanted some assets to go to a family foundation).

Finally, Basques bought insurance to provide for the couple's charitable interests. The end result of all these actions was annual cash flow for Basques that was greater than his rental income had been; the provision of funds for his heirs; and money for the charitable causes that interested him and his wife.

NUAs

Net Unrealized Appreciation (NUA) is a key transfer strategy that wealth managers too often overlook. With so many people now including company stock in their retirement plans, this is very important to know. Most of your advisors won't know to tell you. It allows you to receive an in-kind distribution of your company's stock and only be required to pay income tax on the average cost basis of the shares, rather than on the current market value.

Here is how NUA works: An employee is about to retire or separate service and qualifies for a lump-sum distribution from a qualified retirement plan. Under the more conventional strategy of simply rolling the distribution into an IRA, the investor pays up to 35 percent in ordinary income tax on the stock's value, including any gains, upon withdrawal.

By using the NUA strategy, the investor receives the stock and pays ordinary income tax on the average cost basis, which represents the original cost of the shares. This strategy allows the investor to continue to defer gains on any earnings that accrue from the time that the stock was purchased until it's finally sold. At that point, the investor is taxed on the appreciated value at the long-term capital gains rate, which is currently capped at 15 percent.

CASE STUDY: David Kranig

ATTORNEY

An executive at a Denver law firm, David Kranig was planning to leave the firm at year-end. Kranig had $100,000 worth of employer's stock held in the company's 401(k) plan with a cost basis of $20,000. A local investment advisor recommended that Kranig roll his company stock into a low-cost IRA. He explained the advantages of the IRA and how Kranig's account would grow larger, first because the tax would defer and second because of the hot mutual fund that the advisor was recommending.

What the advisor didn't explain (or possibly didn't understand) was that when Kranig's IRA eventually distributed income, he would not only be taxed ordinary income rates on his $20,000 cost basis but he would also be paying the highest income tax rate on his $80,000 gain, which in Kranig's case would be 35 percent, the highest tax bracket. If Kranig simply took out the stock and didn't roll it over into an IRA, his tax on the $80,000 gain would be treated as long-term capital gains and taxed at a maximum of 15 percent. Of course, the $20,000 basis would be taxed as ordinary income. This tactic resulted in a potential tax savings of $12,000.

One caveat about NUAs is that for the employee to qualify for the NUA tax break, the distribution must be taken within a year of leaving employment in order to qualify as a lump-sum distribution. Also, the distribution must be a lump-sum distribution—*not* a partial distribution—to qualify for NUA.

If you plan to complete an NUA transaction, start early—it may take several weeks to complete. It follows that you should never ask for in-kind distributions of company stock in December; it's better to wait a month until the beginning of the next year. The entire distribution (both rollover and in-kind) must be completed in the same calendar year.

The following is a five-step process designed to help a wealth manager complete a successful NUA transaction:

1. *Determine the amount of gain in the stock price.*

An NUA can be elected on some, all, or none of the shares in an employer-sponsored retirement plan. It doesn't make sense to elect this strategy on shares that were purchased for more than the current stock price. Look for shares that are currently selling for twice the cost basis.

2. *Get your cost basis in writing before starting the rollover.*

Obtain formal documentation from the plan of the cost basis of your employer stock—as well as your employer's promise to make an in-kind distribution of the company shares.

3. *Plan the sequence of transactions when your plan holds employer securities and other assets.*

You can roll the noncompany stock portion of your plan into an IRA rollover account and transfer the company stock portion to your taxable (non-IRA) brokerage account. The company stock still qualifies for the tax break on the NUA. Employers are supposed to withhold 20 percent of distributions from a qualified plan for taxes, unless it's a trustee-to-trustee transfer or when the only remaining asset being distributed is employer stock.

4. *Complete the rollover to an IRA first for all assets except the company stock.*

Then the NUA shares can be distributed in-kind, with nothing to withhold for the IRS from either transaction.

5. *Make sure the money is available to pay taxes on the cost basis.*

You will need to have money on hand to pay the income taxes on your cost basis for the shares that are distributed in-kind. Prepare a tax projection to determine the amount needed—and be prepared to pay the taxes in April.

WEALTH INSIGHT: An NUA may not be the best decision for an investor whose retirement savings are heavily concentrated in an employer's stock. The trade-off is that the NUA doesn't mitigate the risks associated with improper diversification. An investor with 98 percent of his or her retirement account tied up in one stock may want to consider liquidating a portion of his or her stock position and distributing a smaller portion of the stock in-kind. Still, for many investors, the NUA strategy makes sense.

Separation Methodologies

This method involves using leases, rents, and licenses to continually divest the business of assets. Thus, the operating business never accumulates significant value that could be exposed to creditors. The assets that are important to overall business success are spread across the component entities, so that the value and profits in each entity are minimized but, when taken as a whole, the investor is more wealthy and profitable than ever. (See Exhibit 4.1)

The wealth protection landscape includes many structural options as well as landmines. Therefore, invest from the beginning with strong wealth protection structures in mind. The best structures not only put assets out of reach of judgments before the need

Exhibit 4.1 **Unbundling Business Assets**

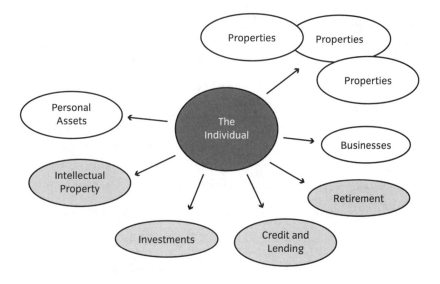

WHAT YOU'RE LOOKING AT: The separation methodology leverages the dichotomy of simple assets versus complex assets. Simple assets are those that cannot be reduced to further component parts, while the opposite is true for complex assets. Unbundling those complex assets is an important part of separation methodology.

WHAT THIS TELLS YOU: One of the primary strategies for unbundling assets is interlocking ownerships. Ideally, you can create interlocking ownerships through a holding company structure. In this simple structure, two tiers of companies exist. The lower tier consists of companies that are actively conducting business, holding business assets, employing people, etc. These are the liability-prone companies. The upper tier consists of one or more companies with few employees that conduct no business other than owning stock in the lower-tier companies.

WHAT THIS MEANS: Holding companies have in the past been used by tax planners to create situations involving interlocking ownership. That arrangement drives down the percentage of ownership held by a taxpayer, yet still allows the taxpayer to retain control. For U.S. citizens, however, the Internal Revenue Code has attribution rules that seriously restrict the effectiveness of these structures.

••••••

MANUFACTURING COMPANY OWNER

William Reilly owned a large manufacturing company in the Midwest; this one asset dominated his net worth. His stock had a very low tax basis, and he therefore had a large tax liability. If Reilly were named in a lawsuit and lost, it would have a major impact on his life and family.

Reilly needed his asset protection structure to address the risks associated with the concentration of that one asset. The collapse of Enron and dot.com stocks had already illustrated the hazards of concentrated wealth. Numerous mainstream, big capitalization, NYSE–listed household names had also seen jarring declines in price of 50 percent or more in recent years.

Risks associated with Reilly's asset included concentration in one company and one industry sector, limited liquidity, and tax ramifications relative to low basis and Alternative Minimum Tax exposure. Concurrent with the growth of his personal taxable wealth, the previous decade had witnessed the creation of innovative strategies for hedging and monetizing restricted and low-cost basis stock positions.

This development created an opportunity for Reilly to look at each component part of his asset in isolation and how those parts might work together. Businesses like his typically have many component assets, including the market value and rental value of real property; company equipment; customer contracts; customer lists; patents; copyrights and trademarks; key employee contracts; and even vendor contracts.

Each of these component parts are assets that can be valued, monetized, and protected separately. For instance, Reilly set up an entity to own a customer list and rented the list to the operating business. He contributed real property and equipment to other entities and leased them to the operating business. He housed trademarks in another entity, and licensed the trademarks to the operating business. Yet another entity contracted with his employees and leased their services to the operating business. Each contract allowed funds to flow from the operating business to each of the separate entities, where those funds were protected from the creditors of the operating business and from the creditors of the other component entities.

arises, but they also provide flexibility to handle changes when they're needed. Focus on what could go wrong and how to fix it.

In Chapter 5, I discuss how to create an all-important Wealth Management Policy—the next step to take after assembling your team and deciding on the ideal structure to suit your needs.

THE WEALTH MANAGEMENT POLICY

At this point, you've likely noticed that *Surviving the Storm* is a progression. I started the book with a broad overview of the background behind why today's most common investment management practices don't work. I then went on to give an overview of what *does* work, and I've used the last couple of chapters talking about how to begin putting your own effective financial structure into place.

Beginning with this chapter (and for the remainder of the book), I'm going to give you more specifics on how to flesh out your structure using the proven tactics that I regularly impart to my own clients. The first of those tactics is The Wealth Management Policy.

WEALTH INSIGHT: My wife Elaine and I were visiting Prague with our daughters when we happened upon the Museum of Communism. This museum provides a historical narrative of the Czech Republic's subjugation by the Soviet Union. Various displays show original artifacts from the communist era, including pictures, reading materials, military objects, and even a reconstructed school classroom. But the relic that literally stopped me in my tracks was a plaque on the wall that read "New York Stock Exchange."

The plaque describes how industry in the former Czechoslovakia reached a peak in the spring of 1929, yet when the New York Stock Exchange collapsed in the fall of that same year, the event triggered an international economic crisis that was deeply felt across Czechoslovakia. By 1931, Czech exports were struck to the ground, inflation and unemployment soared, and businesses closed. Cities that had suffered direct hits became ghost towns. Revenues evaporated, leaving governments without funds to protect their borders.

Of course, I already knew the story of the Great Depression from an American point of view. Back then, the United States had just 5 percent of the global population but produced one-third of the global economic output. Yet that day in Prague, it hit home that when the American economy was out of commission, the global economy fell into utter chaos. This realization really made me think about how fragile the world becomes in the face of an American economic downturn. It simply reaffirms the idea that when the United States sneezes, the rest of the world gets a cold.

Creating Your Wealth Management Policy

If a shift in our economy can bring about such massive (and more corporate than individual) change across the world, imagine what it can do to your own portfolio. Even if you invest in foreign entities, chances are that your overall plan will be intimately tied to the health of the U.S. economy. This is yet another important reason why you need to have a strong structure in place—and a set of guiding principles that can help you keep your structure in focus, no matter how tough times get.

I call this set of principles The Wealth Management Policy—a written statement that sets forth the investment objectives of a wealth management portfolio, along with general guidelines for achieving specific objectives. Think of it as a continuation or crystallization of The Wealth Planning Strategy™ that you outlined for yourself in Chapter 3. In this activity, you'll create a policy statement not for your overall life, as you did with The Wealth Planning Strategy, but for the portion of the solution that specifically pertains to investments.

A common mistake among many wealth managers is that they simply do not take the time to write a Wealth Management Policy statement for their clients. Or, they come up with vague investment policies that state the obvious without giving investors any genuine guidance. Guidelines such as little or no risk, maximize return, or preserve capital are virtually useless unless they are clearly defined and explained.

All serious investors should have a Wealth Management Policy statement that outlines their goals and how their money will be invested to reach those goals. This should also include an exit strategy for businesses you own or a sell strategy for common stocks and mutual funds. Anyone can get caught up in the emotion of the day and make poor investment decisions. It's only through long-term adherence to a sound policy that investors are going to be successful. In the heat of a market downturn, it's critical to have determined your strategy ahead of time.

> **WEALTH INSIGHT:** When people aren't working and don't have any money or opportunity—that is, a guiding plan for their lives—they tend to listen to whatever (or whoever) is out there. Case in point: Adolph Hitler's relatively easy rise to power. There were a lot of idle hands in 1930s-era Germany. All Hitler had to do was recruit those unemployed masses by suggesting that he could make their lives better if they did exactly as he suggested. By the spring of 1941, his Third Reich had overrun France, Norway, Denmark, Austria, Czechoslovakia, Yugoslavia, Greece, and much of Poland.

Some important issues to consider before writing your Wealth Management Policy statement are as follows:

1. What are the real risks of an adverse outcome? An adverse outcome might mean underperforming the market or target rate of return, or producing a negative return.

2. What would be your probable emotional reactions to an adverse outcome? Perhaps you would panic, deciding to radically change your investment policy to ensure fewer sleepless nights, or perhaps you would handle the news calmly, simply asking your wealth advisory team to reexamine your investment policy to confirm that it's sound.

3. Are there any legal restrictions that will be imposed on the investment policy?

4. Are there any potential consequences of interim fluctuations in portfolio value that might affect your policy?

The Wealth Management Policy statement can also be used to provide specific instructions to cover areas such as target rates of return, risk tolerance, desired holding periods for asset classes, restrictions, and distributions. Again, a written policy statement enables you to clearly define your long-term goals and objectives and serves as a guideline for implementing your investment strategy. It helps you to maintain a sound plan over time; without it, short-term market movements might cause you to second-guess your investment decisions and wander off a well-thought-out path toward investment success.

WEALTH INSIGHT: As I mentioned earlier, I grew up in Montana, on a feedlot. One day, I found a strange horse eating the grass on our lawn. No one knew where the horse had come from, as it had no markings by which it could be identified. My dad and I assumed that the horse must have strayed away from its owner someplace out in the country.

There was no question of keeping the horse—it belonged to someone and therefore needed to be returned to its rightful owner. So my dad mounted the horse and led it to the road, where it began walking. He only intervened when the horse left the road to eat grass or to walk into someone's field. Dad would then just guide it back to the road.

Eventually, the horse found its own way back home to a farm several miles from our house. The owner was very surprised to see his horse. "How did you know that the horse came from here or that it belonged to me?" the man asked.

Dad answered: "I didn't know—the horse knew. All I did was keep him on the path."

Seven Steps to Establishing Your Personal Wealth Management Policy

Work closely with the members of your wealth management dream team to devise your Wealth Management Policy, using the following seven steps as your guide:

1. *Write your goals and objectives clearly and concisely.*

Goals can be anything from early retirement to purchasing a new home. One of the most common goals is to be financially independent. If that's your goal, you want to ensure that your investment portfolio will grow to a future value that will provide you with the income stream necessary to maintain your quality of life throughout your life.

2. *Overlay your long-term goals with the three critical wealth factors that were discussed in Chapter 2: birthrates, spending patterns, and the Seasons of the Economy.*

3. *Define the level of risk that you're willing to accept.*

Along the road to reaching your financial goals, there will be bumps caused by the downturn in various markets. It's important for you to understand the amount of risk and volatility you're willing to tolerate during the Seasons of the Economy.

There's a high probability that sometime between 2010 and 2011 we'll experience an economic downturn. When that occurs, most investors will have a hard time maintaining a long-term perspective and staying with the program. If you're working with a wealth advisory team, you can request an analysis of how your portfolio mix will fare during the great winter. Choose the portfolio mix that gives you the most confidence that it'll survive.

4. *Determine the rate of return objective.*

Focus on rate of return objectives rather than on risk. The rate of return is going to be a direct result of your willingness to take risks and the long-term nature of your objectives. In getting started, you should write down a range of returns that would be acceptable. You can use these ranges of returns for each risk level as the framework to determine your return expectation for your portfolio as well as its component asset classes.

5. *Select the asset classes to be used to build your core portfolio.*

If your wealth advisory team understands the three wealth factors, get them to list all the different asset classes that you might want to consider in your portfolio, based on how they might react to the various seasonal changes. You may be surprised by the differences between what you've been told to use in the past and what you should use in the future. Once you've identified the asset classes, you need to determine how you're going to allocate your capital to each asset class based on the Seasons of the Economy (see Exhibit 5.1).

Exhibit 5.1 **Asset Classes and Associated Risks by Season of the Economy**

Level of Decline	Target Growth Rate	Seasons of the Economy	Core Strategy	Riskometer
3%	3–5%	0–6 months	CDs, money markets	
6%	5–6%	3–12 months	Active money markets, CDs, cash	
8%	6–8%	6 months–2 years	Conservative balanced portfolio, bonds, Portfolio 1	
10%	8–9%	Spring/Summer	Balanced fund, Portfolio 2	
15%	9–11%	Spring/Summer/Fall	Conservative equity, Portfolio 3	
23%	10–13%	Summer	Equity fund, Portfolio 4	
35%	11–14%	Summer	Equities, Portfoliio 4	
50%	12–15%	Summer	Equities, Portfolio 4	

WHAT YOU'RE LOOKING AT: The various types of assets you should hold during different economic seasons.

WHAT THIS TELLS YOU: The chart spells out the levels of risk involved in each asset type—with some assets clearly more risky than others.

WHAT THIS MEANS: As you can see in this table, the balmy days of spring and summer call for riskier investments, while the colder fall and frigid winter mean your strategy should be more conservative.

••••••

6. *Key measures:* Watch indicators for changes in the investment seasons.

7. *Rebalance!*

Rebalancing tests everyone's mettle. You've done your asset allocation, but as the portfolio percolates, it gets out of balance because, obviously, some parts of the portfolio do better than others. So, for example, instead of 20–20–20 in each group, now one group is at 30 percent, another is at 10, and another is at 20. Prudence would tell you to take the 30 and make it 20 and take the 10 and make it 20. It's psychologically difficult to take from a portfolio that's doing well and put it into one that's not, but that's what rebalancing is—and it's sometimes a tough decision. Hopefully, you've built your portfolio to have negative correlation which will balance out your risks.

Even if you're working with a wealth advisory team, it's a good idea to familiarize yourself sufficiently with the operating rules contained within this book. Your written wealth management policy statement will enable you to better define your investment expectations and help you to decide how best to implement your asset allocation.

Your wealth management policy statement embodies the essence of the wealth planning process: assessing where you are now and where you want to go, as well as developing a strategy to get there. Having and using this policy statement compels you to become more disciplined and systematic, increasing the probability of satisfying your investment goals.

With your policy down on paper, you can feel confident as you move on to Chapter 6, where we'll talk about how to build the portfolio that will be guided by your policy.

THE WEALTH MANAGEMENT PROCESS

In this chapter, I'll show you how to maximize your returns while minimizing risk. I'll also give you a set of wealth factor guidelines—which I call The Wealth Management Process—that should remove much of the guesswork related to investing. These guidelines will help you comprehend the different types of accounts and how to control the "whole kit and kaboodle."

> **WEALTH INSIGHT:** The word *kaboodle* means a collection of unrelated objects, which I think best describes the world of investment management. The word probably appeared as *boodle* originally, with the phrase being "the whole kit and boodle," but the initial "k" sound was likely added to "boodle" for euphony.

The Principles of an Effective Investment Strategy

The following simple two-step solution will help you execute your investment process in the right order:

1. The very first step is to determine your strategy, which will be based on The Wealth Management Policy that you created in the last chapter. In order to determine a strategy, you must understand the following:

   • Which economic season we are currently in

   • Which season will be next (unlike nature's seasons, economic seasons can occur out of order)

   • What will be the expected returns and risks for each asset class in the new season

   • How to calculate the most efficient frontier

   • How to specify your own asset class mix

2. Once you have a strategy, then you can implement and monitor the process, which includes:

   • Separate money manager or mutual fund money manager selection

   • Asset allocation

   • Appropriateness of chosen investment vehicles

   • Management of fees and costs

As I stated previously, it's been my experience that many advisors get these two important steps in the investment process backwards. As a result, today's typical financial plan is investment-oriented rather than strategy-oriented. The latest solution product has been life cycle or lifestyle funds, which evolved in the 1990s and were seen as a potential solution to the challenges of investment selection for 401(k) plan participants. Most of these funds are poorly engineered by portfolio managers who know more about picking stocks than about true investment strategy, which includes understanding the seasons of the economy. When your process is investment manager oriented in this way, your investment strategy is an accidental by-product of your selection and therefore is inevitably flawed.

Knowing what nuts and bolts go into a complex investment strategy and knowing how those parts all work together are two different matters. Think of this idea in terms of a car engine: You could open the car's hood and look at individual components of the motor for as long as you want, but simply looking at those components by themselves would not give you a clear idea of how they collaborate to make the car go.

To find out how something actually works, you must take it apart and reassemble it, stopping at many points along the way to see if the function has yet been restored. Even this may not yield a clear idea of how the thing operates under extreme conditions, but it does give a working knowledge of which components are critical.

The Right Amount of Risk

Let me begin this section with an analogy that describes the way that most investment advisors manage their clients' money. Picture a train ride in which the passengers change seats repeatedly; lots of movement, shifting, and activity goes on. Yet this movement doesn't change the fact that when the train stops, all of the passengers still end up at the same station, with none ultimately better or worse off than the other.

> **WEALTH INSIGHT:** An asset class is a group of securities that has similar risk characteristics.

Since there is truly no investment advantage to be gained by riding this "train," why are most money managers here? There are two basic reasons. First, many brokers and/or advisors still subscribe to the popular myth that they can win the stock market game by exercising their superior knowledge of stock market moves. Why? Because it's the only way they've been taught to play the game. Second, these managers are scrambling for a seat on the train because, as we discussed in Chapter 1, it's how they earn their living—selling a ton of products that revolve around the market.

Remember Harry Markowitz, the father of Modern Portfolio Theory, whom I mentioned in earlier chapters? He had a keen insight: that risk (which he defined as volatility) must be the central focus for the whole process of investing. What Markowitz found was an investment world blindly living in a paradox: Even though human beings are risk-averse by nature, the interrelationship between risk and return is precisely what drives the effective investment process. To that end, Markowitz discovered that if two investments have the same average rates of return, the one with lower volatility would always have a higher compounded return.

On the surface, this idea seems like such a little thing. But Markowitz's discovery meant that for every level of risk, there's some optimal combination of investments that will provide the highest rate of return with less volatility. If that's true, why does the average risk-averse investor underperform the stock market from as little as 2 percent to as much as 10 percent?

Lest anyone mistake this rate of underperformance for a small number, consider this: $100,000 invested at 10 percent for 30 years grows to $1,744,940, while the same amount invested at 8 percent for the same duration grows to only $1,006,266. The missing 2 percent compounds to nearly three-quarters of a million missing dollars for a hypothetical investor with a 30-year time horizon— roughly the average time between mid-career and mid-retirement for today's long-lived individuals.

WEALTH INSIGHT: Assuming that one's career begins at age 25 and ends at 65, mid-career is at age 45. Workers tend to earn higher incomes in the later years of their careers, but that's at least partially offset by the longer time for which earlier retirement plan contributions are invested. Assuming further that the retiree expends his or her income from age 65 to death at 85, mid-retirement is at age 75. Thus, the average investment-holding period is 30 years (age 45 to 75).

Exhibit 6.1 highlights the findings of the Quantitative Analysis of Investor Behavior Study.[1]

Exhibit 6.1 **Quantitative Analysis of Investor Behavior Study**

Category	Cumulative Return[2]	Annualized Return[3]
S&P 500 Index	793.34%	12.22%
Small Company Stock Index	538.94%	10.25%
Average Equity Fund Investor	**62.11%**	**2.57%**
Long-term Government Bond Index	718.05%	11.70%
Long-term Corporate Bond Index	659.30%	11.26%
Intermediate-term Bond Index	436.40%	9.24%
Average Fixed Income Fund Investor	120.06%	4.24%
Treasury Bills	175.89%	5.49%
Inflation	79.80%	3.14%

WHAT YOU'RE LOOKING AT: This study shows that an average equity investor underperforms the S&P 500 by almost 10 percentage points per year!

WHAT THIS TELLS YOU: The majority of these investors have no idea what their investment performance is.

WHAT THIS MEANS: The reason for this underperformance lies in investor behavior. Average investors likely influenced by "noise" obviously leap to the wrong conclusions, relying on the safe bet of hindsight as their guide.

The problem with hindsight is that it incorporates a cognitive bias—it's a process in which you look at the past and, because you know the past, you think that nothing could have happened other than what actually happened. This leads you to believe that past performance is the factor in predictability. This way of thinking is common and normal for the typical risk-averse human being—yet it's nevertheless wrong. Investing based on past performance is like trying to drive somewhere by looking through the rearview mirror to see where you're going.

· · · · · ·

WEALTH INSIGHT: I was flying into Denver recently, and as we descended to 30,000 feet, two things struck me as I looked out the window. The first was the lack of detail of the towns below. The second was that because I couldn't see the details, a bigger picture emerged. What I *could* see was where each city was located and how they were connected together. As we finally drew nearer to the ground, the detail became clearer—but I lost sight of the big picture. These two observations don't have much meaning when viewed separately. However, when you combine them, you can grasp the big picture and how the detail fits within that picture. This is much like the big picture of the economic seasons and how the investment detail is affected inside the big picture.

Seven Investing Rules to Remember

Now that you know you must invest with an eye toward the future and a certain amount of (healthy) risk, let's get started with the nuts-and-bolts portion of your plan. As a subset to our bigger picture, the seasons of the economy, here are seven rules to remember about investing:

1. *The nature of the markets is that they move in a cyclical manner.*

Many people project that the markets move linearly; hence, they gravely misunderstand the reality that demographics influence investing. They buy at tops and sell at bottoms.

2. *People take the wrong amount of risk.*

Human tendencies cause investors to perceive low risk when risk is actually at its greatest, and high risk when risk is lowest. Many investors allocate their investments in ways that are completely unsuited to the achievement of their investment goals. By far, the most common misallocation is to take too little market risk, with the bulk of one's assets in cash and the rest in stable-value investments. A less common problem is excessive risk taking. A small but visible group of investors seeks extraordinary returns through a 100 percent equity allocation in their retirement plans, often using the plan's fund-switching mechanism to chase the "hot dot" fund of the week (choosing funds based almost entirely on a review of recent performance).

3. *Investors tend to chase the hottest sectors.*

Some misinformed investors will relentlessly pursue hot dot funds and stocks, perceiving that such a strategy will achieve the highest returns, when in fact that approach has proved to be ineffective precisely because investors buy after such investments have already made gains.

4. *For potential higher returns, you must take higher risk.*

The strongest sectors in the last upturn typically suffer the greatest setbacks in the correction to follow. Only by understanding the economy can investors offset these inherent risks to a substantial degree.

5. *The market is not your friend.*

The market is constantly trying to talk you into buying near the top and selling near the bottom, which reduces your long-term returns while increasing your risk.

6. *Costs are hidden or ignored.*

High commissions and fees steal your profits. High costs are a major source of underperformance in most investment plans. Transaction costs have several components, of which direct costs (brokerage commissions and bid-ask spreads) are only a small part. Market impact and the opportunity cost of delays in trading and missed trades are hidden costs that can be a multiple of the direct costs.

7. *There's no such thing as little or no risk.*

Many of the so-called guaranteed investment contracts (GICs) were not marked to the market. As some found out the hard way, the word *guaranteed* was not a guarantee against risk, but merely a guarantee by the insurance company issuing the contract not to reduce the stated rate of return. Guaranteed investment contracts are and were risky, as was proved conclusively by the defaults of Executive Life and Mutual Benefit Life, both major carriers with top ratings.

CASE STUDY: Wayne Grasmere

CARDIOLOGIST

Recently, an advisor friend came to me with a problem. He'd recently created an estate plan for a cardiologist, Dr. Wayne Grasmere, who wanted to shift a significant portion of his investment portfolio to a hot mutual fund manager that Grasmere had seen on a television show.

The doctor didn't see the whole picture. What the fund manager on television didn't explain was that his portfolio had lost 50 percent in year one but doubled in year two. Divided by two years, the manager could honestly tout an average annual return of 25 percent. However, the reality is that if Dr. Grasmere had invested his estate assets of $1,000,000 in the hot fund two years earlier, he would have lost half of its value the first year ($500,000) before doubling the value the following year. At the end of year two, Dr. Grasmere's portfolio would amount to his original investment of $1,000,000. That equals zero growth.

On the other hand, though Dr. Grasmere's actual conservative investment showed a much lower average annual rate of return of 12.94 percent, it was a *compounded* rate of return, and his investment grew to $1,275,544. He actually made substantially more money than the hot manager, and he accomplished this with lower risk.

That said, it seems almost silly that any investor would succumb to advertised returns. Unfortunately, Dr. Grasmere was falling prey to the "noise" that we talked about in Chapter 2—the irrelevant or sensational data (which often emanates from the media) that obscures the facts and manipulates emotions. The vast majority of individuals who are looking for fast-fix strategies give credence to noise without even knowing it. Not surprisingly, when emotions become part of the mix, anyone can make a misguided investment decision.

Controlling the Two Main Types of Investment Risk

We've made the case for why a certain amount of financial risk is necessary for overall gain. At this point, you may be asking yourself: How do I mitigate the risks so that I achieve the appropriate balance? To answer that question, let me start with a short primer about the principles behind the two main types of investment risk: uncompensated and compensated.

Uncompensated Risk

Uncompensated risk, which comprises about 70 percent of total risk, is the possibility that economic (and noneconomic) news may uniquely affect the market price of a particular stock. For example, the price of Ford Motor Co. stock may go down because of the departure of a key Ford executive. Investors who hold only Ford stock can protect themselves against this type of risk by also owning stock in companies that would be unaffected by the departure of Ford executives.

Compensated Risk

Compensated risk, which comprises about 30 percent of total risk, reflects the economic (and noneconomic) news that affects the market price of many (or all) stocks. Since the prices of individual stocks are affected, more or less, by the risk of a general rise or fall in the value of the stock market itself, compensated risk is unavoidable by an investor who invests in the stock market. When investors bear compensated risk, however, they expect to be rewarded for doing so.

In light of these two kinds of risk, the question that you should ultimately be asking yourself is "How can I protect my portfolio from uncompensated risk while in the pursuit of higher returns?" The first method that you should employ is one that you already know: plain old-fashioned diversification.

> **WEALTH INSIGHT:** Although concentrated ownership of founders' stock sometimes conveys fabulous riches on a fortunate few (for example, Microsoft's Bill Gates), it's impossible to know ahead of time which firms will grow from unseasoned start-ups to Fortune 500 companies. In fact, it's reasonable to expect that a great percentage of new companies will fail.

Diversification Keeps Risk Under Control

The object of diversification is to minimize the uncompensated risk of having too few investments. An investor can eliminate virtually all uncompensated risk from a portfolio with proper diversification. A popular definition for diversification is "Don't put all your investment eggs in one basket."

Though almost all diversification is good, the academics have refined the concept to what they call *effective diversification* and *ineffective diversification*. An example of ineffective diversification is the investor who holds Microsoft stock and decides to diversify by investing in Dell and six other computer companies. If anything affects that industry, all of that person's investments could be expected to move together—either up or down. It's almost as if the investor holding Microsoft didn't diversify at all, because his or her investments are so positively correlated with each other. Overall, this investor's attempt to diversify his or her portfolio was particularly ineffective.

On the other hand, effective diversification would be building a portfolio with stocks or asset classes during the growth or summer season of the economy that have dissimilar price movements. And, by creating a portfolio with asset classes that don't move together, you can significantly reduce your portfolio's overall volatility.

WEALTH INSIGHT: A landmark academic discovery showed that when two portfolios have the same average return, the portfolio with smaller up and down swings in value (less volatility) will have a greater compound return. This also explains why Dr. Grasmere's conservative investment grew as described in our earlier example. Consequently, his prospects for a greater compound rate of return over time could also improve.

This reduction in volatility allows investors to be more comfortable and to focus on the long term, and helps them to not be distracted by the noise of the day. It's similar to the story of the tortoise and the hare. The hare races like crazy but is out of control, which allows the slow but steady tortoise to ultimately win the race.

When it comes to asset classes, each class has different types and levels of risk (and return) attached to them. These varying characteristics will cause different asset classes to behave differently over time. Your key goal in this area should be to allocate and diversify your assets to balance out the overall risk for the greatest possible return. The Brinson, Hood, Beebower study illustrated in Exhibit 6.2 supports this idea.

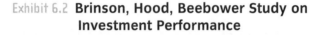

Exhibit 6.2 **Brinson, Hood, Beebower Study on Investment Performance**

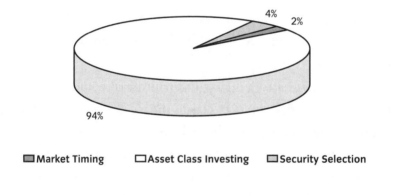

■ Market Timing   □ Asset Class Investing   ■ Security Selection

WHAT YOU'RE LOOKING AT: The results of the Brinson, Hood, Beebower study.

WHAT THIS TELLS YOU: The study showed that 94 percent of performance was attributable to the allocation of the assets. Picking the right individual asset added little value (less than 6 percent).

WHAT THIS MEANS: It was the combination or allocation of asset classes that made the most difference. Demographics—how the spending of large groups of people influenced stock returns—were never factored into the study, but the study itself still stands as a good example of how asset allocation impacts overall returns.

• • • • • •

In a 1991 follow-up to the study, Brinson et al., again showed that more than 94 percent of the rate of return on a portfolio is a result of correct asset allocation and only 6 percent is a result of buying an investment at just the right time or buying the best investment. The study analyzed the three primary investment strategies to determine variations in portfolio performance: asset allocation, security selection, and market timing.

I'm going to ignore the two strategies that had the least impact on performance: market timing and securities selection. One of the study's main findings revealed that most investors spend the bulk of their time on these less important strategies. On average, the strategies don't add value; in fact, they cause portfolios to lose value, because they rely on attempts to predict the future by looking at past performance.

> **WEALTH INSIGHT:**   Ironically, most media recommendations are based on past performance. I'm not saying that the advertisements— which are largely no-load mutual funds that display their latest performance records—in these magazines influence the writers, but the ads have to at least cause some bias. After all, the media doesn't want to bite the hand that feeds it.

It's easy to believe that good past fund performance equates to those funds having great people (fund managers) picking the best possible stocks. You simply have to look at the mutual fund industry's spectacular growth during the 1990s and 2000s, despite the crashing of the tech bubble in the spring of 2000. The total assets under management rose from $1.07 trillion at year-end 1990 to $7.65 trillion by 2004! See Exhibit 6.3.

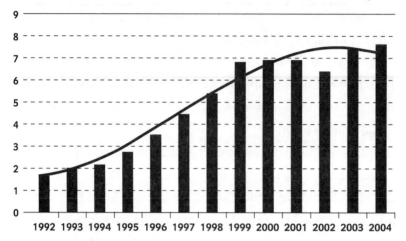

Exhibit 6.3 **U.S. Mutual Fund Assets (in $ trillions)**

WHAT YOU'RE LOOKING AT: Look closely and you'll see that the expansion reflects positive retirement savings flow, with ongoing reinvestment of dividends and interest.

WHAT THIS TELLS YOU: The reason behind this positive retirement savings flow is the large group of baby boomers who had reached their peak spending years and were also moving toward their highest savings rate.

WHAT THIS MEANS: See how you get a different spin on the cause of those growth exhibits when you're looking at the exhibits in a more data-inclusive way?

•••••

As I mentioned before, Wall Street firms spend billions of dollars each year trying to out-guess their competition in market timing and securities selection, because they get paid a commission for selling products. But they don't recommend the management strategy that our study proved to have the most positive impact on portfolio performance—asset allocation—for individual investors. And why not? Because that would mean it wasn't Wall Street's money management people who were responsible for all of the success out there. Instead, it was you! Just one of the 78 million baby boomers, trucking along in our life cycles, was ultimately responsible for the 94 percent of the rate of return performance. And this success was due to correct asset allocation—*not* trying to guess which stock or mutual fund would go up next. In addition, where to allocate is something you would know by watching Wealth Factors 1 and 2: birthrate and predictable spending cycles or patterns (see Chapter 2).

Diversified Asset Allocation

With market timing and securities selection off to the side, I'll now focus on the third strategy—asset allocation—which accounted for over 90 percent of the profit determination in the study. This powerful technique can also be applied successfully to changes in the economy's seasons.

Yet even when investors know and understand the methodology of asset allocation or other strategies, they often fail in their investments. A main cause of this failure involves the Human Model of Forecasting. People tend to forecast trends as straight-line extrapolations from the past, even though trends move in curvilinear or cyclical patterns. This tendency to forecast in a straight line causes investors to be the most optimistic and risk-accepting at the top of a cycle, when likely the greatest risk and negative returns lie ahead. Then those same investors become the most pessimistic and risk-averse at the bottom, when the markets have washed out—discounting that the worst of the risk taking has passed and the longest periods of high returns typically lie ahead.

This tendency to project the recent past into the future not only makes many of us terrible investors but it also causes bubbles to develop near the tops of very robust markets, just as it did in 1987 and 2000. The bubbles with unrealistic valuations develop to the greatest degree in the sectors that were strongest during the up-trend in the cycle. Most investors buy more of the hottest sectors and less of sectors that they may have previously included in their portfolio for diversification of risk. Hence, investors abandon the principle of diversification that actually represents the best single way of reducing risk while aiming for strong, long-term returns. As a result, many investors get into the highest risk positions just before a major correction; they then suffer the worst of the downturn and put themselves in the lowest risk position by selling out just in time to miss the returns of the next rebound.

> **WEALTH INSIGHT:** Confusion often stems from the interchangeable use of the terms *asset allocation* and *diversification*. Asset allocation simply means determining what proportion of your money is going to be invested in each asset class—stocks, bonds, cash investments—in order to maximize the growth of your portfolio for each unit of risk that you take. Diversification is simply adding more names/investments into the same investment category.

So how do you actually determine what percentage of each asset class you should own? Academics have calculated methods to measure correlation in a portfolio, thereby enabling the volatility or risk of a portfolio to be measured with a degree of predictability. Your wealth management advisory team should have access to these types of tools.

Because of these measurement tools, it's possible to combine a portfolio of asset classes that have the potential to generate higher returns due to their volatile nature, but whose market performances have a low correlation to one another. This achieves the result that the portfolio as a whole will actually be less risky than any one of the individual investments, yet it will generate a higher overall return than a portfolio made up solely of low-risk investments. Exhibits 6.4 and 6.5 illustrate inefficient and efficient diversification.

Exhibit 6.4 **Inefficient Asset Diversification**

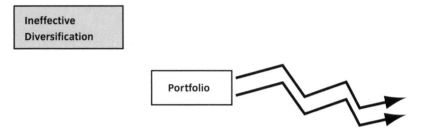

WHAT YOU'RE LOOKING AT: The progression of investments that move in tandem.

WHAT THIS TELLS YOU: Ineffective diversification results when all of your investments move together.

WHAT THIS MEANS: You put your portfolio at risk when you don't diversify well.

· · · · · ·

Exhibit 6.5 **Efficient Asset Diversification**

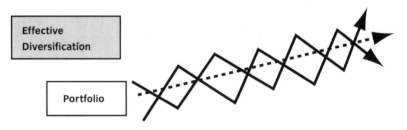

WHAT YOU'RE LOOKING AT: The progression of investments that move independently.

WHAT THIS TELLS YOU: When each of your investment vehicles moves independently, you can accomplish effective diversification of your portfolio.

WHAT THIS MEANS: The idea of effective diversification may seem simple and unimportant, but it can have a big impact on your returns.

· · · · · ·

The Wealth Investment Process

You're now well-versed in the fundamentals of an effective investment strategy, so we'll move on to understanding how those fundamentals relate to the Weath Investment Process.

Understanding the Process

The three-step Wealth Investment Process uses Markowitz's theory of building a portfolio of investments whose returns move in different, noncorrelated patterns in order to lower risk.

Step One: Demographics

This step involves what you've been reading about in the first four chapters—relying on demographic data to determine economic areas with the most growth potential, and then allocating your assets appropriately.

Step Two: Historical Outcomes

In this step, you'll look at historical outcomes and the probability of their recurrence. You also know this as the Seasons of the Economy. Here, you want to see if the life cycles of the industries fit in the current season and what are the chances or probabilities that those cycles will continue in the next season.

Step Three: Fundamental and Technical Analyses

This step can provide you with an indication of a fair market valuation versus simply historical norms. In terms of fundamental analysis, you begin with the earning per share (EPS) of a company. You want to know the expectations for future earnings, also known as its price-to-earnings growth (PEG) ratio. Is the company's current price-to-earnings undervalued or overvalued? Lastly, you'll consider the technical analysis, or the forecasting of future movements in a company's stock price based solely on looking at past price movement patterns. There are no guarantees in this view; the purpose is to estimate a likely outcome based on similar historical activity in the price of the stock.

WEALTH INSIGHT: While technical analysis can be a useful fine-tuning tool, money flow can help in forecasting the future just by reviewing a few key data points such as: Is the average daily price trend ahead of the 10-day moving average? If so, it's right to conclude that more "new" investment money is moving into the company stock. If not, then what else could make the stock go up? Like all items available for purchase, the price one ultimately pays is based on supply and demand. If more people are buying (demand), and the supply is constant (which is a known determination for public companies), then the price will increase.

If the volume also increases, and those increases are in 10,000-share blocks (normal amounts at institutional levels), you have data to make the logical money flow conclusion: that the stock's price is going up (more demand), and the volume is up as are the 10,000-share blocks. Money is flowing into this company! The institutional elephant leaves a clue—the "footprint" of increasing, or, in a downward price movement, decreasing prices on large volume. Observing this data over time frames you choose to look at, you'll see the money flow secret.

Applying the Process

Keeping the three main steps of the Wealth Investment Process in mind, let's examine how to apply the process to an investment portfolio—and how to choose a qualified planning firm to manage it.

An important consideration when applying the process is not just to include all of the economic sectors that will outperform in each season of the economy. You need to determine which sectors have the highest expected returns and which are not affected by news or economic data in similar ways. In other words, find efficient diversification we just discussed.

For example, many sectors, such as retail banks and financial services, have high correlation coefficients, and therefore the returns of these sectors move in step. This in-step movement of returns does not help the portfolio to lower its risk through asset allocation. Sometimes the return from one asset class will be positive when the return from another asset class is negative, and vice versa (see Exhibit 6.6).

Exhibit 6.6 **The Efficient Frontier Curve**

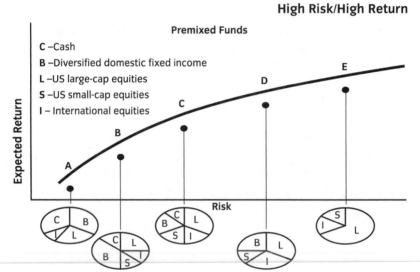

WHAT YOU'RE LOOKING AT: The efficient frontier curve and a mix of five risk choices. The curve is a tool that most advisors use to select your portfolio. The idea is to plot a graph, which shows the highest potential return from a diversified portfolio for a given level of risk.

WHAT THIS TELLS YOU: This efficient frontier curve demonstrates the potential trade-offs between equities, bonds, and cash. You have low risk in owning a money market fund, but you also get a low expected return. The curve also demonstrates that when you choose investments with higher risk, your expected returns also increase proportionately.

WHAT THIS MEANS: As you can see, there's a risk-return trade-off. Understanding how each of these assets correlates with each other is the next step in managing this risk-return trade-off.

· · · · · ·

If the correlation between assets is zero, the movements of the securities are said to have no correlation—it's completely random. If one security moves up or down, there's a good chance that the other will move either up or down, but the way in which they move is random. A perfect correlation is +1, and an opposite correlation would be –1. There's no diversification advantage to be gained by pairing two assets with a +1 correlation.

On the other hand, pairing assets having a –1 correlation could be advantageous. You'd want the one in your portfolio because it provides you with dissimilar price movement. *Dissimilar price movement* is easily defined as the movement of one investment that you're observing (most of the time) in an opposite direction as another observed investment. Or, that as one asset class moves up, the other moves down—over the same time period.

Most people forget that all of our domestic asset classes are in U.S. dollars. They're so highly correlated with each other, it's impossible to be truly diversified. When we get into a winter period, you'll want investments that will be negatively correlated with U.S. investments. As the U.S. stock market and/or the dollar falls, foreign currencies and other international markets will in all likelihood (but not always) increase.

U.S. dollar. By January 2005, the euro was trading at $1.33, an improvement of over 50 percent.

Looking back at the fall of the dollar against the euro—33 percent between 2002 and 2005—it would seem that Buffett's timing was perfect. What he was anticipating was the asset, in this case the euro, responding differently to changes in the U.S. economy and our investment marketplace.

Managed Asset Accounts

Earlier, we discussed how the principle of diversification offers you greater comfort because it disburses your risk. But how do you know you're really diversified? The key is to search out and find groups of investment assets that don't move together in unison, but rather those that move inversely or dissimilarly to each other.

By combining assets and having low correlation, volatility can be lowered for portfolios while enhancing risk-adjusted rates of return. An investor needs to understand, analyze, and select the appropriate type of managed portfolio account based on the current academic research.

The investment business has many names for the various types of managed accounts out there, even though many of these names mean the same thing. I've defined the major types and clarified the differences between them below.

Separate Accounts

These accounts are also known as separately managed accounts, individually managed accounts, or managed accounts. For simplicity's sake, I'll refer to them here as separate accounts. A *separate account* is an investment vehicle in which the investor gives an investment firm full discretion over cash and/or securities to manage according to the investor's specifications. This type of account can also be used inside a qualified retirement plan.

Separate accounts have certain similarities to mutual funds such as professional management, cost, diversification, and liquidity. However, the investor directly owns the individual securities inside the separate account, and investments aren't pooled with those of other investors, as they are in a mutual fund. Also, separate account programs routinely handle specific and unique requests, oftentimes pertaining to tax considerations. Because of their pooled ownership structure, mutual funds cannot take such individual preferences into consideration.

Scalability is a huge issue, one that cuts many different ways including scalability of operations and scalability of client service. One of the reasons that investors use separate accounts is the ability to customize the account for tax efficiency. Two separate accounts started two months apart can have a different cost basis even when the stocks are the same. When December rolls around, you want to be sure that your wealth management team is monitoring all aspects of your account. For instance, are your capital gains or losses being harvested in a way that's ideal for you and your tax rate?

Good wealth management advisors are constantly checking on not just how their clients' portfolios are doing but also on harvesting gains or losses. Rather than having performance seep out, you can add performance by tweaking the account in a way that mutual funds cannot be tweaked. That's the other attractive feature of separate accounts: You know what your mutual fund return is going to be. With a separate account, your wealth management firm can do some things that will make a difference to the upside—or not do things that will lead to performance to the downside.

WEALTH INSIGHT: Before you decide on a separate account, you may want to take some precautions. The following is a strategy that can help to insulate your separate account from the devastation that can transpire during a bear market.

The obvious starting point is your return requirements and risk tolerance. Your wealth management team can help you to determine each of these as part of your comprehensive planning strategy and incorporate the findings into your wealth management policy statement. The wealth management policy statement should be the foundation for allocation, manager selection, and ongoing manager and performance monitoring.

Next, you need to have identified how much risk you're actually taking. Have a methodology in place to determine how changing market conditions affect your investment policy. And finally, you'd better be able to determine if your wealth advisory team is adding value relative to their benchmark and peer group.

You also need to know that any positive results are not simply correlated with normal market fluctuations. By integrating manager returns and the performance metrics of beta, standard deviation, and alpha, your wealth management team should be able to determine the best manager(s) in each style box or market in your asset allocation model. In addition, your wealth advisor should perform normal due diligence on the manager, the manager's tenure, style correlation, and the like before adding the manager to your portfolio.

Multi-Discipline Account (MDA)

An MDA is a popular offering among larger public investment firms that combines several distinct investment strategies in a single account. An MDA manager is really a program sponsor. The program sponsor is the investment advisor and is responsible for establishing and maintaining the program.

Multi-Style Account (MSA)

Cerulli Associates' umbrella term joins the growing list of acronyms used to describe the packaging together of investment styles in predetermined percentages—often with lower investment minimums.

Unified Managed Account (UMA)

This is a centralized platform for brokerages to support a service for financial consultants' fee-based businesses.

Client-Directed, Fee-Based Account

In this type of account, the client directs the investments on a discretionary basis and can trade as much as he or she wants but is charged only one fee. These accounts are rising in popularity and usually contain trading restrictions to control the frequency of trading.

Broker-Directed or Personally Advised Account

This account is one in which the investment advisor and/or stockbroker directs the investments on a discretionary basis. There's no independent money manager. Pioneered at E. F. Hutton, these programs are usually available only through a limited number of experienced, prequalified brokers.

Guided Managed Account

These programs are brokerage accounts that use their research departments to put together "buy" lists and give brokers and/or advisors a choice for clients of one or two securities in each category. These programs are some of the fastest-growing products at many firms. The term "fee-based brokerage account" is used interchangeably with guided portfolio account, which the broker manages on a discretionary basis.

Wrap Fee Account

The original wrap account was an individually managed account run by a professional money manager on a discretionary basis for the client. Mutual fund wraps, or mutual fund managed accounts, consist of a portfolio of mutual funds with an advisory fee overlay. This was the hottest product in the 1990s but cooled down as diversified asset allocation didn't perform well in the technology-heavy bull market.

Core Portfolio Development

Once you settle on the type of managed account that best suits your needs, you must develop the core portfolio of assets that will go into that account. The portfolio's core positions should be representative of a proven investment strategy employing stocks, bonds, and cash that are strategically allocated based on certain factors such as your objectives, return requirements, and risk profile. (See Exhibit 6.7.)

This portfolio strategy will never be concentrated in the top-performing asset class, but that's all right, since every academic study shows that nobody can forecast which asset class will represent the winning strategy with any indication of reliability. Your objective should simply be to build a diversified core portfolio.

Again, keep in mind that we're working beneath the big picture described earlier in Step One: Demographics. For the moment, we're assuming we're in the growth or summer season, where we'd be building a growth portfolio. Obviously, this will change as we move toward the winter season of investing, which I detail in Chapter 10.

Exhibit 6.7 **Core Portfolio Development**

WHAT YOU'RE LOOKING AT: A visual representation of a core strategy.

WHAT THIS TELLS YOU: The core's center is built around what you can't afford to lose within your specified time parameter. You begin at

More Risk/More Reward Potential

the center by assembling a portfolio of lower risk, lower volatility (possibly generating some) investments, then build outward depending on your desired level of risk and growth.

WHAT THIS MEANS: As you move outward from the core, you add riskier investment classes until you capture the exact combination that you desire to protect against both actual investment loss and loss of purchasing power.

• • • • • •

Remember our Morningstar Box Grid in Chapter 1? It is seen again in Exhibit 6.8.

Exhibit 6.8 **Morningstar Box Grid**

Large-cap Value	Large-cap Blend	Large-cap Growth
Mid-cap Value	Mid-cap Blend	Mid-cap Growth
Small-cap Value	Small -cap Blend	Small-cap Growth

WHAT YOU'RE LOOKING AT: A Morningstar Box Grid (see Exhibit 1.2).

WHAT THIS TELLS YOU: This chart includes small-, mid-, and large-cap-italization equities on one axis, and value, blended, and growth equities on the other axis—in addition to multiple classes of fixed-income securities.

WHAT THIS MEANS: Advanced planning strategies depict a core wealth strategy as the center of the style box. The chart shows a series of boxes stacked upon each other, rather than a central investment image around which riskier, more style-specific sectors orbit. The human mind has an easier time grasping a simplistic visual concept rather than the complex depiction of style boxes.

••••••

Everything outside the core represents more aggressive investment strategies or ones in which there's either a higher degree of risk or a lower level of confidence. The outermost ring, representing the portion of the portfolio with the greatest risk, includes various trading strategies, which we determined earlier were quantifiably less productive, as were alternative investments.

The ultimate method of controlling risk in a core strategy is through company stock selection. For example, if a company is high quality, reporting a growing stream of earnings, and the price paid for the stock is reasonable, by definition, the stock should have less risk relative to other stocks. If your portfolio is full of these "excellent" stocks, the relative risk of loss or volatility should be less than other noncore portfolios. This rule applies equally to both growth and value stocks since "excellent" stocks can have either or both growth and value attributes. In essence, *growth* is not necessarily a dirty word to a core value equity manager, and low price is not necessarily an impediment to a core growth equity manager.

A core strategy is generally not bound by capitalization or geographical constraints, since these inherently restrict investment opportunities or cause early forfeitures of gains or forced loss realization if strictly applied. In addition, strict application of these constraints may require you to avoid a cap range or specific country that's in favor while requiring participation in either a range or geography that's underperforming.

> **WEALTH INSIGHT:** Core wealth advisory managers generally don't believe in momentum investing, which in many cases is based on emotion or market psychology rather than investment fundamentals. Momentum investing also often leads to the application of specific rules with little or no flexibility to adapt to unique circumstances. A stock that is sold solely because it has doubled may not become a success story if it thereafter continues to appreciate but at a slower rate.

As I'll discuss in detail in Chapter 7, an experienced wealth advisory management team is a necessary component in building confidence in the core portion of an investment portfolio. Some of the more significant experience factors include a philosophy of investing only in businesses that have a track record of recognizing and correcting mistakes early. Other attributes of character include a natural reluctance to follow the crowd; a tendency to engage in independent thinking; adherence to a fundamental investment philosophy despite changes in market sentiment or falling security prices; and the recognition that the importance of a sell discipline is equal to that of a buy discipline.

Finally, within the core portion of any portfolio, tax management is an important objective. (I also go into more detail on this in Chapter 7.) Regardless of the rate of portfolio turnover, the ultimate result should be a high degree of tax efficiency relative to realized gains and losses. For the core portion of the fixed income portfolio, it is much more desirable to sacrifice minimal amounts of income in return for less market price volatility. The primary purpose of the fixed-income portion of the core portfolio was formerly considered a way to reduce overall portfolio risk, but that hasn't proved to be the case. When interest rates rise, the capital value of bonds will typically decrease to reflect yields that are comparable to those of newly issued bonds.

Once in place, the core can form the foundation of a total investment portfolio designed to meet your investment objectives. This is a place where you should feel comfort and security and never anxiety or panic. It's designed to form the base from which all other investment strategies can be launched, and, at the same time, serve as a safety net in times of economic or financial turmoil.

Monitoring the Process

After choosing managed accounts and putting a core portfolio in place, you can just sit back, relax, and count on your money to grow, right? Wrong! Ongoing monitoring must be done and necessary allocation changes must be made in order to stay invested appropriately. The following are three important points to take into consideration when monitoring the performance of an investment account.

Beta

The first performance metric is beta, which is a measure of the relative risk of an investment compared to that of a market or benchmark, usually defined by an index like the S&P 500. The market or index is assumed to have a beta of 1.00. A separate account manager with a beta of 1.50 would have a relative risk that would be 50 percent greater than the index. By this measure, the separate account manager could be expected to go up by approximately 15 percent if the index were to have a positive move of 10 percent. Conversely, if the index were to have a negative move of 10 percent, you could expect this manager to go down by 15 percent.

Standard Deviation

Standard deviation measures the disbursement of returns or volatility of returns around the mean return that's been achieved by a manager over a trailing period of time. The greater the variation from the mean rate of return, the greater the standard deviation — or the greater the risk the manager is taking to achieve the return. By using standard deviation in the allocation process, you can make sure that you're not creating a manager allocation that will fall outside of your risk tolerance. To determine your tolerance for volatility and risk, you will need to answer questions about how much fluctuation in your account value (volatility) you're willing to experience in order to achieve your required return.

WEALTH INSIGHT: During the mid-1990s, the standard deviation of the S&P 500 hovered around 8 percent on a trailing three-year basis. However, standard deviation doesn't indicate the possible loss of capital for any one particular year. A standard deviation of 8 percent may not sound particularly risky, but in 1987, the S&P 500 had a one-year negative return of 26.7 percent. This absolute decline represented more volatility or risk than most investors were comfortable taking. Many abandoned their investment plans, managers, and advisors during this negative performance period.

From 1995 to 2000, the standard deviation of the S&P 500 continued to expand at an alarming rate, from about 8 percent to more than 18 percent—over a 100 percent increase in volatility. A prudent wealth advisor would assume that the possible declines in portfolio value that an investor could experience had also expanded dramatically. This increase in standard deviation was a very clear indication that the risk investors were taking with a manager who benchmarked against the S&P had, more than likely, increased dramatically.

By using standard deviation in your investment design and management process, you can collar, or contain, your risk by design. In your wealth management policy, you need to define a band of acceptable volatility. You can do this by selecting a market benchmark like the S&P 500 Index as a proxy for the amount of risk that you're willing to assume. You need to thoroughly understand the risk dynamics of the benchmark, including not only standard deviation measures but also its absolute worst one-year performance statistics.

CASE STUDY: Mark and Judy Lewis

CORPORATE EXECUTIVES

In 1995, Mark and Judy Lewis, a 50-year-old couple with $2,000,000 to invest, consulted with a wealth manager and discussed using separate account managers. In filling out the investment questionnaire, the couple indicated that they didn't view themselves as conservative or aggressive but more moderate in their attitudes about risk.

For every level of risk, there's some optimum combination of investments that will give you the highest rate of return. These combinations have risk/reward trade-off and form what we referred to as the efficient frontier. The efficient frontier is determined by calculating the expected rate of return, standard deviation, and correlation coefficient for each investment manager. The efficient frontier lets you visualize who has the highest expected return for each incremental level of risk. Another way to think about the efficient frontier is the point where the maximum amount of risk an investor is willing to tolerate intersects with the maximum amount of reward that can potentially be generated.

The Lewises indicated that they'd be willing to incur 75 percent risk (of the volatility of the S&P 500, as measured by its three-year standard deviation) to achieve an expected rate of return of 10 percent. When they set up their account in 1995, it would have only taken investing 40 percent of the couple's assets with a conservative income fund manager using a balanced allocation of 20 percent with a U.S. large-cap growth manager; 20 percent with a U.S. mid-cap growth manager; and 20 percent with an international manager to reach their goals.

Yet in the end, the large-cap growth manager, the mid-cap growth manager, and the international managers' volatility or risk as measured by standard deviation increased faster than their S&P benchmark. Even though that initial asset allocation fit the couple's risk tolerance constraint, everything changed. Five years later, their same allocation exposed them to more risk. Risk or volatility can be statistically measured using standard deviation, which describes how far from the mean historic performance has been, either higher or lower. The lesson here is: You can't keep your head in the sand; just because your account is growing, don't assume everything is fine.

As the markets became more volatile in the late 1990s, the wealth manager did what the Lewises had paid her to do by rebalancing their portfolio. Rebalancing is the process of shifting percentages of assets between managers in order to maintain the correct balance of stated risk. By increasing the couple's exposure to fixed income, the manager brought the portfolio allocation back within the Lewises' risk constraint parameters that they set forth in their wealth investment policy statement.

During the late 1990s, when the U.S. equity market was flying, the last thing investors wanted to do was move money away from equities and become more conservative. This process automatically reduces risk during periods when markets become more volatile and allows you to increase your risk profile once markets stabilize. You might have had a little bit less upside return when the markets were cooking, but you didn't lose as much on the downside.

Finally, by closely monitoring standard deviation, you can also make changes to your selection of managers if they stray too far from your portfolio objectives.

Alpha

Alpha represents the difference between the manager's actual return and its expected performance relative to the performance and volatility of the market, measured by its beta. The difference is expressed as an annual percentage. For example, assume that risk-free Treasury bills returned 6 percent and the S&P 500 returned 12 percent, and a manager with a beta of 1.2 returned 15 percent. The market excess return is 6 percent (12% – 6%), and the expected return of the manager is 13.2 percent (1.2 x 6%) + 6%). Since the portfolio actually returned 15 percent, its alpha is 1.8 percent (15% – 13.2%), meaning that the portfolio performed better than expected in light of the risk taken. The significant advantage alpha offers over other performance metrics is apples-to-apples comparisons between managers.

When a separate account manager provides a rate of return over and above his or her benchmark, the manager is providing real value and will have a positive alpha. Some managers try to get excess over a benchmark index by taking an inordinate amount of risk. Their return in an up-market may look great when the additional risk that they are taking enhances returns, but when markets turn sour and decline, these same managers are likely to lose your capital at an accelerated rate.

WEALTH INSIGHT: From 1945 to 1965, the markets were in an explosive up-trend. The economy expanded as never before. We experienced the *Happy Days* phase of economic and market growth during the 1950s and early 1960s. The economy was booming; unemployment was almost nonexistent; the markets were flying; and returns were breaking records. Sound familiar? Following this economic boom period and huge bull market, we experienced a significant period of market underperformance.

Beginning in 1965, we witnessed 17 years of significant market underperformance, including the market crash of 1973–1974. In 1965, the Dow hit a high of nearly 1000, but the last great bull market run started in 1982 with the Dow at 777. This is a 70 percent inflation-adjusted loss. We may soon be starting a cycle reminiscent of that 1965 to 1982 period. During an underperformance cycle, you may not be able to tolerate a buy and hold strategy. To survive, you must adjust your strategy based on the current market environment, or risk the potential loss to a significant amount of your capital.

After reading this chapter, you are in a great position. You now know what it takes to build an effective investment process from the ground up, starting with a sound Wealth Investment Policy to all of the components of a strong Wealth Management Process. You're ready to graduate to Chapter 7, where we'll talk about how you can put those lessons to work toward creating your own personal Wealth Management Process.

---

1. Calculated by Dalbar using data presented in *Stocks, Bonds and Inflation 2003 Yearbook*, Ibbotson & Associates, Inc. Based on copyrighted works by Ibbotson and Sinquefield. All rights reserved. Used with permission.

2. Annualized return assumes returns are compounded annually.

3. The rate of return investors earn based on the length of time shareholders actually remain invested in a fund and the historic performance of the fund's appropriate index.

CREATING YOUR OWN WEALTH MANAGEMENT PROCESS

Before selecting a wealth management or investment team, we need to be clear about who's on first—meaning, what are these people called?

Making Sense of Investment Team Titles

In the old days, traditional wealth managers only provided financial services to high net worth individuals and worked for trust companies. They didn't have to be registered investment advisors (RIAs) because they operated under banking rules. But that was then.

Today, just about anyone can call him- or herself a wealth manager. I'm trained as a Certified Financial Planner™ practitioner, but my firm became a wealth management firm...not for marketing purposes, but because it better describes what we do.

I realize there's confusion when I describe the people used in different investment functions. The problem centers around industry shorthand names that everyone uses, and such is also the case with money managers. A mutual fund manager and a separate account manager are both money managers but under different management formats. Some investment advisors and financial planners even call themselves money managers. It creates tremendous confusion.

To make matters even worse, people who were stockbrokers now call themselves financial consultants, and financial consultants are called financial advisors. Some financial advisors want to be called financial coaches. There are over 60 professional delegations in my industry alone!

Get the point? Confusion.

How did it get so confusing? Because we live in a look-alike world of competitors, and our industry decided to call in the marketing experts who said, "No problem; everyone should have his or her own 'brand.'" The result was more confusion.

Now here's the good news. I'm going to help you make sense of the most common names. That way, as I discuss the creation of your personal Wealth Management Process, you'll know who's responsible for each part of the process. The most common names include: Financial Advisor and Investment Advisor, Financial Planner and Certified Financial Planner, Registered Investment Advisor, Financial Consultant, Money Manager, Investment Management Firm, Broker/Stockbroker, and Plan Sponsor.

Financial Advisor and Investment Advisor

These terms are used interchangeably. They may offer many services, but they basically give investment advice in return for compensation.

Financial Planner and Certified Financial Planner

Both will draw up a plan for your financial future. Certified means they have completed a rigorous two-year examination process, passed the final examination, and signed the College for Financial Planning Code of Ethics.

Registered Investment Advisor

Historically, a registered investment advisor (RIA) was someone who managed portfolios, generally with discretion, such as a mutual fund manager or a separate account manager. The definition of the traditional RIA was expanded. Operating as an RIA in order to be able to charge fees was not the original intent of the Investment Advisers Act of 1940. The original intent was to regulate portfolio managers and investment advisors who manage specific portfolios.

Many financial planners have become RIAs because they were making investment decisions and recommendations to their clients, which by definition is acting in a fiduciary capacity. A fiduciary capacity means you can be held personally liable for your advice. But since an RIA can also be an investment advisor, it makes it a bit confusing.

Financial Consultant

These people work mostly with 401(k) plans and large pension plans offering the following services: asset allocation, investment strategy, manager searches, manager evaluation, and performance analysis.

Money Manager

The core function of a money manager is portfolio management at a mutual fund or separate account firm.

Investment Management Firm

This is a company offering mutual funds or separate account management.

Broker/Stockbroker

Most brokers simply buy and sell stocks on behalf of their clients, but they can go by many names: advisor, financial advisor, investment consultant, and some are even called financial planners. Just remember that they represent a brokerage firm while they're working with you.

Plan Sponsor

A sponsor isn't a person but a company—maybe a broker or dealer or brokerage firm that offers an approved list of mutual funds and/or separate account programs. They do the due diligence and background checks.

Okay, now that we have that straight, we can talk about the specific members who should be on your wealth management team who will handle investing. These members will likely include your overall team facilitator (your financial advisor) as well as other potential team members, depending on the type of management team structure that you choose.

Selecting an Investment Management Team

I'm going to start this section with a table (Exhibit 7.1) that demonstrates the two main management approaches.

Either way, manager selection begins with the screening process. The process of qualifying the money manager is better known as due diligence by the investment industry. This simply means that care has been taken to substantiate the suitability of a money manager. But no matter how carefully this process is implemented, the criteria in performing due diligence is subjective in nature, and the process is difficult to learn.

Exhibit 7.1 **A Bottom-Up versus Top-Down Management Approach**

	Strengths	Weaknesses
Bottom Up	Best managers used Smaller stable of managers for the broker to follow Usually allows managers to go to where the performance is	Higher correlation among managers Tendency to have few managers managing most of client assets
Top Down	Each style represented by "best in class" manager Style box–friendly Lower correlation among managers	Managers constrained by style FA has to do due diligence on many different managers

WHAT YOU'RE LOOKING AT: The strengths and weaknesses of the two main management approaches.

WHAT THIS TELLS YOU: Many wealth management teams, like mine, have a stable of mutual funds or separate account managers. Or, as I described above, they have money managers who have an approach the team prefers and who generally have good contacts at the investment management firms as well. Most brokerage firms have an approved list of managers. Some only allow a preselected collection of mutual funds and/or separate accounts. This involves a bottom-up selection process.

WHAT THIS MEANS: Bottom up means first selecting a handful of preferred money managers, then building client portfolios around them. The alternative to this is a top-down approach—that is, first determining which types or styles of money managers are needed for an allocation, then finding the best manager to fill each slot. Both approaches have their strengths and weaknesses, which I've outlined in the table above.

· · · · · ·

Here's a basic outline of the steps involved in the process. (From this point forward, all money managers, including mutual fund and separate account managers, will be referred to simply as managers.)

Preliminary Screen

There are preliminary criteria that must be met before a manager can be considered. Criteria may vary depending on the asset class of the securities. The preliminary screening usually requires:

- *Assets under Management:* At least $300 million under management.

- *Length and Documentation of Track Record:* A verifiable five-year track record, based on Association for Investment Management and Research (AIMR) standards; personnel responsible for the track record should still be at the firm.

- *Consistency of Personnel:* Little or no turnover among the investment professionals.

- *Registration:* Properly registered with the Securities and Exchange Commission.

- *Compliance:* No involvement in any investigation or litigation that's deemed material.

Quantitative Criteria

The next step is to evaluate the mutual fund or separate account manager's style behavior, consistency, added value, and performance in different market cycles. These criteria may change depending on the asset classes under consideration:

- *Predictability of Performance Relative to Benchmark:* Commonly referred to as R-squared; tracking errors are calculated and analyzed over various time periods against an appropriate benchmark.

- *Style Analysis:* Firms take different approaches, which may include return-based analysis, fundamental portfolio analysis and investment philosophy, and process analysis. Some wealth advisory teams use a variety of databases to analyze style by a return-based regression methodology. This analysis can also illustrate the tendency of a portfolio manager to alter his or her investment style over time. This is referred to as style drift.

- *Risk-Adjusted Performance:* An analysis of performance generated per unit of risk taken is performed by looking at the following factors over various time periods: Alpha, Sharpe Ratio, and Information Ratio. These numbers are analyzed relative to the appropriate benchmark as well as to other managers in the same asset class.

- *Consistency:* Along with other indicators, this measures the ratio of the quarters in which the manager outperforms to the quarters in which he or she underperforms, plus the manager's performance over rolling time periods.

- *Seasons of the Economy Analysis:* The performance of the manager may be examined over various economic seasons and cycles when the manager's style is in favor versus when it's out of favor.

Qualitative Analysis

This analysis helps to determine if the factors that contributed to past performance are still in place and are positioned to contribute well into the future. The following components are evaluated:

- *Personnel:* Tenure, experience, depth, continuity, and skill level of key investment personnel.

- *Investment Philosophy and Process:* The portfolio construction process and underlying philosophy.

- *Investment Research:* The generation of earnings estimates, sources of credit research on bonds, the number of industry specialists, and the areas they cover.

- *Implementation of the Investment Process:* The checks and balances in place at the money management firm are examined to ensure that the investment process is implemented uniformly across all accounts.

- *Business Structure:* The business plan and financial condition of the firm are analyzed, as well as the compliance procedures and back-office operations.

Once a manager is approved, your wealth advisory team should monitor the following on a quarterly basis:

- Consistency of application of the stated investment discipline

- Disbursement of returns among accounts

- Reported aggregate performance versus performance in individual accounts

Managers can be removed from the recommended list if deterioration is noted in the qualitative factors mentioned above, or if a manager consistently underperforms his or her benchmark over a market cycle. Some examples of deterioration are as follows:

- *Personnel Change:* The potential for disrupting the investment process increases dramatically whenever a key investment professional departs.

- *Investment Process:* A manager can be terminated if the style and risk posture change from the mandate for which the manager was hired.

- *Consistency:* If a money manager doesn't adhere to the stated investment style, he or she will not continue to be recommended as an approved manager for that style.

- *Inability to Manage Growth in Assets:* If a money manager's corporate infrastructure is unable to provide good operational support, communication, and client service, the manager may be removed from the recommended list.

- *Unexplained Poor Performance:* Persistent, sustained underperformance relative to the money manager's peer group may trigger removal from the recommended list.

WEALTH INSIGHT: The criteria for choosing an investment team are important, but what about performance numbers? We all have individual investment requirements. Individual investment needs often cause managers to handle portfolios in different ways. The way managers choose to report on these portfolios leads to different performance results. Consequently, performance numbers often tell less about a manager than the investor assumes.

In looking at money managers, what you really want is consistency of results. Don't just pick the managers who had the highest rate of performance over the last couple of years; invariably, they underperform over the next couple of years.

SEC Information Provides Additional Insight

You do have other alternatives for gathering information about managers. Because the Securities and Exchange Commission (SEC) regulates investment managers, you can gain access to additional information from the disclosure statements on file with the government.

Form ADV

The most important of these disclosure documents is the Form ADV. By law, the manager must provide Part II of the form (or equivalent disclosure) to prospective investors. While Part II is the only form legally required to furnish to the public, it's a good idea to request both Parts I and II.

The ADV provides basic background information on the manager's state registrations, disciplinary or legal problems, ownership, potential conflicts of interest with fees or commissions, financial condition, and the background of the firm's principals. Investors should keep in mind that the SEC never passes on the merits or accuracy of the information provided in the ADV. Its purpose is to place basic information about the manager on public record.

Having access to an ADV gives you the opportunity to do some basic background checking of your own. Obvious areas of interest are prior employment of the firm's principals and the manager's educational background. When legal actions against the firm are discovered, investors should try to obtain copies of the court-filed complaints. By checking with the SEC's enforcement division, you may uncover actions taken by the SEC against the manager for regulatory violations.

Form 13F Filing

If a wealth manager manages $100 million or more in equities, then SEC regulations require that a quarterly 13F filing be made. This filing states the equity positions and the number of shares in those positions held by the manager. Because the manager submits his or her portfolio positions quarterly, these reports often accurately predict the manager's performance for the coming quarter.

Some wealth managers may argue that, because portfolio adjustments often occur between filings, the 13F is an inaccurate performance measure. Most wealth managers have portfolio turnovers of about 25 percent a year or higher. Even at a 40 percent per year turnover rate, the average quarter has only a 10 percent change in portfolio positions—a relatively small amount. This gives you another way of comparing the manager's publicly reported performance with his or her SEC 13F filings.

What Your Investment Advisor Should Be Asking

Once you've weeded out the first round of investment team candidates through your preliminary research, you can consider interviewing the remaining candidates. A money manager's disclosure is, by nature, a one-sided viewpoint. There are numerous questions that I could list here which would be prudent to ask, but for the sake of brevity, let's address two of the most critical.

1. *What's the history of their money management team?*

As with any organization, an investment team must work well together if it's going to succeed. If there's dissension among those making the decisions, portfolio consistency might suffer.

2. *What's their total asset value and number of accounts they've won or lost?*

The second question, if truthfully answered, is one of the most telling pieces of information about any wealth manager. Ask the manager to state the total asset value and the number of new accounts acquired and lost during the past five years. A good wealth manager has little to fear from this question. On the basis of this one piece of evidence alone, most investors could save themselves a lot of trouble.

Other factors investors might want to know include the size of the firm, how long the firm has been in business, its clientele list, and any referrals the principals might want to disclose. Common sense dictates that these basic questions need to be explored.

Investors should be careful of firms that are growing so fast that service and performance could suffer. These managers must place additional time and attention on the administration of their business. This can sometimes be detrimental to securities research and portfolio performance.

Due Diligence Checklist: Six Steps to Hiring an Account Manager

We'll now go through a checklist of criteria for performing manager due diligence. The key element is to discover if the research provided to you is absolutely independent and conflict-free. Once you're comfortable that the advice you're being given is conflict-free, then you can evaluate their history and experience.

Check 1: Conduct and Manage Interviews

When it comes to interviewing money managers, any question is fair game. Know who is responsible for key decisions such as establishing the level and timing of cash reserves; deciding the emphasis to be placed on themes, sectors, and industries; determining which stocks are to be purchased and sold; developing the actual portfolio; and reviewing portfolio results.

WEALTH INSIGHT: One big mistake is choosing the firm that gave the best presentation. Don't turn the manager selection process into a beauty pageant, which is what happens if you base your decision mainly on the 30-minute or 1-hour marketing pitch each firm gives. One of the key factors in choosing a manager is gaining a solid understanding of the firm's investment process. You won't always get that from a presentation.

Check 2: Dig into the Background of the Money Manager Team

Quiz each candidate about his or her investment style. Part of understanding the investment process requires an assessment of risk at the portfolio level. Among the considerations should be: How is diversification used? How often are strategic changes made? You must understand the relationship between risk and return to make informed and prudent investment decisions in order to properly evaluate money managers.

Check 3: Measure Money Manager Performance against Appropriate Benchmarks

Your money manager should be compared to market indexes, but blend them proportionately to match the composition of your portfolio. If your portfolio is restricted to a specific asset allocation mix, measure the account against the indexes in the same proportions.

For example, if an account has a 40 percent allocation to bonds and a 60 percent allocation to stocks, the bond return should be measured against 40 percent of the return of the Shearson Lehman or Salomon bond indexes or another appropriate benchmark. And the stock return should be measured against 60 percent of the return of the S&P 500 or another appropriate index.

Your investment team must also measure returns against the indexes that match the asset class or substyle in which you are invested. It's a mistake to use the S&P 500 to assess the performance (or lack of) Nasdaq stock positions, and likewise, to measure the performance of an investor's S&P 500 positions against the Dow. Maybe the Dow is up 12 percent but an investor's portfolio gained only 8 percent. The Dow is only 30 stocks; the S&P is 500. If the S&P portfolio didn't own all 30 Dow stocks, how can it be expected to have performed the same way? Or how can an investor's small-cap portfolio measure up against the Nasdaq 100?

> **WEALTH INSIGHT:** The Association for Investment Management and Research (AIMR) Board of Governors has endorsed a set of Performance Presentation Standards designed to raise the ethical and professional practices of the wealth investment management industry. The performance standards provide money managers with a standardized format for calculation and presentation of their performance results for investors.

Check 4: Evaluate the Money Manager Profile

The money manager profile, which explains the investment style, philosophy, and process of each money manager, also gives a snapshot of the manager's performance history and largest current holdings.

Check 5: Read Research Reports

Research reports review the current status of qualitative factors for each money manager. They also explain the market and business cycle factors that affected recent performance.

Check 6: Review Sector Summaries

Sector summaries place the recent performance of each money manager within the context of the relevant investment style sector, and compare manager performance to a peer group. This ongoing oversight can help you identify and evaluate changes in a manager's process or effectiveness.

You really want to look for consistency in the money manager's style and in performance comparisons to his or her peer group. This type of monitoring will help you assess the predictability of the manager's results—a key element of the benefits that the manager will offer you.

> **WEALTH INSIGHT:** These tips will serve as possible red flags when monitoring money managers:
>
> • Your manager does not have a methodology for getting you out of the market when economic seasons shift—what I call the "sell discipline."
>
> • Your portfolio is reassigned to another staffer.
>
> • One or more key members of your money manager team quit or are fired.
>
> • Several major clients terminate their accounts with the manager.
>
> • Assets under management decline.
>
> • Assets under management increase dramatically.
>
> • Such information should be responded to immediately. You can learn about any of these occurrences from competing money managers and from trustees and executives of other funds. Once you learn of the defections, dig for the reasons behind them, and determine the effect that they may have on your portfolio.

After selecting the most suitable money managers, based on your constraints for time, risk, and volatility, it would be beneficial to revisit your wealth management policy statement to confirm that the investment parameters based on your goals and objectives have indeed been followed.

What Will the Investment Process Cost You?

Pricing in the securities industry has been a mess due to the never-ending quest by financial institutions to hide fees. In this section, my goal is to disclose (unbundle) fees and expenses, so that you understand what's going on inside your money management investment program.

Over the last 20 years, rapidly changing technology in the industry has challenged the very premise of the wrap fee structure. The cost of monitoring accounts and of record keeping is dropping. From the wealth manager's side, changes in technology have also led to decreased costs in executing transactions and portfolio management. Many products have hidden many costs—or at least made them less visible. Because the extra expenses are hidden in the net cost, most investors are unaware that they're paying added-on expenses.

Many money managers have minimum account sizes of $1 million or more. But under a brokerage firm's wrap account program, money managers take lower minimums. According to Morningstar, the average expense ratio for a domestic equity mutual fund is 1.4 percent. This expense ratio does not include transaction (brokerage) costs.

For the 10 largest domestic equity funds, the average brokerage charges are 0.13 percent, bringing the total costs to approximately 1.53 percent (an average size fund could have a much higher total cost, as the 10 largest funds enjoy economies of scale in their costs). For a $100,000 managed account, the management, brokerage, and program fees can total approximately 1.25 percent. The media would never advertise this, but it's entirely possible to buy a separate account investment for less money than its mutual fund alternative. See Exhibit 7.2.

Due to the current complexity in pricing, in order to figure out the best way to purchase funds, investors must rely on professionals with specialized knowledge to process all the multiple variables. To add to the confusion, there are management fees and commissions plus combinations of the two. Some brokerage firms offer the choice of either commission or one fee, which includes a certain number of trades. The problem is that each fee structure is designed in a vacuum. The end result is investor confusion and skepticism.

My solution is to spell out everything and break down and list all component parts. Bare-bones management and administrative costs should be detailed. Supermarket charges and mark-ups should be highlighted as additional, as should any distribution charges paid to a financial intermediary. The same applies to wrap account fees. The financial intermediary fee should be set up and declared, with custody fees stated. The investment advisor's fee should also be disclosed. Each component should be broken out so that investors can make a determination of where the value is being added.

Exhibit 7.2 **Unwrapped Pricing for a $100,000 Account**

Assuming the total fee to the client is:	2.50%
Wealth Investment Fee	.45%
Sponsor Advisory Fee	.40%
Clearing/Execution Fee	.25%
Consultant Gross	1.40%
Consultant Net (90%)	1.26%

WHAT YOU'RE LOOKING AT: Most wealth investment accounts have subcategories that can be broken down even further, such as these subcategories.

WHAT THIS TELLS YOU: The first step in understanding pricing is to unbundle the components. This is something that the largest money managers have thus far been reluctant to do. But this is now changing as newer entrants into the field have had to unbundle their programs because they don't have all of the manufacturing components available in-house.

WHAT THIS MEANS: The total costs for the typical money manager account can range from around 1.25 percent to 2.5 percent.

......

WEALTH INSIGHT: In our practice, we charge a fee for advice regardless of whether our investors choose separately managed accounts, mutual funds, annuities, or packaged products. This eliminates any incentive to sell one product over another, which might not be in an investor's best interest.

Disclosing the component parts of the fee to the investor will have the effect of driving costs down, as individual money managers compete for the business on the basis of fees. Finally, fees for each of the components will fall as the accounts increase in value.

Unbundling the Four Main Fee Components

The main fees and costs of the investment process can be broken down into four categories:

1. Money manager

2. Sponsoring brokerage firm

3. Custody, clearing, and execution

4. Advisor consultant

Money Manager

The function of the money manager is the easiest to explain of all the components. This manager's core function is simply portfolio management.

Money managers who don't go through a sponsor can typically charge 1 percent. Managers who participate in a sponsor program are typically paid (for equity and balanced accounts) a high of 65 basis points (BPS), scaling down to 30 BPS.

Sponsoring Brokerage Firm

Brokerage firm services vary to the wealth management team and investor, and to the money managers to whom they distribute assets for management. The most common services provided by a sponsoring brokerage firm are as follows:

- Research on money managers
- Asset allocation
- Separate account generation
- Client reporting (statement/performance)
- Account administration
- Billing
- Consultant interface
- Account setup

Optional sponsor services are:

- Fiduciary responsibility
- Portfolio design teams
- Trust services
- Consultant training
- Portfolio record keeping
- Reconciliation
- Regulatory compliance
- Internet access to account data

Due to the different services, the fees vary but are quoted on an account or household level, not on total assets. Typically, on a $500,000 household, fees will range from 25 to 65 BPS. As account size increases, the fee drops substantially. A wealth management team working directly with the investor, that is, as an RIA without a sponsoring brokerage firm, has to perform the majority of the core services, making it a de facto sponsor or super-manager.

WEALTH INSIGHT: The traditional sponsor will have to go through the most changes of the separate account components over the next decade. The large sponsor will be forced to move from what has been a primarily closed process to an open-architecture platform. Along with an open architecture platform will come unbundled pricing of services.

As this pricing evolves, true value comparisons can be made. Similar to the money managers, sponsors are currently pricing to what the market will bear, not on services provided. This has forced many of the traditional smaller sponsors out of business. They haven't been able to demonstrate superior services that would justify a premium price.

Custody, Clearing, and Execution

Until recently, custody, clearing, and execution services were bundled into the overall sponsor fee, making the actual costs almost impossible to determine. Due to sponsor entrants who do not self-clear, these costs are now being identified. For a typical $250,000 account, clearing, custody, and execution come bundled at between 20 and 40 BPS.

In most cases, the following services are considered a pure commodity:

- *Custody:* The actual separate account fee keeping and official record keeper. Traditionally, this has been the role of the bank.

- *Execution:* Execution of buy and sell orders from the money manager, which has generally been the role of the stockbroker.

- *Clearing:* When the manager executes a block of stock for multiple accounts, it must be delivered to the custodian and placed in the proper account—which is the clearing function.

Clearing, custody, and execution are performed by the separate account sponsor platform. This means that for a money manager in 20 sponsor programs who wants to buy a stock across all accounts, he or she must place 20 orders of the stock at the same time, one at each sponsor custodian. This practice is ripe for change as it's simply not efficient; investors who have the same separate account manager but different sponsor custodians will get different execution prices. As of this writing, the SEC plans to review these trading practices.

In the future, execution will be separated from custody and clearing. The manager will place one block order at the institution that has the best execution, and the 20 smaller blocks will be cleared to each sponsor custodian. This will ensure the best execution.

WEALTH INSIGHT: As separate accounts revamp their trading procedures to this new standard, you'll see commissions on stock trades reappear. The separate account will have come full circle in 25 years. As soon as execution is unbundled, the market for best execution will take off. This market will be trade-by-trade depending on difficulty, making basis point pricing for execution impossible.

This may seem like a step backward, but it isn't. Executions will be better for the investor (the cost of execution is close to zero on big blocks anyway). Also, as execution is stripped from the custodian, the bundled fee will decrease dramatically. One major clearing firm is already doing business with a 5 BPS custody charge and competing for executions at $5 per trade.

Unbundled execution will also solve another problem. Currently, sponsor custodians lose money on some very active managers, but make enough on the lower turnover managers to make the total business profitable. This means that investors with low turnover managers are subsidizing investors with high turnover managers. This is not only unfair to the investor, it creates artificial businesses. There are extremely high turnover managers in the industry that wouldn't survive competitively if the actual trading costs were factored into manager performance. Unbundling execution will solve these inequities and be a major benefit to the investor.

Advisor Consultant

This group is relatively straightforward. The fee for servicing the account in the traditional large sponsor program is wrapped into the bundled fee. In the independent advisor world, the fees are distinct. The typical advisor charges between 40 and 100 BPS, based on household size. The average fee on a $1 million household is 68 BPS.

This fee tends to differ by professional evolution. That is, an advisor who grew up in the brokerage business is on the high end. Advisors who came out of the accounting world are on the low end. If the advisor's core business is investment consulting, he or she tends to charge more than if it's a secondary business to the core business.

Let's look at Exhibit 7.3 and see how all of these pieces add up in the wealth management investment process.

There's an industry trend toward an unconflicted, fee-based consulting process, rather than a transactional commission-based process. This trend is most evident in the financial planning business with the enormous success of Schwab's One Source program, where investors agree to pay a flat fee on top of varying mutual fund expenses.

Exhibit 7.3 Component Pricing of the Wealth Management Investment Process

	$100,000 Account	$1 Million Household	$10 Million Household
Money manager	50 bps	45 bps	40 bps
Sponsor	50	40	30
Custody, clearing, and execution	30	20	10
Total Manufacturing Expense	**130**	**105**	**80**
Advisor/consultant	100	70	40
Total Cost to Investor	**230 bps**	**175 bps**	**120 bps**

WHAT YOU'RE LOOKING AT: A breakdown of what it typically costs you, the investor, to engage in the wealth management investment process.

WHAT THIS TELLS YOU: The total manufacturing expenses fall right in line with no-load mutual funds. In fact, mutual fund expense ratios do not include execution figures, which the figures in Exhibit 7.3 do.

WHAT THIS MEANS: Looking at these fees, it's apparent that the money management investment process is actually very cost-competitive.

• • • • • •

WEALTH INSIGHT: During flat trading periods, a customer might be better off investing on a commission basis. However, in periods of heavy trading activity, the investor would save money using a wrap fee arrangement. Because no one knows when such periods will occur, it might be wise to look past the economics and judge wrap fee programs on more compelling issues—trust, integrity, and your individual needs. The investor needn't fear that the wrap fee broker will do any excessive trades, since all trading is paid for in advance.

Will separate account management prices continue to decrease? Probably not. As the numbers illustrate, the entire expense already mirrors that of mutual funds. As the big mutual fund complexes enter this market, they won't want to cannibalize their businesses, so they won't underprice them. In fact, you may see fees inch back up. As the fund complexes treat the wealth management investment process as a premium service to their mutual funds, they may also charge a premium price, using the logic: Why should a custom suit cost less than one off the rack?

Tax Management: Less for Taxes, More for Compounding

The erosion of returns from taxes happens so gradually over the years that it escapes the notice of many investors. But the impact is there all the same, and it can be significant—even for those investors who are not in the top tax bracket.

I'm going to start off this section by describing the top five most common misconceptions that investors have about tax liabilities:

Misconception 1: Only Wealthy People Should Be Concerned with Tax Efficiency

Many people associate tax-managed investments with tax-exempt investments, whose lower yields are favorable only for people in the highest income brackets.

Misconception 2: Portfolio Turnover Is the Key Indicator of Tax Efficiency

Turnover is certainly easy to measure, but the results of various studies suggest that it's not always a very reliable measure of tax effi-

Exhibit 7.4 **After-Tax Yield Equivalents**

If you file single and earn...	OR file jointly and earn...	you would need pretax returns of...	to match a tax-free yield of...
$0-$25,750	$0–$43,050	4.71%	4%
		5.88%	5%
		7.06%	6%
$25,751–$62,450	$43,051–$104,050	5.56%	4%
		6.94%	5%
		8.33%	6%
$62,451–$130,250	$104,051–$158,550	5.80%	4%
		7.25%	5%
		8.70%	6%
$130,251–$283,150	$158,551–$283,150	6.25%	4%
		7.81%	5%
		9.38%	6%
$283,151+	$283,151+	6.62%	4%
		8.28%	5%
		9.93%	6%

Calculations are based on federal tax rates. State taxes would increase the pretax returns required.

> **WHAT YOU'RE LOOKING AT:** A list of after-tax yield equivalents at different income levels.
>
> **WHAT THIS TELLS YOU:** It's obvious that high-income investors are going to get the greatest benefit from tax-management strategies: the

difference between their income tax rates (as high as 39.6 percent at the federal level) and the long-term capital gains rate (15 percent) is greater. But even investors in the 28 percent federal income tax bracket can gain from tax-management strategies—particularly if the effects of state taxes are included.

WHAT THIS MEANS: It pays to investigate tax-managed investments, even if you don't fall into the highest income brackets.

• • • • • •

ciency. The notion of the link between turnover and tax efficiency got a boost in 1993, when Jeffrey and Arnott concluded that tax efficiency required extremely low levels of turnover. However, these studies were done using hypothetical, rather than actual, portfolios and were based on assumptions that oversimplified the relationship between portfolio turnover and taxable gains.

Other studies, based on actual portfolio data, reached different conclusions. Dickson and Shoven found the statistical correlation between portfolio turnover and tax efficiency to be quite weak. For investors in the lowest tax bracket with portfolio liquidation assumed, some correlations were positive, suggesting that higher turnover actually improved tax efficiency. While the study did show that there's a correlation, it wasn't the strong correlation that the simple equation of turnover with tax efficiency would suggest.

Misconception 3: Indexing Is the Best Approach to Tax-Managed Investing

It's true that index mutual funds have a number of innate characteristics that have tended to foster strong pretax performance along with high tax efficiency. For one thing, index funds have exceptionally low turnover rates, which means that their transaction expenses are generally lower. They're also likely to have more long-term capital gains and fewer short-term gains compared with actively managed funds.

But even with these features, index funds are not the ultimate tax-managed investments, for several reasons. Stocks within an index fund change periodically. Companies may be added or deleted by the firm that maintains the index, in response to changing market realities or events such as corporate mergers. Strict indexing requires portfolio managers to buy or sell whenever stocks are added or deleted from the index. It means they also have to own all companies, even Enron, Global Crossing, and Lucent. This type of trading activity may not lead to a great deal of turnover, but it can lead to considerable recognition of gains.

In addition, timing of sales may be inefficient. For example, in the course of following its passive strategy, an index fund might end up selling stock just days before it would qualify for tax treatment as long-term capital gains. The fund may also have to invest in high-dividend stocks. An index fund cannot limit holdings of a stock just because it pays high dividends. With the most popular index funds investing heavily in blue chip stocks, index funds can generate substantial dividend income, which is taxed at the higher rate for ordinary income.

Moreover, rebalancing can generate capital gains. An index fund's portfolio must be rebalanced periodically, and the manager may need to recognize capital gains to do so. Finally, the fund cannot be managed for tax efficiency when it comes to shareholder redemptions. Because it must maintain its similarity to an index in the proportions of each stock it owns, an index fund can't choose which stocks to sell when handling redemptions. Chances are good that it will end up having to sell many holdings that will generate short-term gains, which will affect the fund's tax efficiency for all shareholders remaining in the fund. And because most index funds are carrying sizeable unrealized gains, this could lead to considerable realized gains if a large number of redemptions take place.

Misconception 4: Any Investment Style Can Be Tax Efficient

Certainly any investment style can be modified to improve tax efficiency. But some styles lend themselves to tax-efficient techniques far better than others. For example, growth-oriented investment strategies seem to be more appropriate for tax-managed investing than value-oriented strategies. This is in part because a growth approach is oriented toward capital appreciation, while a value approach will tend to lead a portfolio manager to select a portfolio that produces comparatively higher rates of income.

The Peters and Miller study of fund groups for the 10- and 20-year periods found that growth managers provided higher average pretax returns, higher after-tax returns, and greater tax efficiency than growth and income managers or equity income managers. Managers that focus on large company stocks are also better candidates for tax-managed investing than small-cap managers. One reason is that small company stock managers have a built-in reason to sell: those that are most successful eventually outgrow the small-cap category, and must be sold. This can lead to a high level of realized capital gains. In addition, small companies are often bought out, leading once again to excessive realization of capital gains.

Misconception 5: All Tax-Sensitive Investors Have the Same Needs

While generalizations can be comforting, it's essential to consider each investor's particular situation. Federal and state marginal rates vary from individual to individual. A growing percentage of taxpayers each year are subject to the federal alternative minimum tax (AMT). This separate tax computation is applied to individuals whose deductions under the regular tax rules might otherwise eliminate their tax liability. Some investors may have other holdings or personal businesses that can provide some offsetting losses. And, as always, it's essential to keep in mind the individual's ultimate investment goal and time horizon. A separate account portfolio manager can tie purchase and sales decisions to the individual's specific tax situation. For smaller investors, though, the costs of managing a separate account generally make mutual funds more appropriate.

Instead of cash when making charitable gifts, consider the use of securities that have appreciated significantly as a technique that can improve tax efficiency. With this strategy, you effectively give away the capital gain. Investors who are planning to leave a taxable portfolio as part of their estate are a special case, thanks to the current tax code provision for a step-up in basis upon an investor's death. This essentially means that when heirs withdraw money from the account, capital gains will be calculated from the basis cost at the time of death. This effectively resets the clock on basis calculations and means that heirs need not pay capital gain taxes on the portfolio's unrealized capital gains.

As these misconceptions demonstrate, you must be aware of the major tax liabilities that will be associated with your investment process. A good place to begin educating yourself about these liabil-

Exhibit 7.5 **Embedded Capital Gains for the Largest Equity Mutual Funds**

Stock Mutual Fund	Potential Capital Gain Exposure (%)
Fidelity Magellan	37
Investment Company of America	5
Washington Mutual Investors	23
Fidelity Growth & Income	41
Fidelity Contra Fund	17
Janus	9
Growth Fund of America	21
American Century Ultra Inv	27
Janus Worldwide	20
American Funds Euro Pacific Growth	15
American Funds New Perspective	25
Fidelity Growth Comp	30
Fidelity Blue Chip Growth	29
Janus Twenty	18
Putnam Voyager A	23
Fidelity Equity-Income	22
Median	(23)

WHAT YOU'RE LOOKING AT: Capital gains percentages for the major equity mutual funds, plus the overall median gain.

WHAT THIS TELLS YOU: If we look back to the beginning of 2001, the average domestic equity mutual fund had a 23 percent unrealized capital gain.

WHAT THIS MEANS: This gain means that an individual investing new money in a mutual fund owes tax on a 23 percent gain that he or she has not received the benefit of. Do you remember how 2000 and 2001 were down in the realm of returns? Yet at the same time, many investors were redeeming (selling). Thus, mutual funds and index funds alike were forced to sell in order to give the sellers their money. It was this selling that caused capital gains to be realized in the portfolio and passed through to the remaining shareholders. Therefore, it was likely in 2000 and 2001 that as a new investor in a mutual fund, be it index or otherwise, you saw a reduction in your money, and you owed capital gains tax on the activity passed to you from activity inside the mutual fund.

· · · · · ·

ities is to become familiar with embedded capital gains for the largest equity mutual funds. See Exhibit 7.5.

You need to be aware that these tax risks are out there, and that if they go unnoticed, they can create an unnecessary tax burden. One goal of risk management should be not to buy into any unwarranted tax liability. As the individual managed account investor, you want to establish your own cost basis at the time of purchase. See Exhibit 7.6.

WEALTH INSIGHT: Mutual funds distribute their dividends and their realized capital gains to all shareholders. Dividends and short-term capital gains are taxed as ordinary income. The current federal rates for income tax range from 15 to 39.6 percent, depending on income level. A mutual fund's distribution of long-term capital gains is currently taxed at 15 percent for most investors.

Exhibit 7.6 Tax-Related Features of Mutual Funds versus Separately Managed Accounts

Tax-related Features	Mutual Funds	Separately Managed Account (Direct Ownership)
Separately Held Securities	NO, investor holds one security, the fund, which in turn owns a diversified portfolio	YES, investor holds securities in an account purchased by the portfolio manager
Unrealized Capital Gains	YES, average U.S. mutual fund has a 20% unrealized capital gain	NO, at the time of purchase, the investor establishes his or her own cost basis for each security in the portfolio
Customized to Control Taxes	NO, most fund managers manage for pretax return without regard for the tax liability they may create for investors. All investors pay their proportionate share of taxes	YES, investors can instruct their portfolio managers to take gains or losses as available to manage their tax liability. Some managers will explicitly manage to control the tax consequences
Gain/Loss Distribution Policies	All gains distributed; losses cannot be distributed	Treated as direct stock ownership in which realized gains and losses are reported in the year recorded

WHAT YOU'RE LOOKING AT: The differences in features and characteristics between mutual funds and separately held accounts.

WHAT THIS TELLS YOU: For mutual fund investors, the tax status of a fund's gains depends on how long the fund held the asset on which it realized the gain (not on how long the investor receiving the distribution has owned shares of the fund). Gains from assets that the fund owned for at least 12 months are distributed as long-term gains; gains from assets sold less than 12 months after the fund bought them are distributed as short-term gains.

WHAT THIS MEANS: Because the classification of distributions is a result of the fund's actions, not the investor's actions, it can to some extent be controlled by the fund's managers, if they so choose. By the same token, investors can be hurt by a fund's lack of attention to tax issues. In addition, new investors in funds with holdings that the fund bought many years earlier at low prices may inherit substantial gains that, as shareholders, they will be taxed on when these holdings are sold.

･･････

For tax-deferred investors, comparing mutual funds is fairly simple, as tax effects don't have to be considered. Net total return (gross total return minus expenses) is the operative basis for comparison. But for the taxable investor, the size and composition of fund distributions make a big difference. After-tax returns are the critical basis for comparing fund performance in any taxable investment situation. See Exhibit 7.7.

Exhibit 7.7 **Real Gains Reflected in After-Tax Returns**

Analysis of Tax Management Potential

Initial Investment: $1,000,000	Without tax-management techniques:	With loss matching, loss harvesting, and managed tracking:
After-tax ending value	$3,551,000	$3,756,000
After-tax return	13.5%	14.2%

WHAT YOU'RE LOOKING AT: The effects of tax-management techniques applied to a hypothetical $1 million investment in an S&P 500—based index portfolio:

WHAT THIS TELLS YOU: A $1 million investment stands to grow by nearly 1 extra percentage point when exposed to tax management methods.

WHAT THIS MEANS: Tax management can literally add up to huge gains.

･･････

Six Tips for Managing Taxes

As you can plainly see, income taxes can kill wealth accumulation. Every dollar paid in taxes today is a dollar that is lost to future compounding. Taxes and expenses can rob you. So what can a separate account manager do to help? Make sure your manager is aware of the following tax tips for managing your account taxes.

Ability to Accept Low-Cost-Basis Stock

The majority of separate account managers accept only cash. This has to change. Most high net worth investors have low-cost-basis stock, and they're beginning to understand the inherent risk in holding the stock and the tax implications of selling it to diversify. They're looking for managers who can propose solutions for the investor from total sale, to partial sale, to holding the stock and diversifying around it using other money. The manager should develop a working knowledge of collars and put and call strategies to hedge positions. Accepting low-cost-basis stock is one of the basic tenets of true separate account management.

Tax-Lot Accounting

The fundamental technique to gain tax efficiency is to employ tax-lot accounting. Among other things, this allows the manager to respond to withdrawals and required turnover by selling higher cost basis stock first.

Tax-Loss Matching and Harvesting

This strategy seeks to realize losses within a portfolio to enhance after-tax return through (1) matching gains with losses when the realization of gains is either desirable or unavoidable; and (2) creating an inventory of losses to offset gains elsewhere in an investor's portfolio. The extent to which tax-loss harvesting can be exploited is partly determined by overall market returns and individual stock volatility. In periods of lower market returns and with asset classes of greater stock volatility, the after-tax value of this technique increases.

Tax-Lot Optimization

Most money managers use some form of portfolio or security optimization — that is, calculating how to mix your holdings to get maximum return for varying levels of risk. The roots of optimization lie in modern portfolio theory. The simplest models look at historical price volatility versus future projections. To manage after-tax money effectively, you have to add another variable: the tax-lot cost of the securities purchased.

This makes the optimization process far more complex. Not only will different clients have different cost bases, making optimization necessary on an account basis rather than firm portfolio basis, but individual clients will have different tax lots of the same securities. Adding to an already complex process, clients will be at varying tax levels. Sales and replacement purchases that make sense for one client may not make sense for another. Again, disbursal among clients should be expected and accepted. This process sounds daunting, but new technology, available now and in the future, makes this level of management possible even today.

Year-End Loss/Gain Request

Besides harvesting losses to reposition the portfolio internally, the money manager should entertain requests from the investor to offset realized gains and losses outside his or her portfolio. For example, an investor realizes a big gain from the sale of a condo.

The manager should attempt to harvest losses to offset the gain as far as possible. This is an incredible value-added service, especially in poor equity markets. Rather than being admonished for poor performance, the manager is congratulated for saving the investor from writing a big check to the IRS. That is tangible value-added and will guarantee a long-term relationship between the manager and the investor even in performance downturns.

An extension of this service is to work with the other money managers in a multi-manager household, creating communication links with the other managers to make the overall account more tax-efficient. The instigation of this type of communication usually falls to your wealth management team, but the money manager should be responsive.

Managed Portfolio Tracking

Over time, a portfolio built to mirror an index will develop return differences (tracking) as the index constituent's change. For many investors, taxes incurred by a portfolio manager attempting to fully replicate all index changes represent unnecessary costs. By accepting a small degree of tracking difference (that is, portfolios may replicate the benchmark closely but not exactly), investors can improve their after-tax performance but at the same time incur a risk of underperforming the index.

We're coming into the home stretch, now that you're well-versed in the fundamentals of wealth management in general and investing in particular. Let's move on to Chapter 8, where you'll learn how to tweak your process to fit the specific season.

8

TWEAK YOUR PROCESS TO FIT THE SEASON

At this point, you have the information and resources necessary to build and maintain a solid wealth management framework. You've become aware of the three factors that really matter in the overall wealth management picture, as well as how to create the preliminary wealth strategy that will guide your in-depth wealth management planning; how to devise a Wealth Policy Statement and subsequent Wealth Investment Process; and, finally, how to develop a strong investment management plan as a part of the larger Wealth Management Process.

What you need to know now is how to tweak this information to fit the current Season of the Economy. As you're well aware by now, the economic seasons come and go, and you must be ready for their challenges to be a successful investor. So let's jump right in to a discussion of how to fine-tune your plans according to the contemporary economic climate, beginning with a look at the common threads that run through all economic seasons.

What Lies in Store for Any Season

What's true about life is equally true about wealth management: sometimes you're thrown a curveball (or two). However, there are certain factors that are virtually guaranteed to occur, no matter which economic season you're currently in. Here's a summary of the three most important guarantees:

Guarantee 1: Bubble Follows Bubble

Go as far back in our economic past as you like, and you'll notice that a constant presence exists in each phase: the bubble-after-bubble concept. Nothing can disrupt this concept—not even something as big as the 1987 crash or 1990 recession. The only thing that changes about the concept is that we keep seeing bigger and bigger bubbles—first it was energy in the 1970s, then housing in the early 1980s, then stocks in the late 1980s, and now back to higher highs in all three areas in the 2000s.

One of the reasons that these bubbles, such as housing (which I discuss in more detail in Chapter 9) and commodities, have continued to grow larger and larger of late is that the baby boomers with retirement money and pension plans have more and more money to chase the hot sectors of the economy as they come into sight. This is the case even though there's significant evidence pointing to a slowdown in both housing and commodities. There's still one quantifiably undervalued asset class where I think people can make a great deal of money: ownership in corporate America through ownership of common stocks and common stock mutual funds.

Certainly, housing and commodities appear overvalued, but corporate America has continued to grow in this environment of expanding consumer spending. With the growth in revenue, these companies as a whole represent some of the fairest values today, even though most stock indexes are near or above all-time highs. This is mostly because corporations are likely to use leverage and economies of scale to move into new areas where they can add value. Commodity-based investments can't do this.

Guarantee 2: Demographics Don't Change

This guarantee ties into the theme that runs throughout the entire book: the base is demographics, and demographics don't change. No matter which curveballs are thrown to us, people will always recover and do what they do. It doesn't matter if rising oil prices take a little more out of their budgets—people will always find a way to feed and clothe their kids, get them into college, etc. Since the baby boomers now have kids in this family cycle, the economy is going to be strong until the kids leave the nest to go to college or enter the workforce.

Guarantee 3: Inflation (and Deflation) Happen

There's no disputing the fact that our economy needs money to survive. As the economy grows—and it is growing—it requires more available money. Therefore, the U.S. government is going to continue to create money and, at a minimum, that's going to cause modest inflation, at least in the short term.

Most people don't understand that inflation is a requirement for any growing economy. If there isn't any inflation, the economy is contracting, not expanding. The important thing is to keep inflation at a modest growth rate. The best you can hope for is what we have now—a 3 to 4 percent gross domestic product (GDP) growth rate with a modest 2 percent inflation rate. This tells us that our baby-boom generation is doing a good job at work—that they're productive, that is, producing goods and services efficiently.

Unlike inflation, deflation is seen less but is also a natural mechanism in our economy. Deflation shakes out a lot of growth from our expansion, down to the survival of the fittest. It creates fewer but stronger companies as a result. The most recent example of this is the dot.com and/or telecom bust of the early 2000s. We're now left with fewer providers, yet these providers are strong, well-capitalized companies with insightful business platforms to expand from. Many grew to this level by acquiring competitors for cents on the dollar during the deflationary technology shakeout.

WEALTH INSIGHT: Though the Federal Reserve usually fails to see it, it is doing the wrong thing when it comes to inflation. They tend to increase short-term interest rates in an attempt to slow economic growth. The Fed is reacting to events just like many of my clients tend to do with their investments or businesses. Instead of seeing what's really happening and why, the Fed and economists are still reacting to the inflationary period that occurred mostly in the 1970s. This period was largely caused by the education and placement of the boomers into productive business. Even though the boomers were in their most expensive years at that time, requiring a lot of investment to get up and running in their new careers, they've been paying off this debt to society ever since, with productivity. Unfortunately, the Fed doesn't consider productivity in the economy when making interest-rate decisions—just growth.

How to Ride the Seasonal Roller Coaster

Throughout this book I've talked about how to anticipate seasonal fluctuations. (Remember the Early Warning Indicators of Winter that I gave you way back in Chapter 2 that culminated with the pointers on what to expect from any season?) So by now, you should be pretty good at sniffing out changes in the air. Specifically, you can probably notice investment bubbles in areas of the economy, general spending patterns at your local mall (watch your boomer friends), and the overall growth or contraction in the economy by noting inflation versus deflation.

How should you handle your wealth management plans when you sense that the season is on the verge of a transformation? I've provided various, seasonally based answers to this question below.

Fall and Winter Lows

When faced with an economic fall or winter season, most people move from stocks and real estate to a long-term fixed annuity or other form of fixed income, simply paying themselves the interest earned for the rest of their lives. Bonds and cash also play prominent roles in this scenario.

Bonds: Corporate versus Government

In terms of bonds, high-quality corporate bonds should be a better investment than government bonds in a longer-lasting, difficult environment. This is because the government will likely have significant debt as well as a meaningful budget deficit in a down economy. In addition, weak economies tend to generate less tax revenue. On the other hand, the largest companies that lead their industries should benefit from the demise of their smaller, weaker competitors as the economy slides. These large companies will be the ones to survive with positive cash flow, which will enable them to pay off their bonds (debt) even as their earnings and stock prices are likely to be going down.

> **WEALTH INSIGHT:** When talking about how to manage wealth in a down economy, I tend to like the example of General Motors in the 1930s. The company had a positive cash flow every year from 1930 to 1942, despite the worst times in U.S. history. So would you rather have had General Motors bonds during that period—or 30-year government treasuries, when the government ran huge deficits trying to bail out the economy?

In a general sense, we should be trying to prevent inflation and deflation. But let's say the government is in a deflationary cycle, running huge deficits. You wouldn't want to be holding a lot of government bonds. (We're not seeing this yet in our current economy—compare budget deficits and overall debt to our ability to pay it off from our now $13 trillion plus GDP.) However, if you do see and hear about deflation and higher deficits on government debt, you'd want to focus on short-term government bonds. In this example, a better choice might be holding medium-term bonds from AAA or AA companies in which you have a high level of confidence.

Let's look closer at this. If you saw better economic growth and less of an impact on Asia from the weakening U.S. economy, and you also have a few really conservative countries in Europe like Switzerland and Austria whose bonds you could own, then you could buy government or corporate bonds from those countries. It's likely that some of those countries will do well whether or not there's a downturn in the United States. You wouldn't want to buy in France, Italy, Germany, or England, because in many ways, they're going to be affected by the same circumstances as the United States. By investing in the more fiscally conservative countries like those listed, you're diversified and protected against the likely decline in the U.S. dollar. These and other currencies would be expected to maintain or increase in value during an economic downturn in the United States.

WEALTH INSIGHT: For some time now, the dollar has been going down versus other currencies. As our economy continues to strengthen over the next few years, we'd expect this trend to reverse. Perhaps we could see a 20 percent or more increase in the U.S. dollar versus the other currencies in the basket. Then the dollar will likely go down, much like it did in 2000 and 2002. In fact, the dollar will probably go down more than most other currencies. Thus, by having your money invested in non-dollar-denominated investments, you add an extra level of protection and potential source of growth to your portfolio as we move into the economic winter.

Cash in the Short Term

In today's very strong economy, some investors attempt to weather what they perceive as a bad economic season by converting a portion of their holdings to cash. I advise most of these folks to fight their instincts to convert and just stay put until they see the beginning of the seasonal changes in the economy. These are detailed in Chapter 10 as the Seven Warning Signs of Winter. But, if you're one of those investors, and you still insist on converting to cash temporarily, then I recommend waiting for a clear signal.

Whether you hold 10, 20, or 50 percent in cash depends on your tolerance for risk. No matter which percentage you choose, you must remember that even cash isn't a guarantee. You could convert to cash, the economy could get thrown another curveball, perhaps a positive curveball, and the market could subsequently take off without you. And believe me, the market wants nothing more than to do that. I think it'll continue toward all-time highs until at least mid 2009 or 2010.

Historically, during periods of extended uncertainty in the stock market, shares tend to transfer from the weak to the strong investors. Usually, that means from individual investors to institutional investors. In 2006, there was nearly $1 trillion in buyout and merger activity. Also in 2006, we saw one of the lowest money flows from individuals to large growth companies—a perfect example of the weak to the strong process. I recommend that if you are going to convert to cash, do it when the odds facing you are formidable.

Spring and Summer Highs

I've devoted so much space to talking about down markets and risk protection that it's easy to forget that the economy has its upswings as well. Let's go back to the scenario we posed in the last section, and consider what would happen after the initial, but significant, sell-off (which, in relation to our present economic circumstances, should happen somewhere between mid 2010 and 2012).

This is the point at which you begin to anticipate an initial stabilizing and possible upsurge into spring. You subsequently begin to systematically liquidate your cash and fixed-income investments so you can start your reinvestment using a dollar cost averaging technique, buying back corporate America a little at a time. Some areas that could offer value might be health care and strong companies in the Asian sector and, to a lesser extent, technology and biotech (which I talk about a bit more below). You'll find sectors that should still be experiencing strong revenue growth and earnings but whose stock values are greatly reduced after the crash primarily due to the fear-motivated seller. Start to reconstruct your stock portfolio slowly using these types of companies.

Small Companies versus Large Companies

A discussion about stock investment revolves largely around small versus large companies. Our small-cap model is literally two things put together. Half of it is the normal consumer spending wave, the same one that we used for large caps. The other half is a 23-year lag for the peak of innovation in new products and industries.

Young people cost money and are therefore inflationary. They're also the people from whom innovations emanate. We found a 23-year lag period that corresponds to young people, and we coined it the yuppie index—young, educated people coming out of college who start technology and social trends (for example, the iPod). According to this creative innovation cycle, they rebel and do things that create new growth markets for small companies, not big companies.

At the top of the boom, big companies are going to be dominating mass markets, using their mass marketing skills and economy of scale to generate tremendous earning power. So while we expect that the reduced consumer spending wave will hit both large and small companies, the innovative index will favor small companies, making them both good trends. The overall question then becomes not one of small versus large, but of the best possible investment based on valuation.

What's on Tap for the Major Sectors

The current spring season is going to affect the major sectors in various ways. I've summarized below what I think these effects will be.

Technology

In technology, we had a boom, we had a shakeout, and we're slowly coming out of it—making us due for the next, perhaps stronger, boom in tech stocks. Being a contrarian investor at heart, I notice most people believe that technology stocks will never go back up. Thus, they're probably the single best place to be.

We're coming into what many are calling the second Internet revolution. There's certainly been a great deal of new venture capital (smart money) coming to this area. This investment capital will support a whole new level of innovations—putting tech stocks in a good position to lead in our current spring season. Biotech and health care should follow close behind.

Health Care

Like many sectors, health care has several subsets. Generally, the entire sector would be expected to grow. One thing we're assured of is that as we age, we increasingly need some or all of the products and services provided in the health care sector.

Even though more people will have a need for products from this area, other external factors play into the model. First, insurance companies are usually responsible for some or all of the patient's bill. It's likely that these companies exert influence on pricing in an effort to support their profit structure versus that of the supplying health care provider. Second, the government is responsible for paying all or part of health care–related bills via Medicaid and Medicare.

In addition, the government is responsible for many aspects of new product, processes, and procedures approval. Because of these two powerful outside influences, the health care industry, even with growing demand for its products, could turn out to be a challenged sector. At the very least, it's not the easy money you might initially think—though it's certainly worth thinking through.

Perhaps a directly related sector that isn't influenced as dramatically by these powerful external influences is a better choice. One area that comes to mind is publicly traded retirement homes—or a REIT (real estate investment trust) that represents the same investment.

Financial Services

Financial services have seen many changes, both good and bad, from changes in the government regulations. Banks have done well from the tremendous mortgage underwriting associated with the residential real estate boom, and again in the "cooling off" period as they rewrite some of the same loans again and again. In addition, the credit card business has been very profitable, with fewer bad credit lines than the press implies.

Brokerage firms have also benefited as our economy has rebounded and continues to grow since the market lows of 2002. The brokerages have benefited from increased trading and company buybacks and buyouts (a record high was set in 2006 of nearly $800 billion in buyout deals, and that amount is on track to double in 2007). The sector clearly has a leveraged benefit in an economic rebound such as we are seeing now and expect to continue into 2010. This sector has just as powerful an effect on your portfolio, or downside leverage, in a slowing or—worse yet—a contracting economy. If you have investments in this area, you'll want little or no exposure as we get toward the end of the summer season in 2009 and 2010.

WEALTH INSIGHT: Though emerging markets can be a great play, remember to exercise a high degree of caution: They're highly volatile.

International

Investing outside the United States will continue to offer opportunity. Like the economic leverage I just mentioned in the Financial Services section (both positive in an up economy and negative in a down economy), the international area has similar effects on the portfolio. During the period from 2000–2006, the dollar was going down versus other currencies. So for those who invest outside the United States, they had a "double gainer" at that time—for example, 10 percent from the foreign stock account plus 10 percent more when they converted back to U.S. dollars. Of course, this is due to the fact that the dollar dropped against the other currencies in that portfolio. In their 401(k) plans at work, most people buy an international fund and have no idea how this works or what happens. As the U.S. dollar gains in value with our stronger economy, this can actually work in reverse. The international stock portfolio can go up 10 percent, the dollar can go up 10 percent, and after adjusting, they gain zero. I suspect that these international markets will do very well between now and 2010–2011, but so will the United States, making our dollar more valuable (higher) and the ability to get easy double-digit returns from international portfolios at least a bit more difficult. After 2010–2011, if our scenario plays out and our economy weakens, the dollar drops and you'd think it's "game on" again for international. But remember, when the U.S. economy sneezes, the rest of the world gets a cold.

If you think China is too big for that, remember that all of the GDP (goods and services produced) is less than California alone. Also, think back to the Asian Contagion of 1998 and the foreign currency meltdown that came with it. It'll remind you to reduce exposure here if you see the seasons of winter start to kick in.

You're approaching the end of your wealth management journey. But before I put the brakes on this eventful trip, I want to spend one of the final chapters discussing the current direction of the three hot topics that remain in the front of everyone's minds: real estate, the stock market, and new businesses. So turn to Chapter 9 to learn more about the state of affairs in these three important areas.

CHAPTER

9

SPECIAL SECTION: WHAT'S IN STORE FOR REAL ESTATE

Most of this book has dealt with how to manage your wealth in terms of the stock market. I'd like to use this chapter to discuss another topic that typically plays a major role in an investor's overall wealth portfolio: real estate. As you'll read in the succeeding sections, the three primary wealth factors that we've discussed throughout this text—birthrate, spending patterns, and seasons of the economy—have considerable influence on this important topic.

What about Real Estate?

Housing prices are now in a downturn that actually began in 2004. According to an October 2006 CBS News report, the median price of a new home plunged in September 2006 by the largest amount in more than 35 years. It was also the biggest single drop on record.

These declines in prices underscore the severity of the correction in the once-booming housing market, which had seen sales of both new and existing homes soar to record levels for five consecutive years, propelled by the lowest mortgage rates in more than four decades.

The same CBS News report stated that more than 300,000 U.S. properties entered foreclosure during the third quarter of 2006—up 43 percent from the same period in 2005. According to the Center for Responsible Lending (CRL), 2.2 million households have either lost their homes to foreclosure or hold sub-prime mortgages that will fail over the next few years costing homeowners as much as $164 billion in lost home equity.

Further estimates indicate that more than $1 trillion in adjustable-rate mortgages (ARMs) will be reset from 2006 until the beginning of 2008. What does that mean for homeowners with ARMs? Perhaps an increase of between 20 and 50 percent in their monthly mortgage bills. Depending on when the refinancing takes place, the increase could be a meaningful one in their monthly payments.

CASE STUDY: The Colorado Housing Market

I currently live in Colorado, where my neighbor and I were recently talking about a piece of property that she had for sale. She bought the property in the midst of the state's real estate boom, with no down payment and an interest-only loan. I told her about some of the factors that will cause real estate to drop over the next couple of years. Her response was, "Well, that's your opinion."

"No, it's just spending patterns," I replied.

"Didn't you read how we just passed the 300,000,000 population mark? All of those people are going to need a place to sleep—you'll see," she added.

I saw her again a few months later. She had had no bids on her property and was worried about the impending increase of her ARM.

"It was like somebody turned off the lights," she told me.

Unfortunately, I had nothing positive to tell her. Until 2004, Colorado was one of the hottest housing markets in the country, but oversupply and rising mortgage interest rates then torpedoed the market—and we have likely not hit bottom yet.

The problem is that homeowners with ARMs have begun to face payments that many may not be able to afford. In Colorado, many homeowners have been forced to put their properties on the market, yet because many haven't been able to find buyers, they may have to default on their loans. As a result, several of Colorado's counties lead the nation in foreclosures. For instance, one in every 168 households in Weld County is in foreclosure, a rate that's 700 percent higher than the national average.

Just like my neighbor, you may be asking yourself, "How on earth could this be happening?" The Consumer Expenditures Survey (remember this from Chapter 2?) gives four general factors that affect real estate behavior and therefore drive home price appreciation (or depreciation):

1. *Predictable Spending Trends by Age and Income:* Demographic spending trends (for example, birthrates and spending patterns) are the largest factors behind home building and home appreciation rates over time. As people and households age, they spend more on housing to a point, at approximately age 43 (of course, this spending peak is highly affected by their income level as well). After that age, we tend to have the house we want. Also, it's usually the largest and most expensive house we'll ever own. From this age forward, money spent on housing drops.

2. *Mortgage Rates and Affordability:* The lower inflation rates are, the lower mortgage rates will be. More people can afford larger houses and can qualify for home purchases and mortgages as mortgage rates fall.

3. *Overbuilding Cycles:* In response to growing demand, developers cause overbuilding cycles that tend to create overcapacity, causing prices to decline, often in advance of such a peak. This decline will continue until the excess inventories of housing are sold off.

4. *Overall Economic Trends:* When the overall economy grows, employment grows with it. As employment grows, people's incomes grow—and the propensity to buy housing or trade up to a better or larger house grows right along with the other trends.

The Demographic Impact on Real Estate

While all of the charts and newspaper headlines may be hyping our growing global population, what they typically don't show are how the four reasons that I just mentioned affect this burgeoning population. In particular, they overlook birthrates and spending patterns—two of the most important wealth factors that we've discussed throughout this book.

If you were to overlay these factors onto the U.S. population today, you'd see a quite different picture of the real estate bubble in America than my neighbor does: the largest single group of Americans (the baby boomers), 77 million strong, have already surpassed the age at which most people buy the most expensive home they will ever purchase, which is, again, at age 43.

These demographics of real estate spending strongly suggest slowing and even mildly declining home prices for high-priced markets over the rest of this decade, despite an increasingly booming economy. So today, we're seeing upper-end homes begin to peak, flatten, and fall substantially in a number of high-priced markets. More upscale areas can be expected to follow the same price flattening to declining pattern as we go forward.

WEALTH INSIGHT: Real estate declines tend to start in highly valued luxury markets and then spread over time to lesser degrees down into broader markets.

What all of this means for you is that in the next few years, your upscale real estate is likely more at risk than your stock and mutual fund portfolios. As we mentioned, we are predicting modest gains in the stock market between now and 2010, with very little in the economic expansion to worry about on the downside.

WEALTH INSIGHT: Real estate foreclosures have grown so numerous in Colorado that the state just established a first-of-its-kind foreclosure help hotline. More than 1,400 calls were received on the first day. Call 1-877-601-HOPE (4673) to access the hotline.

Let's look at Exhibit 9.1 to see the impact of demographics on home-buying trends.

Exhibit 9.1 **First-Time versus Repeat Buyers[1]**

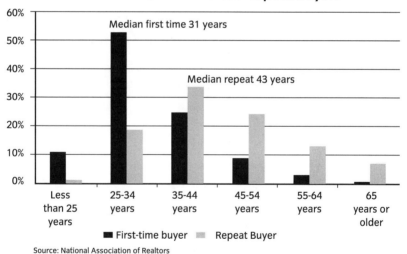

Source: National Association of Realtors

WHAT YOU'RE LOOKING AT: Predictable spending patterns—how trade-up buying in homes peaks around age 43; total home purchasing peaks at about age 37; and downsizing occurs at approximately age 54.

WHAT THIS TELLS YOU: You want the part-to-part bars that are much taller than the others, which means that most of the variation is from the true differences in the items being measured. Less than 10 percent means little variation in data; 10 to 30 percent indicates large variations.

WHAT THIS MEANS: That housing is in its Autumn Season and is about to enter the Winter Season. Autumn is a period of slow or no growth. Winter is a contracting price structure. Overlay the large baby-boom generation, which is more than four times the magnitude of past generations and so massive that every spending stage it moves through affects the economy to extremes. Baby boomers are in the initial stages of downsizing, and the age group behind them is two-thirds of their size, which means that supply will outpace demand and, as you know, when there are more sellers than buyers, prices will fall.

• • • • • •

The histogram in Exhibit 9.1 represents the count within different ranges of data rather than plotting individual data points. When you see a number of distributions that are skewed, it means that most of the numbers or so-called data values pile up toward one end and tail off toward the other end, as in the case of the graph in Exhibit 9.2. This histogram illustrates that the greatest numbers of first-time buyers (data values that you see forming the bubble on the left side) occur between ages 25 and 34 and then drop off dramatically.

Exhibit 9.2 **Number of Home Purchasers by Age[2]**

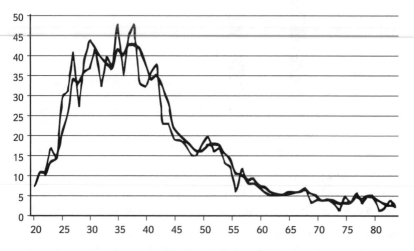

Source: Consumer Expenditure Survey, 2000; US Bureau of Labor and Statistics

WHAT YOU'RE LOOKING AT: The horizontal bar represents age of population. The vertical line represents numbers of homes purchased in thousands.

WHAT THIS TELLS YOU: The data show the percentage of households that are first-time or starter-home buyers and repeat buyers or trade-up buyers. The median or typical first-time buyer is age 31 and, again, repeat buyers peak around age 43.

You can see that the general prime time for volume of home buyers is between ages 25 and 42.

WHAT THIS MEANS: The peak numbers of baby boomers in our population today would have been progressing through that cycle from 1986 to 2003. Note that there's a very steep dropoff in the volume of buyers after age 42—which would have equated to the year 2003 for the peak in baby boomers.

••••••

To sum up, the current demographic trends are projecting a marked slowing in growth after 2003–2006 (which we've already seen) and an overall peak in housing demand by 2011, with a much larger drop to follow in demand and prices.

Smart Post-Peak Real Estate Moves

Now that you know when the housing market will go through its own winter season, during which prices will most likely drop off dramatically, you can begin to prepare for how you'll handle the downturn.

In the post–2011 real estate world, there will be greater strength in apartments and multifamily dwellings; vacation, resort, and retirement areas; and lower income segments of the residential market.

Vacation, Resort, and Retirement Areas

Six percent of all homes—and a growing percentage of home sales—are second or vacation homes. New data from the Consumer Expenditures Survey strongly suggest that instead of simply peaking at around age 50, there's a dual surge in vacation home buying, with a first peak in the late forties and a second, higher peak in the late fifties and mid-sixties.

With many baby boomers now in their sixties, this market clearly has much stronger demographic growth in store over the coming years. The survey also shows that vacation home buying is not largely an affluent market but is spread across the income spectrum. This is probably due to the popularity of timeshares. See Exhibit 9.3.

Exhibit 9.3 **Major Retirement Havens**

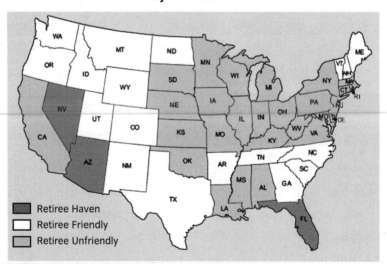

WHAT YOU'RE LOOKING AT: The three key states that are major retirement havens: Arizona, Nevada, and Florida.

WHAT THIS TELLS YOU: These have been the greatest magnets for retirees for decades due to their warm weather and (at least so far) lower costs of living.

WHAT THIS MEANS: The three states shown here will be good real estate investment targets going forward.

••••••

WEALTH INSIGHT: Other retirement-friendly states include: Washington, Oregon, Idaho, Montana, Wyoming, Colorado, Utah, New Mexico, Arkansas, Tennessee, North Carolina, South Carolina, Georgia, Delaware, New Hampshire, Vermont, and Maine.

Note that only about 28 percent of retirees relocate to a different area, with the remaining 72 percent staying in their local areas to be close to family and friends and/or to continue to be at least partially active in business or other pursuits. But the relocation of 28 percent of the baby boomers, no insignificant number in itself, over the next two decades will still cause major growth pressures in the retirement areas that they move to.

Apartments and Multifamily Housing

The baby boom–generated children (the echo baby boom) are moving into their marriage and family formation cycle—and that correlates with a peak in rental apartments and multifamily housing. See Exhibits 9.4 and 9.5.

Exhibit 9.4 **Rental Housing Spending by Age**

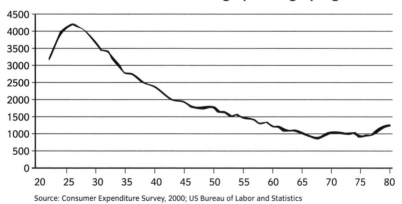

Source: Consumer Expenditure Survey, 2000; US Bureau of Labor and Statistics

WHAT YOU'RE LOOKING AT: How spending on rental housing peaks between ages 24 and 26.

WHAT THIS TELLS YOU: Demand for rentals will drop as people move into their family formation and marriage cycles.

WHAT THIS MEANS: Rental property investments will lose momentum when echo boomers begin to marry and have families.

••••••

Exhibit 9.5 **Multifamily Housing Patterns**

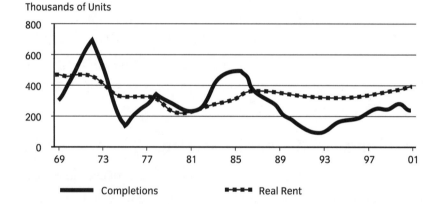

WHAT YOU'RE LOOKING AT: How multifamily housing peaked in 1985 and then declined despite a booming economy and falling mortgage rates.

WHAT THIS TELLS YOU: The multifamily housing peak in the baby-boom cycle would have hit by 1980 and peaked in 1986 on a 25-year lag to the peak births in 1961.

WHAT THIS MEANS: We should see the echo baby-boom effect on multifamily housing from 2006–2015.

••••••

Lower Income Residential Market

Spending patterns for lower income home buyers differ from those who fall into the high-end home market. Among the less affluent, we typically see that the average home value climbs steadily to age 67, the age that shows the greatest difference in this market.

> **WEALTH INSIGHT:** A recent AARP survey showed that 45 percent of baby boomers plan to work beyond age 65 and that 25 percent plan to work into their 70s.

These folks simply keep trading up into retirement, as they gain higher discretionary incomes and receive inheritances. This segment of many rising immigrants and ethnic groups also demonstrates a stronger motivation to improve their living standards over their life cycle and become middle class. Their mortgage interest has a dual peak at ages 41 and 48 before falling off.

Although this is currently the smallest and lowest price-point market and would have peaked in growth momentum between 2000 and 2002, the market historically grows the most as new generations age. Looking ahead, this segment will represent better growth and price appreciation than the middle and upper segments. I expect the segment will also help to keep the lower and middle-priced housing markets stronger during the contracting price period. This market, coupled with the rising tide of starter home buying by the echo boomers, will represent the strongest and most buoyant market in the downturn after 2010 or so.

Four Effective Real Estate Tools

There are a number of resources out there that can help you get a handle on the current state of real estate affairs. Here are some of my favorites.

Fidelity Hansen Quality

Fidelity Hansen Quality has created a series of valuation tools. The automated process assigns a risk rating to the underlying valuation of a subject property. Their proprietary system is based on public databases, appraiser performance, area history, foreclosure data, and regional economic risk indicators. Before investing hundreds of thousands of dollars in a leveraged real estate transaction, investors could purchase a report such as this to assist in predicting the possible reward versus risk in each transaction. The Fidelity Hansen Value provides a quantification report that scores one valuation versus undervaluation of a subject property. Investors can use a report such as this as a first broad stroke valuation (over/under) before deciding to continue their due diligence or to move on to the next possible investment. For more information, check out the Web site at www.hanqual.com.

John Burns Real Estate Consulting Database

This new database from John Burns Real Estate Consulting projects opportunities in maturing buying segments as the baby boomers age. The database can be found at www.realestateconsulting.com, where you can use it to look ahead to the local areas that are likely to attract the 45- to 64-year-old demographic buyer for late stage trade-up, vacation, and retirement housing in the coming years and decades.

A July 2006 special newsletter on real estate reported that the buying level for family homes (ages 37 to 42) peaked between 2002 and 2003. There will be lower levels of buying to come, but they will come from baby boomers aging into their late forties, fifties, and sixties, and the fastest growth rates will come from the first half of the baby-boom birth wave (born between 1937 and 1947) that is now in their sixties.

John Burns Real Estate Consulting offers the ability to buy the full statistics on the United States for $4,995, or by region, state, county, or metro area ranging from $95 to $995. These reports give you a wealth of data ranging from age distribution by area, to propensity to buy by age cohort versus average, price trends, age of housing stock versus average, forecasts of retirees, and ratings for propensity to attract retirees by county. You can order this in the On-line Store.

The John Burns model also rates states and counties by their past propensity to attract retirees and breaks them down into four categories: Retirement Havens (13 percent greater growth than average); Retirement Friendly (0 to 13 percent greater growth); Retirement Unfriendly (0 to 13 percent lower growth); and Retirement Exodus (more than 13 percent lower growth). Go to our Web site (www.wealthstratgroup.com) for updates and more information.

www.Neighborhoodscout.com

This Web site revolves around lifestyle models for scouting out compatible areas for relocation and retirement. It applies to people who are looking to relocate to another area either for business and/or career opportunities, or for retirement. For $9.95, you can compare your local neighborhood with neighborhoods in the area that you're relocating to and determine which are the best match in lifestyle, demographics, and quality-of-life factors.

www.Zillow.com

Finally, this Web site provides free real estate information including homes for sale, comparable homes, historical sales, home valuation tools, and more. In various comparisons, the research that we pulled from the Web site was incredibly accurate on description and valuations. Just plug in your own address and see for yourself. At the same time, become the social scientist that I described earlier and ask the "what if" question: What if I could shop for my next home, tour it, finance it, and buy it—all without leaving my home office? What would this mean to me in terms of time and money saved? What would it mean to the real estate industry? If you're a consumer, it's likely a good place to be. If you're in real estate sales, it could be a signpost of changing trends that you might want to watch!

(Incidentally, www.Zillow.com now has competition from Real Estate ABC, which has a Web site in beta test at www.realestateabc.com/home-values/).

Now, you have just one more chapter to go before you can begin to implement all of your new methods and strategies in your everyday life. With this final chapter, I've saved the best for last— because the information that it imparts is critical to protecting your wealth during the great winter that looms large on our horizon.

---

1. National Association of Realtors, 2002.

2. From the 2000 Consumer Expenditures Survey and the U.S. Bureau of Labor Statistics.

IMPLEMENTING A WINNING WINTER STRATEGY

Try as we might, we can never predict precisely what the future will bring. But as we've discussed throughout this book, educated calculations of demographic trends can help predict how these trends will affect our economy. This chapter will help you devise strategies for coping with the most drastic and difficult changes that can occur when our autumn economic season moves into a long, cold, harsh Great Winter.

The Seven Winter Warning Signs

Way back in Chapter 2, I gave you a short list of warning signs that indicate the economic Great Winter is on its way. As promised, I'm now going to explain each of the items in this list in a bit more detail.

> **WEALTH INSIGHT:** At www.wealthstratgroup.com, my company's Web site, you'll find a constantly updated checklist of the Seven Winter Warning Signs, data points, a systematic liquidation strategy, and an action list. See Exhibit 10.1. By checking the Web site each month, you can monitor events as they begin to unfold and then tweak your plan of action based on these events.

Exhibit 10.1

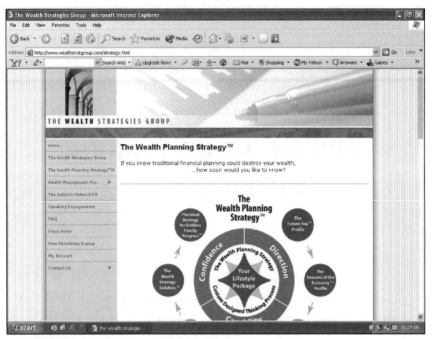

The Seven Winter Warning Signs are listed here in order of priority.

1. **Indicator:** Personal Consumption Expenditure Survey (PCE)

Where to find it: www.bea.gov

What to look for: Consumer spending drops for three consecutive months

Warning number one is when you see any reduction in consumer spending. Three consecutive monthly drops is a concern. However, if there are two consecutive down quarters (six months) in the Personal Consumption Expenditure, you should consider this a significant event. When you start to see consumers purchasing less, you have your first indication that the overall economy is starting to weaken—meaning that consumer spending has likely peaked, is beginning to flatten, and is perhaps beginning its likely long-term descent. Watch this especially closely as we move into the middle of 2009 toward mid-2011.

2. **Indicator:** Institutional Money Flow

   Where to find it: www.wordenbrothers.com or www.barrons.com/convictionoftraders

   What to look for: Decreasing prices on high volume of large block trades

The second warning sign will be when you see institutional money flowing away from common stocks. This is usually reflected by large institutional investors reallocating away from the investment market, and it's generally difficult to see. Although this development could possibly have nothing to do with the large group of people moving through the economy and may be due to investors liquidating their portfolios, it is still an indication that change is in the air. There are many ways to notice this change:

- The most obvious clue is when equity prices start to go down, that is, there are more sellers than buyers. This should be accompanied by a significant increase in volume.

- You may notice large increases in institutional transactions, which are at least 10,000 shares each.

- You might simply follow the price trend of three exchange-traded funds (ETFs): QQQQ (Nasdaq 100 Trust Shares); DIA (DIAMONDS Trust, Series 1); and SPY (S&P 500 Index), noticing volume trends in all three.

- Track price and volume. I use Telechart Gold from Worden Brothers (www.wordenbrothers.com). You could also use www.bigcharts.com or www.finance.yahoo.com to track volume and price trends.

- Watch the S&P 500 futures contract. Institutions will use the futures market vehicles to hedge their portfolio versus buying and selling large blocks of stock. Each S&P 500 futures contract covers roughly $250,000 to $300,000 in S&P 500 stock value. If a large institutional money manager, like a mutual fund or public pension fund, for example, wanted to protect a million dollars on the downside, it could sell one S&P 500 contract short to cover roughly 25 percent of its market exposure. If it was really concerned about the downside, it could get 100 percent hedged by selling roughly four contracts short, thus, never having to sell its portfolio. You can watch the number of contracts traded, plus long versus short, to get an idea of how bullish or bearish these institutions are. These numbers are posted in *Barron's* each week.

The big beasts (institutions) do leave footprints. Follow them! In your casual observation of transaction volume, you may also notice money moving and flowing from more aggressive sectors, like small-growth companies or technology companies, toward the value style of management. Value investing is historically perceived as less risky and less volatile. Thus, when investors aren't sure about what's happening in the environment, they tend to switch to a more conservative investment strategy. You could see a growth index dropping and the value index increasing as the money leaves growth going to value. Also, you may notice money flowing away from equity and toward fixed income.

3. **Indicator:** Leading Economic Indicators (LEI)

   Where to find it: www.businesscycle.com or www.newyorkfed.org/research/global-economy/globalindicators.html

   What to look for: Trends down for three to four months

This point is a bit subjective, but if you see the weekly leading economic indicators down for about three to four months, combined with the Personal Consumption Expenditure declining for two quarters, this would be an indication that change is in the air. A normal decline may go on for several months; a fair estimate could be six to eight months. However, at three to four months and with Personal Consumption in a decline, you may want to begin moving forward with your systematic liquidation plan (which I cover in detail below under "Seven Basic Strategies for Weathering a Great Winter") in an effort to deemphasize your equity investments. You should then consider moving toward paying down debt with the cash raised in your systematic liquidation. Start to invest the excess and any new cash savings in supersafe, income-oriented bonds (preferably denominated in currencies other than the U.S. dollar).

WEALTH INSIGHT: Leading economic indicator information can be found on www.businesscycle.com. This service monitors over 100 proprietary cyclical indexes for major economies covering more than 85 percent of world GDP. The Economic Cycle Research Institute (ECRI) interprets this data and makes forecasts available by subscription.

For those who enjoy looking at the global perspective, you can also reference the global Leading Economic Indicators (LEI) from the Organisation for Economic Co-Operation and Development (OECD). There's plenty of information at www.oecd.org or www.newyorkfed.org, the Web site for the Federal Reserve Bank of New York. That said, it's important to remember that the United States exports only about 9 percent of our GDP. Japan exports about 30 percent of their GDP. When Japanese consumers stopped spending in 1990, the Nikkei peaked and dropped for approximately 14 years. If Japan couldn't count on exports of 30 percent to support their economy, it seems reasonable to expect that we will have difficulty supporting ours with only 9 percent of GDP in exports. Conclusion? Our U.S. LEI will still indicate a great deal more than the global LEI data.

4. **Indicator:** Employment rate and after-tax personal income

Where to find it: www.bls.gov

What to look for: A flattening, then downturn trend in non-farm employment with a flattening to decreasing after-tax income

Jobs growth is very important to the economy. A person who doesn't have a job will, without question, spend less. Since we have already discussed the importance of consumer spending in Indicator 1 above, it is easy to connect the dots from jobs and job growth to spending. Over the last several years, the U.S. economic growth has been quantifiably the largest and broadest in history. This can be seen in the employment numbers. Over the last 45 months (as of June 1, 2007), employment has consistently increased. However, to have economic impact it is important that job creation also brings moderate increases in after-tax income. Why? This allows more people the opportunity to work, earn, and spend, which in turn creates more earnings in corporations, which drives their companies' values higher. It is this upward spiraling effect that represents a wonderful economic environment to invest in until that point in the near future where we may see a lull before the downward spiral into the economic Great Winter.

5. **Indicator:** Durable goods spending

Where to find it: www.census.gov/indicator/www/m3

What to look for: A decreasing trend, especially a downward trend of four to five months out of six

Durable goods are items that aren't consumed or disposed of very quickly. Generally, a durable good is any item that's as good three years from now as it is today. These are items that can be in inventory as parts or supply for a final product. It could even be a final product, like envelopes or underwear—areas where not much changes, except (key point coming up…) supply and demand!

If demand slows at the consumer level, it starts to immediately back up the food chain, so to speak. It seems fair to conclude that if consumer purchasing slows in the store, then new orders and shipments for durable goods would be directly and immediately impacted, as in "Stop filling the inventory in the warehouse because distribution has slowed."

Durable goods are affected by the influence of seasonal shopping. As such, it's not out of the norm to see new orders down two or three months in a row. However, at four consecutive down months in new orders and new shipping, I'd have to conclude the warehouse is backing up. This is a pretty good indicator that consumer spending is slowing, and when combined with the other Seven Winter Warning Signs, suggests that you should keep your plans for systematic liquidation of U.S. equities on track and in motion.

> **WEALTH INSIGHT:** The inventory story is critical. Inventory can be backed up quickly. Retail stores no longer have a large inventory where they can "check in the back" to see if they have what you are looking for. Today's inventory systems know how fast a product turns over on the shelf. Big box retailers keep about three days of sales on the shelf because they know in this "overnight economy" that FedEx can have more of the product on the shelf in two days.

6. **Indicator:** S&P 500 earnings per-share growth

   Where to find it: www.standardandpoors.com (a McGraw-Hill company)

What to look for: Two down quarters of S&P 500 earnings per-share growth

This is also a subjective data point. When a company's earnings per share drop for two quarters in a row, it may just be a blip caused by any number of changes in the company strategy. However, if the collective 500 companies in the S&P 500 have, on average, a reduction for one quarter, this would raise eyebrows. However, two down back-to-back quarters mean that something's probably up. This means that sales would likely have been less. The reduced sales would be a result of the two down quarters of consumption reflected in the Personal Consumption Expenditure Report. Hence, the two down quarters of the S&P 500 earnings would be lagging behind the two down quarters of Personal Consumption Expenditures. As a comparison it is the opposite of today's spiraling up economy. Personal Consumption Expenditures have gone up the last 20 quarters. S&P 500 corporate earnings were also up—and at an all-time high: in addition to having just experienced the longest string of quarterly earnings growth on record.

7. **Indicator:** Inflation/deflation numbers

   Where to find it: www.bls.gov/ppi/ or www.bls.gov/cpi/

   What to look for: An interruption to the consistent but modest increase in the cost we all pay for goods and services.

Inflation is the best indicator of economic growth, period. If the economy is expanding, it means people have jobs, are productive and earning money, and are then spending that money in the economy. It's this velocity of money going through the economy that causes the economy to expand and grow.

If you look back in our nation's history, we've had two periods of high inflation. The first was after the Civil War, and the second was in the late 1970s to early 1980s. Both periods had an expanding population (from immigration after the Civil War and from the peak of the baby boomers' entry into the workforce in the late 1970s to early 1980s). In the latter case, the costs were related to training, hiring, and placing these people—an expensive process that produces very few immediate results in the economy. Thus, the costs associated with these people entering the workforce were part of what caused the inflation.

Today, those same workers are mature, established, and their cost is known and predictable. They're very knowledgeable, skillful, and (key point...) *productive*. However, as they age and retire, they'll consume less. We already know from the birth stats that there are fewer consumers coming into the economy behind this generation—because those consumers were never born.

The conclusion is pretty straightforward: There won't be as many dollars spent on hiring; training; setting up; buying new cars, houses, etc. Thus, it's more likely the economy will grow at a considerably slower rate or even contract as we move past 2010–2011. And contracting means we could experience a period of reduced prices or deflation. When there are fewer buyers and the same supply, the prices will go down, or deflate. Nearly all areas of investment (stocks, real estate, private business, etc.) do poorly during a period of deflating prices, so watch this closely. It's tracked and reported in the national press via the business section of the local papers, as well as on the Web sites mentioned above.

WEALTH INSIGHT: Inflation is certainly an indication of economic growth. Perhaps more so are the tax receipts by the U.S. Treasury. In the economic recovery of 2002 through 2006, many investors questioned the "quality" of reporting by corporations. This was a fair area to question after the corporate maleficence of the period. However, during the same period the U.S. budget deficit went from approximately $500 billion to a projection of under $150 billion in early 2007. The Treasury can't reduce a deficit by approximately $350 billion without some serious revenue inflow. Serious inflow can only come from taxation and collection of tax on revenue earned. Granted, it didn't all come from corporations, as they are only 15 percent of the tax revenue, which means people had jobs, earned money, *paid taxes* (individuals make up 78 percent of tax revenue when social insurance is included), and then consumed goods and services. The goods and services consumed allowed the corporations to earn a profit and *pay taxes*. Watch the total tax receipts to the U.S. Treasury as they are true indicators on how the economy is really doing.

WEALTH INSIGHT: As we get into the Great Winter, it's my opinion that investments for which the underlying currency is the U.S. dollar will be adversely affected. (I'll elaborate later in the section "Seven Basic Strategies for Weathering a Great Winter"). Of course, if you live, work, earn, and spend money in the United States, the value of the dollar doesn't really affect your day-to-day life. It does if you buy foreign products or decide to travel internationally, but that's beyond the scope of our discussion here.

Each of us would be positively affected by foreign investors who convert their currency to U.S. dollars to buy investments in U.S. companies—the same ones owned by your mutual fund in your 401(k) at work. They'll likely buy more of these investments going into the end of this decade, as our economy is quantifiably doing well. What happens if these foreign investors decide to sell their investments and convert their U.S. dollars back to their home currency? Your investments could then drop from their selling, and the U.S. dollar would also drop as it's sold and converted to the investors' respective home currencies.

By paying attention to the Seven Winter Warning Signs, you might anticipate this and become a bit more of a worldly investor. How? By converting some of your U.S. investment dollars to the currencies of other countries before those foreign investors do. This can be a money market or Certificate of Deposit (CD) denominated in another currency (go to www.everbank.com, which I discuss in greater detail later in this chapter, to find out more). You could also invest directly in other countries' bonds, like Iceland, Austria, Switzerland, Australia, and New

Zealand. The dollar versus other currencies is quoted in all major papers, or just Google on U.S. Dollar Conversion, and it takes you to several sources for trend observation. Remember—a downtrend is not your friend!

The Fallout

When you witness a trend change happening inside of the Seven Winter Warning Signs that I just described, you can anticipate that the economic storm is brewing, and the change is likely a turn for the worse. The overall scene could resemble something like the following:

In a deflationary economy, bond values would likely go up, at least initially, due to two factors: a flight to safety and a desire for income. After this initial lift up, the frenzy from foreign selling pressure could take over, pushing prices down. By this point, the already flattening real estate prices should begin to drop in value, and all financial assets will likely follow suit—especially common stocks.

In this environment, there isn't as much demand for base or core commodities; therefore, these are negatively affected. Obviously, when a company is selling less and earning less, the company doesn't need as many employees. There are subsequent layoffs. With fewer jobs offered, unemployment starts to climb. When companies sell less, they make less, and since earnings are what drives the stock value up or down, the company stock starts to drop. Bank loans become a bigger problem, and there are likely defaults on individual real estate, as many people will have lost their jobs, and/or businesses. Some homeowners may even be forced to start giving houses back to the banks and mortgage companies, as they can't afford the mortgage and can't sell in an environment of fewer buyers and no speculators. Some may have to move in with other family members, creating even more housing supply in a market with already significantly decreasing demand. The excessive supply means home prices will likely begin to come down in price even more.

Yet another real estate–related issue is that many home builders must complete their developments and/or projects in order to be paid—even when there's a measurable decrease in demand. Thus, they continue to build into an oversupplied market to fulfill their contracts, providing even more supply.

These factors, combined with the historically increasing property tax rates, and the additional cost of second or third lines of credit, will no doubt force many more people into default and possibly bankruptcy. This, of course, will feed on itself causing prices to continue spiraling downward.

Seven Basic Strategies for Weathering a Great Winter

After reading about the dreary environment just illustrated, the average investor would likely panic. You, on the other hand, are calm. You should have tremendous clarity and confidence, because you've read this book, developing your wealth investment strategies and plans all along the way. Now, you can use the seven strategies that follow to tweak your well-defined core investment plans, ensuring that you'll survive the economic winter as comfortably as possible.

Strategy 1: Systematically Divest Yourself of U.S. Assets

In approximately March 2010, I would encourage taking out 20 percent, making you either 80 or 100 percent out of equities,

Exhibit 10.2 Timeline for Divesting U.S. Assets

Approximate Date	Percent Approximate Out	Percent Totally Out
April 2008	10%	10%
January 2009	15 – 20%	25 – 30%
April 2009	15 – 20%	40 – 50%
December 2009	20 – 30%	60 – 80%
March 2010	20%	80 – 100%

WHAT YOU'RE LOOKING AT: The dates and percentage amounts by which you may want to consider divesting your U.S. assets. (Watch the Seven Winter Warning Signs at www.wealthstratgroup.com.)

WHAT THIS TELLS YOU: Since no one knows the future, how it will unfold, or when a catalyst may cause the next up or down bump, we need to timeline our plan to deal with these unknowns. The first thing you can do to protect your wealth during the economic winter is to systematically divest your holdings over time. This is the opposite of the popular dollar cost averaging strategy which is used to buy similar dollar amounts of an investment over time.

WHAT THIS MEANS: For the Great Winter in our midst, this means that by the end of April 2008 ("Sell in May and go away"), you may choose to liquidate approximately 10 percent of your equity positions. In January 2009, you could liquidate another 15 to 20 percent, which would make you 25 to 30 percent out of the equity markets. In approximately April 2009, liquidate an additional 15 to 20 percent, so that you're 40 to 50 percent divested in common stock. Around December 2009, liquidate 20 to 30 percent, bringing you to 60 to 80 percent out of equity.

• • • • • •

depending on how aggressively you sold along the way. You could choose to leave the 20 percent remaining if you used the least aggressive exit strategy. If you do, I'd suggest that you use stop orders or hedging techniques to protect the downside of your principal during this period.

Strategy 2: Invest in Non-U.S. Equities

China currently holds approximately 16 percent of outstanding U.S. treasuries, with a total of $345 billion USD; Japan holds 30 percent, for a total of $641 billion USD. (*Source:* U.S. Treasury Department, October 2006). These two countries hold a whopping 46 percent of all outstanding U.S. treasuries.

Let's say we enter a slowing U.S. economy—the Winter Season—and you notice the economy begin to weaken. If you were Japan and China, what would you do? You'd likely sell. Under normal trading conditions, selling 46 percent of anything would create more sellers than buyers. Now suppose you're the Federal Reserve chairman, and you see the economy slowing. What would your reaction be? You would probably want to reduce short-term interest rates in an attempt to induce economic growth.

But what might happen next? Interest rates could actually start to climb up, which could cause the opposite effect than the Federal Reserve would like and actually reduce economic growth. It would also cause the price of bonds to go down. How could this be? Once again, supply and demand caused by the potential large sales of U.S. government bonds by Japan and China. In addition, bond buyers who thought they were playing it safe by buying U.S. Treasuries could see 15 percent, perhaps even 20 percent, of their principal value eroded. And if they have to sell before maturity, they'd have a realized loss in principal. Yet another consequence of Japan and China selling U.S. Treasuries would be that they would then convert their U.S. dollars from the sale of their U.S. Treasuries back to their own currencies, putting downward pressure on the U.S. dollar. (Lots of supply (selling), not as much demand (buying).

Suppose you had seen the economic seasons starting to change, and you had some of your money in non–U.S. assets—like equity investments in Korea, China, or India. Now should the U.S. dollar drop 15 to 20 percent or more (which is realistic), you'd be getting your dividend income from your investments, plus you'd realize appreciation of a like percentage from your ability to convert back to now depreciated dollars. This combination could produce low double-digit returns in an environment where stock portfolios are likely being decimated.

Strategy 3: Use Nondollar-Denominated Income Investments

The Internet-based EverBank (www.everbank.com) is an international bank that is also FDIC insured for up to $100,000. The bank has CDs in various currencies that are guaranteed up to the $100,000 limit set by the U.S. government. It was also voted Kiplinger's Best Checking Account (November 2006) and Best of the Web by www.Forbes.com (2000–2006).

EverBank offers WorldCurrency Access deposits and CDs that are U.S. bank deposits denominated in foreign currencies of your choice. Access accounts are demand deposits that can be added to or withdrawn from at any time. The account can earn interest depending on the size of the deposit balance and the currency of the funds held. WorldCurrency CDs are longer-term deposits that generally earn a higher level of interest, as you'd expect. In both cases, the interest is paid in the foreign currency.

As a part of the nationwide division of EverBank, your deposits held at EverBank World Markets are FDIC insured. However, unlike other bank accounts, WorldCurrency deposits have currency risk. The FDIC insurance only insures against losses related to bank insolvency; it doesn't cover any risk associated with changing currency prices. As with all investments, investors can lose money, including principal. That said, it's also the reason to consider this alternative. If you think, as I do, that the dollar would drop and other currencies, like the Chinese yuan or Swiss franc, would appreciate, then a nondollar-denominated CD or non–U.S. government bond could be useful strategies.

Strategy 4: Invest in Kiwi Bonds

New Zealanders—known as Kiwis throughout the world—offer a great wealth protection strategy in their government bonds. These bonds aren't affected by a drop in the dollar, except from a positive standpoint.

WEALTH INSIGHT: You can learn more about New Zealand's wealth protection options at the New Zealand Debt Management Office (NZDMO) Web site: www.nzdmo.govt.nz/aboutnzdmo/.

The New Zealand Debt Management Office (NZDMO) is responsible for managing the Kiwi crown's domestic borrowing program. The Reserve Bank undertakes the tenders of, and transactions relating to, treasury bills and government bonds. It also publishes information on domestic government securities that supports the market in these securities.

The Reserve Bank manages New Zealand's foreign-exchange reserves. These reserves are included in the government's total portfolio and integrated into NZDMO's asset and liability management process. This is done by NZDMO directly financing the Reserve Bank's foreign exchange reserves through foreign-currency deposits with the Reserve Bank. Under this structure, the Reserve Bank's task is to manage its position between its foreign-currency liabilities to NZDMO and the foreign-currency assets that make up the foreign-exchange reserves. Thus, each of the parties—NZDMO and the Reserve Bank—has a well-defined task, the net result being that the financial assets and liabilities of the government are taken fully into account in debt management.

Here's a scenario that illustrates how Kiwi bonds could benefit you during an economic winter. Assume you get 6 percent from a New Zealand bond, and the U.S. dollar drops 10 percent. Because of the currency conversion, you could possibly maintain your principal and, if you add in a 6 percent income stream, you could look at the situation as a total return of 16 percent.

Strategy 5: Protect Your Assets from the New Sport in America: the Frivolous Lawsuit

The key to protecting each of your assets from frivolous lawsuits is to *deter* the lawsuit. Unfortunately, these lawsuits really do happen. Take the case of a friend of mine, who pulled into a restaurant parking lot with his wife one night during a slight snowfall. Two young men came out of the restaurant, sliding and having fun. One of the young men slid by the front of my friend's car—which had stopped so they could have their fun by sliding by—put his hands on the hood of the car, said "Boo!" to my friend inside the car, and then kept running. My friend and his wife proceeded to have dinner (no alcohol), returned to their car, and drove home. Uneventful, right? Wrong!

The next day, the local police called and asked my friend to come in for questioning about a hit and run in the restaurant parking lot the previous night. My friend had witnesses inside and outside the restaurant, the time-stamped bill showed no alcohol, and the car had no damage. The police eventually discovered that the people making the claim had made over 50 such claims. Based on this, the police dropped the hit-and-run allegation. But the group's attorney did not!

It turns out that this group also included an attorney and a chiropractor who, acting on behalf of the two young men, claimed that the hit-and-run "victim" had hurt his back. The group had pulled this same stunt in many different ways and places. This time, they were suing my friend for $25,000 in damages. My friend's insurance company decided to settle, because as you would guess, $25,000 is a lot less than the cost of preparing a defense and going to trial. Not a bad profit for a few moments of sliding and having fun—and that's in a good economy. Wait until we have a not-so-good, or perhaps terrible, economy and see how creative groups like this can get.

The key is to deter. Your first line of defense against situations like this is to have an umbrella liability policy. These are generally inexpensive and can be purchased from your insurance provider. I personally have a $5,000,000 liability policy.

Second is to structure your assets so that you become as much of a *human zero* as possible. You can have pools of assets paying you income or holding assets, but that doesn't have to mean you're the legal owner. Trusts are already a familiar topic to you, after having read Chapter 4 where I talked about them in detail. As you know, you can have your assets put into a trust so that if you're sued, and found to be liable, you don't really own any assets. They are instead owned by the trust. There's nothing of yours to attack ... you're a human zero.

There are also various structures of ownership, such as a Family Limited Partnership (FLP), General or Limited Partnership (GP or LP), Limited Liability Company (LLC), or Limited Liability Limited Partnership (LLLP), as well as various layering techniques of corporate ownership (more detail of each is outlined in Appendix C). All of these types of structures will have a deterring effect on groups like the one in the example above. These can also be legitimate tools for business ownership and, where appropriate, estate planning. Talk with your estate-planning attorney to ensure that your assets are structured to deter this type of frivolous lawsuit.

Strategy 6: Make a Conscious Decision to Keep or Sell Your Business

If you don't really love your business, sell it. In fact, I would advise most people to sell their small businesses during the period of economic strength that we expect to see over the next three to four years. By roughly 2010–2011, many business owners will be faced with the decision to increase the size of their business by either merging with a larger business or selling their business outright to large companies. In the solid growth summer economy that we expect until then, there will be a race for leadership to see who will dominate major growth industries in the future. Commoditization in most businesses means the race will likely not be won by small companies.

While we'll probably see economic strength over the next few years, we'll also see some challenges for small businesses. Overall, the next few years could be very good financially. Know that and plan around it. With the likely arrival of The Great Winter, you should take a moment to look at your business and determine where it fits in the industry and where it stands next to your competition. Perhaps you'll conclude that it does make sense to monetize (sell) and implement some of the ideas that I've presented. Then, during The Great Winter, maybe you'll buy your old business back for less than you sold it—or buy a prior competitor for 10 or 20 cents on the dollar, who has too much debt in a now contracting business environment.

In the 1970s, small companies could take years and years to grow. Today, this process has to happen exponentially faster: You must launch something, grow it, and prove it in your market, all in the blink of an eye. Forget about going public with your small business; it would be too expensive. Simply consider selling it to a bigger company that needs your niche market to build their fortress for The Great Winter.

> **WEALTH INSIGHT:** The consumer spending during the next eco-nomic stage should be starting to look obvious. Just like coonskin caps in the 1960s, bicycles in the 1970s, BMWs in the 1980s, and massive con-sumption of all kinds of consumer goods in the 1990s, the future of the consumer is likely to revolve around everything related to health care and resort travel. These are the areas to position your business in as we go forward.

Strategy 7: Sell Mortgage Company-Related Investments

Fannie Mae has more than $1 trillion in assets, and it may well be that its accounting problems will be the first blip on the mort-gage crisis radar. Why? Think about what will happen to mortgage pools when the mortgage bubble really does burst. Many of those owner-occupied homes, financed with variable-rate mortgages, may prove to be both overpriced and overfinanced. Lenders, always looking for profits from new loans and from refinancing, hire appraisers to look at properties. If the lender wants to write the loan, you can be sure the appraisal will come out at the level that meets with institutional loan approval.

The lenders make their profit short term and then sell the debt to Fannie Mae and other mortgage pools. These pools, with potentially growing numbers of loans based on inflated or exaggerated values, are packaged together and then sold to investors. As interest rates begin creeping upward, borrowers with adjustable-rate mortgages (ARMs) will have monthly payments that follow suit. Many home-owners, only marginally qualified to begin with, may find them-selves unable to keep up. If the market-value bubble also bursts, many borrowers will find themselves with zero equity—or even neg-ative equity—in their homes. It doesn't take much effort to make the leap from here to what could happen to the mortgage company sector and those invested in their income products—and it doesn't take a genius to realize that it probably won't turn out very well.

Four More Aggressive Winter Strategies

Investors looking to take their wealth protection up a notch beyond the basics can consider the following strategies:

1. *Buy long-term put options.*

An option is simply a contract. It can be more risky or less risky, depending on how you choose to use it, that is, as a hedge (less risky) or as speculation (more risky). Put options rise in value as the underlying stock price falls, so the long-term put would be a good position for protection against future price declines. In its most basic form, this would be like buying car insurance. If you cause damage to your car, the insurance makes you whole, less any deductible. The put option goes up in value at a rate that's likely to be about the same as your portfolio might go down in a poor per-forming stock market environment. It's like the insurance example, helping to keep you whole, less any transaction costs. These are useful and effective strategies, but be sure to do your homework before you implement them. When used incorrectly, they can cause a serious case of heartburn.

The U.S. Dollar Index (USDX) trades on the New York Board of Trade under the symbol DX. Using a base of 100, the USDX measures the market value of the dollar versus the trade-weighted geometric average of six currencies. (Seventeen countries are represented in the index, but 12 countries use the euro.) The six currencies are the euro, the Japanese yen, the U.K. pound, the Canadian dollar, the Swedish krona, and the Swiss franc.

Why these particular countries and currencies? First, the six currencies constitute most of America's international trade (except with Mexico and China) and have relatively well-developed foreign exchange markets. Most importantly, the values of these currencies are, with the exception of central bank intervention, freely determined by market forces and market participants.

Purchasing put options on the USDX is the most direct way to capitalize on the dollar's decline. You pay the price—known as the *premium*—to have the right, but not the obligation, for a fixed period of time, to be short of the dollar index at a specific level. Should the dollar fail to fall, or should it even go up in value (which from our 2010–2011 time frame would be highly unlikely), you would simply not exercise your right to be short the dollar—forfeiting the premium paid for the put option, but no more. Your maximum risk is the price you pay for your options plus transaction costs.

2. *Buy euro call options.*

Buying euro call options is almost identical to buying puts on the Dollar Index. Consider buying euro FX call options dated at least four months into the future. If the dollar drops, it would be likely that the euro would rise. Buying calls on the euro, therefore, is a more focused trade. Because the euro-block countries produce a current account surplus, there's an automatic, natural demand for euros. Call options on euro currency futures are promising ways to benefit from a decline in the U.S. dollar. The euro index has been rising steadily since the dollar peaked in February 2002. I suspect that as we move toward the 2010–2011 time frame, the U.S. dollar will have trended up and the euro down. Based on our outlook, these two currencies would then reverse.

3. *Buy foreign currency CDs.*

Invest directly in strong currencies and their CDs. By doing this, you reduce your risks considerably, because you're dealing with a single investment that you own outright and can easily monitor. You can be certain to receive whatever exchange rate advantages or disadvantages may develop between your foreign currency and the U.S. dollar. As you now know, I expect the U.S. dollar to peak with the U.S. economy. Then, as our consumer spending slows and our economy slows with it, the dollar would be expected to start cycling down under the scenario already outlined. Keep in mind that as more boomers retire, they'll pay less income tax and demand more entitlement, such as social security, Medicare, and Medicaid. That means less revenue and increasing expenses in Washington D.C. When combined with expected debt and deficit levels, the solution to economic weakness going forward wouldn't be a big leap, and it is higher taxes. All of this thought process adds fuel to the fire of a spiraling down U.S. dollar.

WEALTH INSIGHT: Until recently, opening a foreign currency account could be done only through an offshore bank. Many countries don't make it easy for their banks to deal with Americans. Offshore bank accounts have led to additional paperwork with the IRS and an increased chance for an audit. Fortunately for U.S. investors, foreign currency accounts are now easily available.

4. *Buy Commodity Index CDs.*

The Commodity Index CD is comprised of the Australian dollar, New Zealand dollar, Canadian dollar, and South African rand. These currencies are grouped together because their economies are all driven by commodities exports. Yet remember the old adage, "If the U.S. sneezes, the rest of the world gets a cold," meaning, if the world economy slows, the demand for commodities won't be as large, and, therefore, these countries may also suffer. As likely as that is, there are still countries that have currencies that will perform well against the dollar in this type of environment.

I've listed this more aggressive strategy last, as I clearly think a pure play using a Swiss franc, Icelandic krona, Australian dollar, and New Zealand dollar is more productive. However, this does give you a basket of currencies (diversification) versus a single currency, which can be good, but the single currency investment has the risk of concentration in the portfolio.

So here's our last short list of the book, summarizing what I just described about assets to sell and hold in preparation for a Great Winter.

Summary: What to Sell and What to Buy

SELL

1. Start to systematically liquidate about 10 percent of your equity portfolio (don't forget your retirement plan at work, if you have one) in April 2008; another 15 to 20 percent in January 2009; 15 to 20 percent in April 2009; 20 to 30 percent in December 2010; and then 20 percent or the remainder of the portfolio by March 2011.

2. Sell holdings in finance, bank, brokerage, and mortgage company investments as we move toward 2010.

3. Move out of real estate (you haven't lived until you lose market value with leverage). Skip the "good debt" versus "bad debt" lecture. In a contracting economy, all debt is bad debt.

4. Watch for business opportunities during the fallout; businesses with too much leverage (debt) are likely to fail. Be sure to have cash and credit lines available to buy these businesses or perhaps buy out competitors in your industry for pennies on the dollar.

HOLD

1. Types of investments to own are CDs and nondollar-denominated government bonds from countries such as Iceland, Austria, Switzerland, Australia, and New Zealand.

2. Countries that should have above-average equity performance based on strong demographic trends are Singapore, Korea, India, and China.

3. If you choose not to liquidate some or all of your portfolio, have at least some portfolio protection with a hedge like the S&P 500 put option strategy presented earlier in this chapter. You could also use a separately managed account that implements this strategy in client accounts.

4. Keep it simple. Find companies that you know will survive. AAA-rated corporations in the United States are likely to have excellent bond income and the ability to return your principal at maturity.

5. Use tax-deferred annuities that allow you to reallocate to different investments during difficult economic environments, plus make use of other currencies.

Congratulations—you made it! It's been an incredible journey. We truly covered all the bases of a great wealth management process, beginning with a primer on the three wealth factors, where you learned that what's behind us determines our future! We also talked at length about wealth structures and risk management strategies, plus how to put those together in a comprehensive wealth management plan.

You know by now that 70 percent of the economy is driven by consumer spending, and that your assets can grow during all seasons, no matter how good or bad the season is. Your overall objective is to protect what you have and not lose principal during any one season. You also understand that assets must have an advantageous configuration—meaning that you can own, title, and control your assets in a tax-advantaged way. Structure is also the key to how those assets flow or transfer in the most efficient way to your family's next generation. Correct structure also has the power to deter frivolous lawsuits.

But all of this information is worth very little if you don't know how to put it to work for you. It's up to you to continue to study beyond this book. At the end of the day, you must establish a list of criteria for your specific needs. Ask your advisor, or group of advisors, the appropriate questions. If any answer is unacceptable, go on to the next advisor. Take your time. It's an investment in your future—and your family's. Don't be pressured. Find the right people for your team—people that you're comfortable with and, most of all, people that you can trust.

Above all, don't be afraid to plan for fear that you might get locked into something for too long. You can always change or adjust your plan if need be. What's most important is to decide what to do today. In the end, the bull's-eye of financial freedom might be a moving target—but you still need a plan, a team, and a structure to give you the confidence to weather all seasons of the economy.

THE LIFE PLANNING STRATEGY MODULE—LEGAL TRANSFER STRATEGIES

This is the last step based on the Future You Profile that you established. It's a structure for the most efficient legal transfer of wealth to those you love.

You can have your assets put into a trust so that if you're sued, you could be found liable, but you don't really own any assets. Since they're owned by the trust, there's nothing to attach. And yet, an irrevocable trust is a vehicle over which you have control. You pay taxes on it, and you can choose to receive money from it—but you don't own it. You're merely the trustee.

When your investment strategy works, but you haven't properly planned for future tax liability, you'll be happy you read this section. If you're an average investor who owns your own home and a life insurance policy, a few minor (but key) structural changes in titling and ownership could save you many thousands of dollars in unnecessary taxes.

Tax Reduction Tool

To remedy that, we plug in the "tax reduction tool," which is a process that involves five levels of estate planning depending on your particular objectives and circumstances.

Level 1: Basic Plan

Level 1 planning is for the person who has no wills or trusts in place, or whose existing wills or trusts are outdated or inadequate. This person's planning should be designed to:

- Reduce or eliminate estate taxes

- Avoid probate

- Protect heirs from their inability, disability, creditors, and predators

To accomplish these objectives, you'd create a will that directs assets you designated in life to a trust at the time of your death (a pour-over will). You could also create a revocable living trust that allocates the decedent's estate between a credit shelter trust and a marital trust. A basic or level 1 structure should also have current general powers of attorney, and durable powers of attorney for health care and living wills.

Level 2: Irrevocable Life Insurance Trust (ILIT)

Level 2 planning is for those people whose estate is projected to be greater than the $2 million estate-tax exemption (unified credit) for 2006 through 2008 ($4 million for the properly titled "structured" assets of a married couple). In this case, you can make cash gifts to an Irrevocable Life Insurance Trust (ILIT) using the $12,000 per person or $24,000 per couple annual gift-tax exclusion in order to buy an adequate amount of life insurance coverage to offset the future tax liability. Think about this. *You have a chance to turn a liability into a tax-free benefit!*

Level 3: Family Limited Partnerships

Level 3 planning is for the person who has a projected estate-tax liability that exceeds the life insurance purchased in Level 2. If your gift-tax exemption is used to make lifetime gifts, the gifted property and all future appreciation and income on that property are removed from the donor's estate.

Many people would be more willing to make gifts to their children if they could continue to manage the gifted property. A family limited partnership (FLP) or a family limited liability company (FLLC) can play a valuable role in this situation. The donor is typically the general partner or manager and in that capacity, continues to manage the FLP or FLLC's assets. The donor can even take a reasonable management fee for his or her services as the general partner or manager. Moreover, by gifting FLP or FLLC interests to an ILIT, the FLP or FLLC's income can be used to pay premiums, thereby freeing up the clients' $12,000 or $24,000 annual gift-tax exclusion for other types of gifts.

Level 4: QPRTs and GRATs

Level 4 planning is the additional need to reduce your estate's total value after correctly structuring the transfer of your unified credit amount as detailed above in level 2. Each citizen can transfer $2 million or $4 million per couple to a nonspouse beneficiary in life or after death. Although paying gift taxes is less expensive than paying estate taxes, most people will not want to pay gift taxes. There are several techniques to make substantial gifts to children and grandchildren without paying significant gift taxes.

One technique is a qualified personal residence trust (QPRT). A QPRT allows the grantor to transfer a residence or vacation home to a trust for the benefit of his or her children, while retaining the right to use the residence for a term of years. By retaining the right to occupy the residence, the value of the remainder interest is reduced, along with the taxable gift. If the grantor survives the term, the residence (and the future appreciation thereon) is entirely removed from the grantor's estate.

Another technique is a grantor-retained annuity trust (GRAT). A GRAT is similar to a QPRT. The typical GRAT is funded with income-producing property such as subchapter S stock or FLP or FLLC interests. The GRAT pays the grantor a fixed annuity for a specified term of years. Because of the retained annuity, the gift to the grantor's children is substantially less than the current value of the property.

Both QPRTs and GRATs can be designed with terms long enough to reduce the value of the remainder interest passing to the children to a nominal amount or even to zero. However, if the grantor does not survive the stated term, the property is included in the grantor's estate. Therefore, it is recommended that an ILIT be funded as a "hedge" against the grantor's death prior to the end of the stated term.

Level 5: Zero Estate-Tax Plan

Level 5 planning is a desire to disinherit the IRS. The strategy combines gifts of life insurance with gifts to charity.

With the typical marital credit shelter trust, when the first spouse dies, a portion of the estate is allocated to the credit shelter trust and the rest is allocated to the marital trust. No federal estate tax is due. However, at the surviving spouse's death, a large estate tax is due.

The net result is that the inheritors receive much less than they would have.

With the zero estate-tax plan, a couple gifts some of their assets during their lifetime (using their annual gift-tax exclusions) to an ILIT (with generation-skipping provisions) funded with a tax-free life benefit second-to-die life insurance policy. These gifts reduce the estate value. In addition, the couple's living trusts each leave the amount exempt from estate taxes to their children upon the surviving spouse's death. Also, the balance of their estate passes to a public charity or private foundation—estate tax-free. To summarize, the zero estate-tax plan delivers money from the ILIT and from the living trusts to the children; the charity receives a portion of the estate instead of nothing; and the IRS receives nothing.

A CASE STUDY
IN FINANCIAL PLANNING

Every aspect of the planning process depends on the answers to critical financial planning questions. As an example, a simple question such as how to title the accounts depends on an understanding of the estate plan, not just as it exists, but as it should be. Trust planning is becoming an important issue, and we see major errors being made.

Information Gathering

There is a big difference between consulting to institutions and advising to a higher net worth (HNW) individual or couple. With individuals there may be "fuzzy goals"—uncertainty as to concrete objectives or disagreement among family members as to specific needs. There may be tax issues (income and estate taxes); varying time frames related to multiple objectives; ownership issues; risk management questions; insurance matters; legacy and succession concerns. Asset management decisions and Investment Policy Statements must be framed within an overall financial planning context.

Data gathering can be a daunting task. Both the financial advisor and the client must know "where and what all of their stuff is." Often the client does not know. Thus, each advisor should have a method in place to organize data and the patience to wade through it.

In many cases, no single advisor "owns the client relationship." Money, securities, and other assets may be on deposit at multiple institutions. No one understands the big picture. The advisor must have a *process* to accomplish that objective.

Many advisors employ an abbreviated data sheet up front, which is completed by a potential client and submitted prior to the first meeting or brought to the first meeting. Initial data is a "first cut" used to get a sense as to whether the advisor and the client have a basis for a long-term, mutually satisfactory relationship. Most financial planners offer a no-obligation initial interview. The objective is to gather enough information to determine the scope of the engagement as well as get an opportunity to define their *process*.

Often a more detailed data sheet is completed after the engagement has been accepted and construction of the financial plan has begun. Clients are given checklists and questionnaires. Staff members, associate planners, and interns often work with clients to assemble the data. Patience is required, especially when affairs are complex. "Scattered assets" are the norm, and often it may take more time to gather the requested data than it does to do the planning.

Basic data gathering would encompass but should not be limited to the following:

1. *Family census.* Names, residential and business addresses, contact data (phone, fax, e-mail), names of children, ages and dates of birth of all family members, social security numbers. Are children married? Grandchildren? Health status? Special needs?

2. *Net worth statement.* Determine ownership for all assets, that is, ownership by client, spouse, or partner; joint ownership (define such as JTWROS, TIC, community property, etc.); trust (define); other (define, such as accounts held for minors). Request copies of all statements.

3. *Checking and savings accounts, money market, CDs* (show maturity date).

4. *Stocks, bonds, mutual funds* (list or provide brokerage or custodial statement). Include data on U.S. savings bonds. Obtain tax basis for all securities.

5. *Annuities (fixed and variable).* Obtain copy of policy and recent quarterly and annual reports. Determine owner; annuitant; primary and contingent beneficiaries; tax status.

6. *Life insurance.* Request copy of policy, original proposal, last annual report. Determine type of policy, face amount, the insured, owner, beneficiary (primary and contingent), premium payments, adequacy of payments (how long will the policy carry given current assumptions?), purpose of the coverage, cash values if applicable (current value, surrender value, loans outstanding). Include data on group insurance and any coverage tied to employer benefits or business arrangements such as buy/sell agreements. Determine all sources of death benefits.

7. *Real estate, including residence, vacation home, rental properties.* Identify owner, purchase price, current value, mortgage terms and current balance, cash flow from rental properties.

8. *Partnership investments* (obtain copy of recent quarterly or annual report). Determine cash flow, tax benefits, estimated values, liquidity, if any.

9. *Business interests.* Name; type of business; form of ownership (C-Corp., S-Corp., sole proprietor, partnership, LLC); percentage of ownership; value of interest; buy/sell agreement or succession plan.

10. *Personal assets.* Description (car, boat, aircraft); value; debt. List value of other assets such as jewelry, household furnishings.

11. *Retirement plans.* Obtain statements for all pension/profit sharing plans; IRAs; 401(k); 403(b); 457 plans; deferred compensation plans, etc. Specify primary and contingent beneficiaries.

12. *Stock option plans.* Obtain complete description; type of options; number of shares; exercise price; current stock price; vesting.

13. *Education planning.* Section 529 Plans, Education IRAs, other.

14. *Tangibles.* Type of asset (precious metals, gems, coins); date of purchase; original investment; current value.

15. *Other insurance.* Copies of homeowner, rental, auto, umbrella liability policies; personal and group disability policies; long-term care.

16. *Copies of legal documents and other key documents.* Will(s); trusts (including revocable or irrevocable living trusts, charitable trusts); durable powers of attorney for assets and health care; divorce decrees, alimony and child support agreements; prenuptial agreements; stock purchase agreements; business buy/sell agreements; family limited partnerships; most recent tax return.

18. *The Advisory Team.* You want to know the name, address, and contact information for other key advisors such as a CPA or other tax advisor; attorney, banker, trustees, insurance agents, brokers, etc.

19. *Anything else the client(s) thinks is important* to his and/or her life and future.

Beyond the Financial

For most affluent clients, investing and financial planning aren't just about making money. They are about the meaning of money as related to one's psyche, one's mission in life, and one's final legacy.

For example, it is easy to run a retirement planning calculation targeting X dollars by a certain date to fund retirement. The advisor may use linear assumptions or Monte Carlo simulation to come up with a hypothetical result. But is that enough?

What does *retirement* really mean to the client? Or to both clients, if a couple. Will one or both work part-time? Will a hobby become a source of income? Do they want to sell a home and relocate? Rent or buy a boat and sail away? Travel? What are their longevity assumptions? Do the husband and wife agree? (Is there harmony or conflict?)

The client may have achieved financial success. Is there more to it than that? Bob Buford, in his meaningful book *Half Time: Changing Your Game Plan from Success to Significance* (Zondervan Publishing, Grand Rapids, MI, 1994), noted: "One of the most common characteristics of a person nearing the end of the first half [of the game of life] is that unquenchable desire to move from success to significance."

Significance in Buford's book reflects the client's vision of a legacy during his or her lifetime and after one transcends at death to, hopefully, a higher order where character counts and net worth means nothing. A man or woman of true depth recognizes that all earthly blessings are merely loans. All must be left behind.

Significance is a desire to give back now and beyond death, to make a difference.

A trusted advisor needs to know more. What does the client want to do in terms of lifelong learning, a second career, spiritual or ministerial goals, charitable desires, and legacies for survivors as well as yet unborn generations? Clients may wish to fund trusts, endow causes, build cultural edifices, create foundations, educate, enlighten, inspire. Addressing these issues will make The Wealth Planning Strategy™ significant in their lives.

These are the "soft issues" regarding money. Proper questioning and exploring in the deeper areas beyond money and surface simplicities will set great advisors apart from the crowd and from those looking for quick sales. Matters of significance require money, but money is not the point.

Beyond the Questionnaire

"Information gathering" means going beyond the data sheet. An understanding of the client's core values and objectives comes out of face-to-face conversations over coffee or other refreshments, over lunch or dinner, in relaxed atmospheres, in unguarded moments. It is the exercise in human communication, verbal and nonverbal, that leads to important discoveries and creative solutions. This is why most of our clients become true friends.

"What If?" Questions

As we approach the formulation stage of writing an Investment Policy Statement for a client, we explain the three phases of "money life": accumulation, preservation, distribution.

In a similar fashion, here is a very straightforward thought process that can be used for an effective approach to strategic estate planning based on only three possibilities. The client is either:

1. O.K.

2. Not O.K.

3. Dead

Clients often find the above statement to be amusing, but it does help to clarify thinking. When most prospective clients come in for the first meeting, they are O.K., at least from a health standpoint. They may be under stress from a divorce, death of a spouse or other loved one, or a forced retirement or other kind of job loss. Or they may be looking to the future, in a positive mode, wanting to better deploy capital, set goals, and operate from a defined plan. The point is, they are not incapacitated. They can think, study, learn, and make logical and informed decisions.

But what if at some point they cannot make good decisions? They are incapacitated due to illness or accident? They are comatose or suffering from a mental impairment? Who is empowered to make decisions for them?

Often clients will say, "My executor will make decisions."

Unfortunately, this is an incorrect assumption. The client is not dead. The client's will is not in effect. The client's life insurance has not paid off. The client is suffering a "living death," which may or may not be permanent.

I believe it makes sense to discuss a worse-case scenario in order to motivate clients to create a plan that will fulfill their wishes. "You have been in an accident or had a stroke and you are in a coma. Who has the authority to deal with your investments? Your rental properties? Business interests? If an asset is titled in your name, did you know that neither your spouse, your adult child, nor your business partner has the authority to act in your behalf? There is a legal proceeding that can be invoked to have a court declare you incompetent, but do you really want to put them through that?"

This opens the door to a discussion of the pros and cons of Durable Powers of Attorney for assets, Revocable Living Trusts, and strategies to protect business interests. Yes, these are legal matters, and I am not a lawyer. But clients must be aware of these issues, and I urge them to consult with an attorney or we can recommend one from our stable, The Solution Network™.

The best idea is to have a savvy estate and tax attorney on our team. But if the client has an attorney that he or she values, I strive to preserve existing relationships.

Continuing with our "what if?" questions, in case of incapacity, I will ask, "Who has the authority to make decisions regarding your most precious asset—your body?" This statement triggers a discussion of Durable Powers of Attorney for Health Care and Living Wills. How does the client feel about endgame intervention—about being kept alive artificially?

A Will Is Not Enough

It is very common for people with significant wealth to have no wills, old wills, or insufficient wills. Estate structures that *maximize* taxes and administrative costs are the rule, not the exception.

A will is only a *part* of an estate plan. Everyone has a will. If clients have not drafted a will, their state of residency has done it for them. It's called "intestacy," but it is a poor substitute for planning.

A will governs distribution of property. You need to know what you are dealing with. Is the will a simple "I love you" will, in other words, "I give it all to her, she gives it all to me" or vice versa? Is the will more complex, containing various trust provisions? Is the will tied to a Living Trust, that is, a pour-over will? Define the functions of all trusts in the will or independent of the will.

However, some property may not be subject to the will. If property is owned jointly with right of survivorship (JTWROS), unless disclaimed, the property goes to the survivor at the death of the first owner.

In similar fashion, contractual designations (beneficiary designations on insurance contracts, annuities, retirement plans, benefit plans, buy-sell agreements) govern distribution. If the beneficiary is not the "estate of the decedent," the asset will pass to the named beneficiary independent of the will.

It is not uncommon where most investments are held jointly (JTWROS) and where the primary beneficiary on insurance policies and retirement plans is the surviving spouse, to see the bulk of postmortem liquidity pass outside of the will. In other words, you may have a will that is legal and valid, but it will not work because of the way you own assets and have designated beneficiaries. Work with a qualified attorney. Estate planning is not just about estate taxes—it is also about *distribution*.

Who Gets the Money?

Tax issues cloud rational thinking at times. Forget tax laws for a minute. Make believe that there are no ordinary income taxes, capital gains taxes, or estate taxes. Ask the client: "If there were no tax laws, what would you like to do with your money and your assets?"

I then tell my clients: "Once we figure out your true wishes and core values, I as your advisor, work with other members of your Advisory Team. Our team, The Solution Network™, includes CPAs and attorneys (as well as other advisors) to minimize taxes and maximize your legacy."

How does the client feel about his or her children as heirs? Are there minors in the picture? If heirs are adults, are there health issues, immaturity factors, spendthrift concerns?

If any of my clients are planning for a noncitizen spouse, I tell them that to qualify for the Marital Deduction at the death of a spouse, the surviving spouse must be a U.S. citizen. Specialized trust planning is necessary for a spouse who is not a U.S. citizen.

As baby boomers age with prospects of greater longevity, albeit with increased likelihood of old-age infirmities, a greater emphasis will be placed on trust planning, both living trusts and testamentary (postmortem) trusts. For the larger estate, advance estate planning strategies may be called for. Life insurance will continue as a tool to leverage legacies. Our role as the advisor, in concert with technical specialists well versed in advanced planning alternatives, is to help the client achieve his or her goals in the most efficient way possible. How can we propose investment strategies for significant monies without a deep understanding of the client's quest for significance—in life and thereafter?

The number of choices and distribution channels can be overwhelming.

An advisor should have an integrated, holistic financial planning and asset management process. The key word is *process*. It is this process that separates great advisors from average advisors: how they blend the precepts of estate, tax, and investment planning into a strategic overlay.

Family (or individual) security and estate planning issues as we have described may be viewed as the first phase of a two-phase strategy. Once there is a mutual understanding of the structure required to actualize security and legacy objectives, then it makes sense to move to the second phase, Investment Planning.

A great place to start is to organize the existing accounts in two "buckets," based on ownership and tax status. See the following table.

Taxable Monies	Tax-Deferred Money
1. Yours	1. IRA (Traditional or Rollover)
2. Your spouse's	2. Roths (Tax Free)
3. Jointly Held	3. SEP-IRA
a. JTWROS	4. Pension Plan
b. TIC	
c. Other	5. Profit Sharing Plan
4. Community Property	6. 401(k)
5. Living Trusts	7. 403(b); TSA
6. Kiddie accounts	8. 457 Plan
a. Under age 14	9. Education IRA
b. Over age 14	10. Section 529 Plan
7. Sub-S Corp/Sole Prop.	11. Non-Qualified Annuities
8. Other Trusts	12. Life Insurance Cash Value
	13. Non-Qualified Deferred Comp.
	14. Stock Option Plans

It is also useful to discuss each registration to determine the original objective in setting up the account. Are those goals being served? What has been the experience with the account? If a change is being contemplated, does the client feel the need for change? An understanding of subjective issues can be useful in establishing the Investment Policy.

Does the individual have sufficient personal liquidity outside of tax-deferred accounts? Based on projected cash flows and expenditures, how much money should be held in reserves such as money market funds?

Identify "sleep-at-night" money. Identify "no-risk" or "low-risk" alternatives. What are the current yields on Treasury bills and shorter-term government paper, money market accounts, CDs? Is that enough? What are the "real return" needs over and above inflation and taxation? Answers will depend on a variety of factors including the client's age and longevity assumptions, sources of cash flow independent of investments, size of the capital pool, and psychological factors relating to risk/reward tradeoffs.

Consider whether the fixed-income allocation should be placed within one or more of the tax-deferred buckets such as a retirement plan or nonqualified tax-deferred annuity. The goal is to defer lesser yielding ordinary income events to the retirement side of the ledger, as they will ultimately be taxed as "ordinary" taxable income. On the personal taxable side, capture and harvest capital gains and losses employing effective tax and investment management. This is a simple but powerful idea.

I always make sure investors understand the interest rate yield curve and the inverse relationship between interest rate movements and bond prices. In 2001, a leading mutual fund group surveyed investors in their bond funds. Less than 30 percent understood that when interest rates rise, bond values decline, and vice versa. Client should understand "total return" and the difference between income and tax-efficient cash flow.

A Matter of Safety

Most advisors have a way to explain "risk," using various measures of historical volatility to classify asset classes and managers. However, as we saw in the rocky markets of 2000 through 2002, linear projections of wealth accumulation based on a specific assumed rate of return are spurious. Since the future is an unfunded liability, various disciplines such as Monte Carlo simulation or other mathematical and statistical machinations should be used to estimate a range of probabilities relative to success or failure of a strategy.

If "reversion to the mean" has more relevance following the growth stock and Nasdaq drubbings of 2000–2002, and we wish to factor in periods of low performance as a possibility, each client will have to understand that an increase in contributions to savings and/or lengthening time horizons could be necessary.

Concentrated Wealth

Are there any "sacred cows" in the portfolio? Does the client own stocks that carry "emotional baggage"? Perhaps the stocks were gifts or bequests from a spouse, parent, grandparent, or other relative and the client feels guilty about selling. Or the stock may have a very low tax basis and the client is intimidated by the tax liability.

I have found one key question to be useful in creating a resolution. I ask the client, "If instead of the stock, you had cash, would you buy the same stock today?" If the answer is "no," liquidation alternatives and efficient tax strategies should be discussed.

By engaging experienced advisors who employ covered call writing strategies, significant cash flows can be generated from sacred cows and low-cost basis stocks. By letting stock get called away at defined higher prices over time, a phased diversification element can be introduced while controlling tax events.

Suppose an investor amassed significant wealth by not diversifying. This investor owns a stock that in hindsight has been a winner, and it now dominates the net worth statement. The stock might constitute from 50 to 90 percent or more of the total net worth. In effect, the client succeeded because he or she rode a winning horse.

I like to ask, "If your liquid wealth increased by 50 percent, would that have a major impact on your lifestyle?" Most likely, the answer will be "no."

Then I ask, "But if your wealth *decreased* by 50 percent, would that have an impact on your lifestyle?"

Quite likely, such an event would be disturbing, or perhaps, devastating. Strategies to deal with the risks associated with concentrated wealth are increasingly important.

Executive and management compensation programs continue to involve significant measures of stock options, stock bonuses, and restricted stock for many high net worth clients. The boom in mergers has also created unprecedented equity wealth concentration. Risks associated with such holdings include concentration in one company and one industry sector, in some cases limited liquidity, and tax ramifications relative to low basis and Alternative Minimum Tax (AMT) exposure. Concurrently, with the growth of personal, concentrated, and taxable wealth, the past decade has witnessed the creation of innovative strategies for hedging and monetizing restricted and low-cost basis stock positions.

All sophisticated wealth management solutions seem to involve an experienced team of professionals who have mastered the complexities of various techniques. If you are a high net worth investor, you should have a solution network with a group that can evaluate various solutions and clearly explain the pros and cons to you and the other advisory team members such as your tax advisor and your attorney.

Your goal is:

1. To know what you own

2. To know where you want to be in one, three, or five years and beyond

3. To understand your assets structure

4. To have a process for distributing your wealth to those you want to have it in the most tax-efficient way

Planning is about process and a full recognition that investment management and wealth management tools are part of a bigger picture.

C

ASSET PROTECTION STRATEGIES

I begin this appendix with (in my opinion) the weaker protection strategies and structures.

Homestead Exemption

Congress recently closed the Homestead Exemption loophole. The homestead exemptions, once considered the strongest bastion against creditors, are now subject to exceptions under the new Consumer Protection Act of 2005.

The new law was ultimately designed to protect abuses made by corporate executives charged with financial crimes. But a last-minute revamp of the rules concerning asset protection now affects innocent investors as well as corporate criminals.

Before the act was passed, Wall Street crooks could defraud their investors, causing huge financial losses for their own employees as well as their investors, then file for personal bankruptcy. But instead of making their investors whole at that point, the criminals were able to move away to Kansas, Florida, Iowa, South Dakota, or Texas (which have unlimited homestead exemptions) and buy huge homesteads, using the homestead exemption as justification.

This ultimately enabled crooks to have all of their debts discharged while retaining their wealth. This loophole was closed when the new act was signed into law.

Avoid the aggressive asset planning tactics you see in seminars on family limited partnerships, offshore trusts, and do-it-yourself kits produced for the masses. Before you answer an asset protection ad or rush to the back of a hotel room after the seminar to buy the secret blueprints for a bulletproof asset protection plan—stop! The only thing most of these do-it-yourself kits accomplish is to generate millions of dollars in needless tax liabilities for investors and exorbitant fees for the promoters.

Foreign Asset Protection Trust

Although offshore trusts are mass-marketed as asset protection tools, they work very poorly. They work only if you are prepared to flee the United States.

For nearly two decades, the U.S. government has attempted to discourage people from hiding assets offshore, and the Treasury Department requires that offshore asset protection strategies be as transparent as possible. There are still several options available which can place assets beyond the reach of investigators and creditors, while complying with U.S. tax and reporting laws.

The primary benefit of "offshoring" derives from jurisdictional immunity. This means, essentially, that courts in other countries do not recognize U.S. legal judgments. Those trying to seize an individual's offshore assets must litigate in the country where their target has his or her money. They must hire a legal team in that country and navigate the entire administrative process of presenting a case from scratch. By the time they litigate their claim in the other jurisdiction, they will likely have spent all the money they might have received. Instead, they may be motivated to negotiate a settlement.

Offshore trusts *do not* protect assets from creditors, but they do shield money from the gaze of perfunctory investigations while providing jurisdictional immunity. The offshore trust is the investment vehicle that the fewest number of creditors are going to go after because they know it's going to cost time and money.

You should own enough vulnerable assets to justify spending the $20,000 or more in fees for the legal structures. Perhaps more significantly, this type of protection is often the target of the IRS. If you established a trust, you are required to notify the IRS. That action alone may make you a target for examination by the agency. The IRS takes the position that an offshore asset protection trust means that the owner is trying to hide something. Finally, you must ensure that the country in which you establish the trust does not honor U.S. judgments. Countries like Liechtenstein, Nevis, Belize, and the Isle of Man currently have laws that are more favorable to the individual who created the trust than to the person or entity that is trying to access the assets.

The problem for most high-risk professionals such as physicians is, of course, that their practices are in the United States, and they probably couldn't make anywhere near the revenue outside the country that they do in it. Thus, although lots of physicians have been sold offshore trusts, what happens in real life is that the physicians don't want to either flee the country or spend time in jail. As a result, when litigation arises, they end up abandoning the offshore trust that they spent so much money for. In other words, when push comes to shove, the offshore trust is worthless unless you are willing to flee the country.

Businesses Registered Offshore

The premise behind establishing businesses in certain foreign locales (which are known as international business companies, or

IBCs) is that it is a method of keeping information confidential. For example the Cayman Islands touts that they offer secrecy of owner-ship. The truth is any U.S. citizen can start up a foreign corporation as long as it is lawful to do so in the country in which the corpora-tion is established. But as with offshore trusts, income from the business *must still be reported* and is taxed in the United States. However, these are a waste of money unless you intend to live in the same country as your business.

The Spouse Defense

Married professionals occasionally put all their worldly goods in their spouses' names for safekeeping. That tactic may or may not work, depending on where you live. In many states, signing prop-erty over to a spouse is better than owning it together, because a creditor can force a couple to liquidate jointly held assets to collect the debtor's share. Of course, letting a spouse own everything puts the other spouse in a vulnerable position if the couple later gets divorced. If the spouse is merely holding assets that the other spouse still controls—by writing checks on a bank account, for example—a creditor still has a good shot at those assets. To qualify for protec-tion, the transferred assets must truly become the spouse's property.

Shifting assets to a spouse may be in vain in states that have com-munity-property laws, such as California and Texas. In these states, a married couple jointly owns all property acquired during the mar-riage, even if the property is titled in only one spouse's name. Exceptions are made for gifts, bequests, and the like. Generally, a creditor of one spouse can pursue the entire value of community property to satisfy a judgment.

In Florida, Ohio, Pennsylvania, and a number of other states, an option is a formidable version of joint ownership known as "tenancy by the entirety." In most states that offer this option, a creditor can't grab property unless there is a judgment against the spouse, too. However, this protection disappears if the couple gets a divorce or if the spouse dies.

Family Limited Partnerships

If you are in family limited partnerships (FLPs) or are contemplating using them, be aware that the IRS has lately been quite successful in attacking them. It is of the utmost importance to have them regularly reviewed, especially if you have an old partnership.

An FLP has traditionally been one of the popular ways to hold real estate, mutual funds, bank accounts, and other possessions. One spouse may be the general partner with a 1 percent interest and managerial rights, while the couple would own the remainder as limited partners. Or one spouse may be the general partner, with the other spouse and the couple's children serving as limited partners. The general partner may then reduce the estate by gradually transferring assets to heirs in the role of limited partners.

Before you implement a family limited partnership, however, consider the following scenario. Say, your spouse retains control of the assets. If you die, her partnership interest could be discounted for tax purposes. For one thing, it's not marketable. So $500,000 in FLP assets might be taxed, for instance, as only $300,000. The same principle also applies to gifts made to limited partners to avoid or reduce gift taxes.

On the other hand, to reach your partnership assets, your creditor must obtain a "charging order" from the court. This order entitles the creditor to any income generated by FLP assets and paid to you. However, you or your spouse as the general partner aren't obligated to distribute this income to a limited partner and won't be in any rush to do so. So the creditor must wait. Plus, the creditor may be stuck with the tax bill for your FLP income!

Family limited partnerships and, more recently, family limited liability companies (FLLCs) are receiving increasing attention. The main idea behind these strategies is to insulate assets from other assets. But if you put all of your properties into one LLC, it could cause a domino effect. In other words, if a creditor can get to one of the properties, he can get to all of them. Conversely, if you insulate each asset, you might lose one property but likely won't lose all of them.

Limited Liability Companies

For ultrawealthy investors—those worth $10 million or more— state law exemptions have their limitations. These investors aren't going to put all of their wealth into a life insurance contract or even a homestead exemption; instead, they often turn to limited liability companies (LLCs) and limited partnerships.

LLCs and limited partnerships closely mirror FLPs in form and function. Instead of general partners and limited partners, LLCs have managing and nonmanaging members. But LLCs also force creditors to obtain charging orders. A creditor can't take an asset that's already encumbered. If you own an office building in your name, for instance, a victorious plaintiff can claim it. But beware that both FLPs and LLCs carry hefty fees. You can count on spending $2,000 to $10,000 to create one and $500 to $2,000 every year afterward to maintain it.

Irrevocable Trusts

With an irrevocable trust, you must truly give up control of your assets, making them judgment-proof. Many wealthy people already have revocable living trusts for the sake of avoiding probate. However, you must understand that these trusts offer no defense against creditors, because whoever puts assets into the trusts can take them back out, if necessary, to pay a judgment. So if you set up a trust that names you as a beneficiary, creditors can help themselves to it in the end.

Self-Settled Trusts

In this type of trust, you make yourself a beneficiary—then transfer your assets to the trust. The Consumer Protection Act 2005 has a fraudulent transfer provision that attempts to thwart this benefit. The transfer will be deemed fraudulent if your transfer was made with the intent to hinder, delay, or defraud creditors (even those that may come along in the future), or if you file for bankruptcy within 10 years of making the transfer. Previously, the statute of limitations was four years in 42 states, while other states had slightly different periods. In the past, you could use self-settled trust laws in eight states—Delaware, Alaska, Nevada, Rhode Island, Missouri, Oklahoma, Utah, and South Dakota—to squirrel away your wealth and then declare bankruptcy and avoid making good on any claims against you. Those days are gone.

State-Based Asset Protection Trusts

Various rules apply in community-property states, where creditors can reach all the assets of a married couple to satisfy the debts of either spouse, regardless of how the assets are titled. An asset-protection vehicle available in many of these states is the option for spouses to hold property as tenants by entirety. When assets are held this way, only the couple's joint creditors have access to them. Creditors of just one spouse can't collect on the debt unless a divorce occurs or one spouse dies.

In January 2004, an asset protection trust law took effect in Utah, enabling people to put money in an asset protection trust in the state. The trust document is drafted in such a way that creditors cannot gain access to the money. Since then, other states— including Oklahoma and Alaska—have joined the party, putting similar trust laws on the books.

There are still 30 states that permit this form of ownership but only for real estate, not for assets such as stocks and bank accounts. Florida and Texas allow it for both real estate and other assets. However, many financial advisors question whether this is the best route when it comes to asset protection. For starters, all assets must be of that state and managed by an advisor in that state. Plus, the trusts are capped at $1 million. In addition, state-based asset protection trusts are relatively new and, as such, untested. In the case of the Utah trusts, for instance, no one knows what a judge in Utah will do. The same holds true for the new widely touted Alaskan trusts.

Domestic Asset Protection Trusts

Domestic asset protection trusts (DAPTs) have been neutered by bankruptcy reform. The 2005 changes to the Bankruptcy Code have created a new 10-year limitations period for transfers to self-settled trusts which are meant to hinder, delay, or defraud creditors. This effectively means that all transfers to domestic asset protection trusts will be suspect for the 10 years prior to the date that a bankruptcy petition is filed. Because of this, domestic asset protection trusts should not be considered for asset protection planning and, indeed, in most circumstances it might be malpractice per se for an advisor to form a DAPT for his or her client if asset protection is a concern.

Several states have recently legalized domestic asset protection trusts, which purport to thwart creditors while allowing investors to be beneficiaries. Some estate-planning experts shy away from DAPTs because they haven't yet been seriously tested in the courts, although other experts say they're sound. The big question remains whether a plaintiff who wins a judgment in New York, for example, can enforce it against a DAPT drafted in Alaska. After all, Article IV of the U.S. Constitution says states should honor other states' decisions. DAPTs also cost $10,000 or so to set up, making them rather pricey.

Beneficiary Defective Trust

A beneficiary defective trust is one in which the trust's beneficiary is treated as its owner for income tax purposes. Unlike most asset protection vehicles that concentrate on existing wealth, this tool focuses on planning for future business opportunities. The trust is creditor protected because it is set up not by the beneficiary but by a third party, such as a family member, who can form the trust as a favor to the beneficiary who is looking to shelter his or her assets. Although the person setting up the trust, known as the settler, can fund the trust in any amount, the sum tends to be small— $5,000 is fairly common. To make the trust effective, the settler gives the beneficiary the power for a limited time, such as 30 days, to withdraw the greater of a percentage of the trust assets or $5,000. A close family friend is typically named the distribution trustee, and the primary beneficiary is the investment trustee. Since the primary beneficiary has no control over distributions, the trust assets are protected from creditors.

But as the trustee in charge of investments, you play an important role in the second part of this strategy—to grow the assets in the trust and in effect create a nest egg, which will be creditor protected. For instance, you could use the trust funds to start a new business, or make a loan to the trust so it could enter into a larger transaction such as a large block of publicly traded stock. The advantage of this type of trust is that you can sell assets to the trust income tax-free and thereby convert assets into things that could be more easily protected.

The legal codes of popular offshore asset shelters such as Switzerland or Panama favor asset protectors. For example, the country may simply not recognize a case brought by a foreign person trying to get at assets domiciled there, or it may have a short statute of limitation period. In the Cook Islands, for example, a plaintiff must initiate a claim within one year.

Offshore Bank Accounts

The offshore bank account is a great tool for people who want to protect their assets. With an offshore bank account, you can use your bank as an investment service. The bank can buy in your name, and you get around all the SEC rules that restrict Americans' rights to buy foreign stocks, mutual funds, or bonds directly.

Swiss bank accounts, once synonymous with wealth, mystery, and individual sovereignty, today—along with similar strongholds in other offshore havens—are under siege. With broad powers borne out of policy wars against drugs, terrorism, and money laundering, the United States can now unearth and examine the most private financial matters of its citizens almost anywhere in the world. Yet, despite its best efforts, the government has either failed to infiltrate or chosen not to eliminate some of the safe harbors. Despite the crackdown, legal options abound for those seeking to shelter assets abroad.

The Swiss bank account remains the classic offshore device. Switzerland has a long history of respecting individual financial privacy, and its legal and financial systems are renowned for their stability.

Income from Offshore

All U.S. citizens must pay taxes on their worldwide income, and that specifically includes income from offshore investments. The law says that no matter where you live in the world or where your income is sourced, you are liable every year to file your 1040 form. That means the IRS has to know about your offshore investments.

If you have an offshore bank account that has had more than $10,000 in it at any time over the tax year, you must declare it on Schedule B of your income tax return. You also need to fill out a more detailed form—TDF 90-22.1—and file it with the Treasury Department by June 30 of the year after your reporting.

The United States, working in tandem with a coalition of European tax authorities, established several treaties with the governments of tax havens that soften privacy rules and force banks in those nations to give up tax evaders or freeze accounts when faced with a court order from the U.S. Justice Department. The IRS also signed qualified intermediary (QI) agreements directly with banks doing business in offshore havens. In return for collecting and filing information on their U.S.-based customers with the IRS, QI banks gain several regulatory advantages in their dealings with the IRS and the Treasury Department. QI banks also have access to the U.S. financial markets.

By December 2000, almost every financial institution in some four dozen tax refuges—including the Caymans, the British Virgin Islands, Switzerland, and Liechtenstein—had signed on. Between the tax treaties and the QI agreements, the Treasury Department has effectively extended the know-your-customers provisions of the Bank Secrecy Act into the world's erstwhile tax havens. With a court order or a money laundering conviction in hand, a U.S. government official can freeze virtually any account almost anywhere in the world.

In 2000, the IRS asked Visa and American Express to release information on U.S. citizens who hold credit cards issued by offshore banks. After a token squabble in the courts, the card companies complied and allowed the IRS to search transactions of those cardholders suspected of evading taxes or of living beyond their means.

The Bush administration quickly connected clandestine worldwide banking activities of any kind with terrorism. It was easy to link terrorism to money laundering, and the step from money laundering to offshore tax havens was a small one. The new emphasis on security set the stage for the Patriot Act, which requires financial institutions, now broadly defined, to file a Suspicious Activity Report whenever anyone makes a transfer of more than $10,000 to or from certain banks in certain countries. These institutions must provide information on those transfers but cannot tell any customer that he or she is under investigation.

Today the United States can unearth and examine the most private financial matters of its citizens almost anywhere in the world. Before you move your assets offshore, get up-to-date advice and don't believe everything you read on the Internet. If you need help, contact us at www.wealthstratgroup.com.

GLOSSARY

Arithmetic and geometric annualized return
The total return on an investment or portfolio over a period of time other than one year, restated as an equivalent return for a one-year period. The formula is as follows:

$(1 + r) (1/n) - 1$, where r is the cumulative return in decimal form and n is the number of years.

Balanced account
An account that includes two or more asset classes other than cash. In a typical balanced account, the asset classes are equities and fixed income securities.

Balanced index
A market index that serves as a basis of comparison for balanced portfolios. The balanced index used in the Monitor is comprised of a 60 percent weighting of the S&P 500 Index and a 40 percent weighting of the SLH Government/Corporate Bond Index. The balanced index relates unmanaged market returns to a balanced portfolio more precisely than either a stock or a bond index would alone.

Basis point
One basis point is 1/100th of a percentage point, or 0.01 percent. Basis points are often used to express changes or differences in yields, returns, or interest rates. Thus, if a portfolio has a total return of 10 percent versus 7 percent for the S&P 500, the portfolio is said to have outperformed the S&P 500 by 300 basis points.

Bear market
A prolonged period of falling stock prices. There's no consensus on what constitutes a bear market. SEI, one of the most widely used performance measurement services, normally defines a bear market or bear leg as a drop of at least 15 percent over two back-to-back quarters.

Benchmark
A standard by which investment performance or trading execution can be judged. The most widely used performance benchmark is the total return of the S&P 500.

Beta

A measure of the sensitivity of a stock or portfolio to the movement of the general market. By definition, the market, usually measured by the S&P 500 Index, has a beta of 1.00. Any stock or portfolio with a higher beta is generally more volatile than the market, whereas any with a lower beta is generally less volatile than the market.

In theory, a portfolio with a beta greater than that of the S&P 500 should outperform that index in a rising market and underperform it in a falling market, but in the real world it doesn't always work that way. A stock's historical variability is not always a good predictor of its future variability.

Book value per share

The net worth per share of a common stock, on the basis of generally accepted accounting principles. Book value is calculated by taking total assets, subtracting all liabilities and the par value of preferred stock, and dividing by the number of outstanding common shares.

Bull market

A prolonged period of rising stock prices. SEI, one of the most widely used performance measurement services, normally defines a bull market or bull leg as a rise of at least 15 percent over two back-to-back quarters.

Commissions

Fees a broker charges for buying or selling securities. Before May 1, 1975, minimum brokerage commissions were fixed by the New York Stock Exchange. After "May Day," brokers were allowed to compete on commission rates, and institutional rates declined. Current rates are often quoted in terms of a discount from the pre-May Day rates.

Consultant

Consultants in the investment industry offer a wide variety of services, including asset allocation, investment strategy, manager searches, manager evaluation, and performance analysis. Some consultants serve only sponsors, and their databases are generally not available to investment managers.

Consumer Expenditure Survey (CES)

An ongoing study conducted by the U.S. government that measures (down to the penny) how much people spend on over 1,000 different items per year.

Consumer Price Index (CPI)

Maintained by the Bureau of Labor Statistics, the CPI measures the changes in the cost of a specified group of consumer products relative to a base period. Because it represents the rate of inflation, the CPI can be used as a general benchmark for gauging the maintenance of purchasing power.

Contrarian

An investment approach characterized by buying stocks that are out of favor.

Correction

A correction is a reversal in the price of a stock, or the market as a whole, within a larger trend. While corrections are most often thought of as declines within an overall market rise, a correction can also be a temporary rise in the midst of a longer-term decline.

Current yield

A bond's annual interest payment as a percentage of its current market price. The current yield is calculated by dividing the annual coupon interest for a bond by the current market price. The coupon rate and the current yield on a bond are equal when the bond is selling at par. Thus, a $1,000 bond with a coupon of 10 percent that is currently selling at $1,000 will have a current yield of 10 percent. However, if the bond's price drops to $800, the current yield becomes 12.5 percent. (As a bond's price falls, its yield rises, and vice versa.)

Efficient market theory

The theory behind indexing that holds that stock prices always reflect all known information and that it's therefore impossible to outperform the market without taking on more risk than the market. The implication is that, on a risk-adjusted basis, an investor will do just as well by throwing darts at the financial pages of a newspaper as by analyzing the fundamentals of potential investments.

Equities

Generally refers to common or preferred stocks. Claims of both common and preferred stockholders are junior to claims of bondholders or other creditors of the company. Holders of common stock assume the greater risk but generally exercise a greater degree of control and may gain the greater reward in the form of dividend growth and capital appreciation.

ERISA

The Employee Retirement Income Security Act of 1974. The stated purpose of ERISA is to protect the interests of workers who participate in private pension and welfare plans and their beneficiaries. The law governs
how funds are administered and managed.

Excess return

Returns over and above a benchmark rate of return. For purposes of com-
puting risk-adjusted returns, the benchmark rate would be the risk-free
rate of return as estimated by the U.S. government Treasury bill rate.

Fourth market

The relatively new institution-to-institution trading networks. The first, or
primary, market is for new issues, including initial public offerings. The
second, or secondary, market generally refers to trades on the various
exchanges. In the third market, sometimes called the upstairs market, a
buyer or seller asks a broker to find the other side of the trade without
shopping the order on any exchange. Such trades do appear in the day's
trading statistics on each day's closing composite, but with a "T" after
them to indicate they weren't done on any exchange. The fourth market
is simply a more technologically sophisticated version of the third market.

Fundamentals

Refers to the financial statistics that traditional analysts and many valuation models use. Fundamental data include earnings, dividends, assets
and liabilities, inventories, debt, and so on. Fundamental data are in contrast to items used in technical analysis—such as price momentum,
volume trends, and short sales statistics.

Index fund

An index fund is a passively managed portfolio designed and computer-
controlled to track the performance of a certain index, such as the S&P
500. In general, such funds have performance within a few basis points of
the target index. The most popular index funds are those that track the
S&P 500, but special index funds, such as those based on the Russell 1000
or the Wilshire 5000, are also available.

Industry sectors

Accounting systems and Wall Street research firms break universes of
stocks into two main categories: macroeconomic sectors and industry
groups. Typically, the energy sector will include stocks from four groups—
domestic oils, international oils, oil service, and natural gas producers (but
not natural gas distributors, which is in the utilities sector).

Investment styles (active managers' marketing styles)
Value—In this instance, the manager uses various tests to determine an intrinsic value for a given security, and tries to purchase the security substantially below that value. The goal and hope are that the stock price will ultimately rise to the stock's fair value or above. Price to earnings, price to sales, price to cash flow, price to book value, and price to break-up value (or true net asset value) are some of the ratios examined in such an approach.

Emerging Growth—Here, a manager is looking for industries and companies whose growth rates are likely to be both rapid and independent of the overall stock market.

Emerging, of course, means new. This implies such companies may be relatively small in size with the potential to grow much larger. Such stocks are generally much more volatile than the stock market in general and require constant, close attention to developments.

Quality Growth—This term implies long-term investment in high-quality growth stocks, some of which might be larger, emerging companies while others might be long-established household names. Such a portfolio might have volatility equal to or above that of the overall market, but less than that of an "emerging growth" portfolio.

Balanced—This term can be applied to any kind of portfolio that uses fixed-income (bonds) as well as equity securities to reach goals. Many "boutique" investment managers are balanced managers, because it permits them to tailor the securities in a portfolio to the specific clients' cash flow needs and objectives. Balanced portfolios are often used by major funds and charitable endowments, as well as by individuals. They provide great flexibility.

Income Growth—The primary purpose in security selection here is to achieve a current yield significantly higher than the S&P 500. The stability and the rate of growth of the dividends are also of concern to the income buyer. These portfolios may own more utilities, fewer high techs, and may own convertible preferreds and convertible bonds.

Fixed Income—This term largely speaks for itself. Fixed-income managers invest in bonds, notes, and other debt instruments. They have a broad range of styles, involving market timing, swapping to gain quality or yield, setting up maturity ladders, and so on. A typical division of the fixed-income market is between short (up to three years), intermediate (3 to 15 years), and long (15 to 30 years). Managers that specialize in each can be obtained.

Sector or Industry Rotators—These managers attempt to be invested in specific industries or specific economic sectors they believe will outperform the general stock market during specific periods. An example would be the recognized switch on behalf of many managers, from "growth" to "cyclical" stocks, since they believe the cyclicals should benefit from an economic pickup, whereas growth stocks have moved up sharply over the past period.

Cash Management—Cash managers invest in short-term fixed instruments and cash equivalents. These instruments make up the portfolio and their objective is to maximize principal protection. Even though these accounts have short-term (one-day) liquidity, they typically pay more like 90- to 180-day CDs versus passbook or one-week CDs.

Junk bonds
Think about the term *Junk bonds*. The definition will give us a clue. Look it up. *Junk* is defined as "rubbish, garbage, trash, and useless items." Now why would anyone buy something like that?

Market capitalization
The current value of a company determined by multiplying the latest available number of outstanding common shares by the current market price of a share. For example, on December 29, 2006, IBM had about 1,366 million shares outstanding, and the stock closed at $97.15. Thus, its market capitalization was approximately $132 billion. Market cap is also an indication of the trading liquidity of a particular issue.

Market capitalization-weighting
As opposed to equal-weighting or manager-weighting, market cap-weighting maintains a stock's weight in a portfolio equal to the percentage of the stock's weight in the S&P 500.

Market cycle
A period of falling prices followed by a period of rising prices, or vice versa. Cycles are measured peak-to-peak or trough-to-trough. The rising leg (called the bull market) and the falling leg (the bear market) make a complete market cycle. The major performance measuring services, such as SEI, do not measure from a precise peak to a precise bottom, but use the nearest complete calendar quarter. The start or end of a market cycle is not known until after the fact.

Market impact

The pressure a manager's trading can have on a stock's price. A manager trading $10 million of IBM, a stock that has an average daily trading of nearly $1 billion, will probably have little market impact. By contrast, a manager who sells $1 million of a smaller stock—for example, with average daily trading of only $1.5 million—can move the price of the stock considerably.

Market timing

The attempt to base investment decisions on the expected direction of the market. If stocks are expected to decline, the timer may elect to hold a portion of the portfolio in cash equivalents or bonds. Timers may base their decisions on fundamentals (for example, selling stocks when the market's price/book ratio reaches a certain level), on technical considerations (such as declining momentum or excessive investor optimism), or a combination of both.

Market value

The market or liquidation value of a given security or of an entire pool of assets.

Market volatility

The size of daily price shifts in the S&P 500, as measured by the standard deviation. *See also* Standard deviation.

Noise

A statistically insignificant difference. Noise can also refer to the difference in performance between two portfolios resulting from a large number of very small timing, weighting, or selection differences at the individual stock level.

Nominal return

The actual current dollar growth in an asset's value over a given period. *See also* Total return and Real return.

Passive manager

The opposite of an active manager. The ultimate passive portfolio is an index fund. Changes in such portfolios are triggered by changes in the index being tracked, often the S&P 500. If a stock is dropped from that index, the passive manager drops it from his fund and replaces it with the stock the S&P 500 uses for a replacement. To bring an indexed portfolio in line with the target index, other major weighting changes are made to rebalance the portfolio. *See also* Index fund.

Price/book ratio (P/B)

The ratio of the current price to the book value per share (the company's common equity divided by the number of shares outstanding). *See also* Book value.

Price/earnings ratio (P/E)

The current price dividend by reported earnings per share for the latest 12-month period. For example, a stock with earnings per share over the trailing year of $5 and currently selling at $50 per share has a price/earnings ratio of 10.

Real return

The inflation-adjusted return on an asset. Inflation-adjusted returns are calculated by subtracting the rate of inflation from an asset's apparent, or nominal, return. For example, if common stocks earn a total return of 10.3 percent over a period of time, but inflation during that period is 3.1 percent, the real return is the difference: 7.2 percent.

Rebalancing

The process of bringing individual issues in a portfolio back to essentially equal weight (or for a balanced portfolio, back to the target stock/bond ratio).

Risk

A portfolio has two types of risk. The first, called *market risk*, captures the amount of portfolio variability caused by events that have an impact on the market as a whole. The second is called *investment risk*, which is the actual variability or expected uncertainty of investment returns over a given period of time. This variability or uncertainty causes "rational" investors to expect higher returns on investments where the actual timing or amount of payoffs is not guaranteed.

Risk-adjusted return

Shows the performance of a portfolio adjusted for the level of market risk taken by the portfolio. In a period when the S&P 500 is up 10 percent, a portfolio taking 20 percent more risk than the market would have to be up 12 percent to hold its own on a risk-adjusted basis. If the portfolio took only 80 percent of the market's risk, it could be up only 9.6 percent and still be in line with the market after adjusting for the risk taken (as measured by the portfolio's beta).

Risk-free rate of return

The return on an asset that is considered virtually riskless. U.S. government Treasury bills are typically used as the risk-free asset because of their short time horizon and the low probability of default.

S&P 500

The performance benchmark most widely used by sponsors, managers, and performance measurement services. This index includes 400 industrial stocks, 20 transportation stocks, 40 financial stocks, and 40 public utilities. Performance is measured on a capitalization-weighted basis. The index is maintained by Standard & Poor's Corporation, a subsidiary of McGraw-Hill, Inc.

Standard deviation

A statistical measure of the variation or dispersion of a sample from the average of the sample. The sample can be one of price moves, total returns, or other groups of observations. The standard deviation is calculated as follows: Standard Deviation = $(xi - x)?$ / $(n - 1)$. The expression within the square root is essentially the average of the squared deviations of each observation from the average of the total sample. The deviations are squared to eliminate the effects of negative differences. As a rule, approximately two-thirds of the sample fall within one standard deviation (plus or minus) around the average of the sample, and 95 percent of the observations will fall within two standard deviations. One example of how standard deviation might be used as an indicator of risk is found in Ibbotson Associates' Stocks, Bonds, Bills, and Inflation Database. In most cases, the higher the return, the higher the standard deviation. This underscores the fact that, in general, higher returns are accompanied by higher risk.

T-Bills

Promissory notes issued by the U.S. Treasury and sold through competitive bidding, with a short-term maturity date, usually 13 to 26 weeks. The return on T-bills has almost no variation, so it serves as a proxy for a riskless investment.

Target-risk funds

A subset of life cycle funds offered in a 401(k) plan as a method of matching the fund risk level to the level of risk a 401(k) participant feels comfortable with. The problem is participants often pick the same amount of risk regardless of their age with no consideration for the three key wealth factors detailed in this book.

Technical analysis

Any investment approach that judges the attractiveness of particular stocks or the market as a whole based on market data, such as price patterns, volume, momentum, or investor sentiment, as opposed to fundamental financial data, such as earnings or dividends.

Time-weighted rate of return

The rate at which a dollar invested at the beginning of a period would grow if no additional capital were invested and no cash withdrawals were made. It provides an indication of value added by the investment manager and allows comparisons to the performance of other investment managers and market indexes.

Total return

A standard measure of performance, or return, that includes both capital appreciation (or depreciation) and dividends or other income received. For example, Stock A is priced at $60 at the start of a year and pays an annual dividend of $4. If the stock moves up to $70 in price, the appreciation component is 16.7 percent, the yield component is 6.7 percent, and the total return is 23.4 percent. That oversimplification does not take into account any earnings on the reinvested dividends.

Tracking error

A measure of how closely the performance of a manager is to the performance of the market. The tracking error is the standard deviation of the differences between the manager's and the market's quarterly returns. If a manager is tracking a given index closely, then there'll be a low tracking error.

Trading costs

Total execution costs (the cost of buying and selling stocks) have three components: (1) the actual dollars paid to the broker in commissions; (2) the market impact—that is, the impact that a manager's trade has on the market price for the stock (this varies with the size of the trade and the skill of the trader); and (3) the opportunity cost (positive or negative) that's the result of not executing the trade instantaneously.

Transaction costs

Another term for execution costs. Total transaction costs (or the cost of buying and selling stocks) have three components: (1) the actual dollars paid to the broker in commissions; (2) the market impact—that is, the impact that a manager's trade has on the market price for the stock (this varies with the size of the trade and the skill of the trader); and (3) the opportunity cost of the return (positive or negative) given up by not executing the trade instantaneously.

Turnover
The volume or percentage of buying or selling activity within a portfolio in relation to the size of the portfolio.

Volatility
The extent to which market values and investment returns are uncertain or fluctuate. Another word for risk, volatility is measured using methods such as beta, mean absolute deviation, and standard deviation.

Weighting
A measure of the contribution made to total return in a portfolio by over-weighting or underweighting a position, an industry group, or a sector relative to the comparable weight in the S&P 500, or other benchmark.

Wrap account fee
A single, all-encompassing fee based on a percentage of assets under management. This is a management fee that covers all charges, including advisor fees, commissions and other transaction charges, and reporting.

Yield (current yield)
For stocks, the percentage return paid in dividends on a common or preferred stock, calculated by dividing the indicated annual dividend by the market price of the stock. For example, if a stock sells for $40 and pays a dividend of $2 per share, it has a yield of 5 percent (that is, $2 divided by $40). For bonds, the coupon rate of interest divided by the market price. For example, a bond selling for $1,000 with a 10 percent coupon offers a 10 percent current yield. If the same bond were selling for $500, it would offer a 20 percent yield to an investor who bought it for $500. (As a bond's price falls, its yield rises, and vice versa.)

Yield to maturity
The discount rate that equates the present value of the bond's cash flows (semiannual coupon payments of the redemption value) with the market price. The yield to maturity will actually be earned if (1) the investor holds the bond to maturity and (2) the investor is able to reinvest all coupon payments at a rate equal to the yield to maturity. When a bond is selling at par, the yield to maturity and the coupon rate are equal.

INDEX